European Administrative Governance

Series Editors

Thomas Christiansen, Luiss University, Rome, Italy
Sophie Vanhoonacker, Maastricht University, Maastricht, The Netherlands

The series maps the range of disciplines addressing the study of European public administration. In particular, contributions to the series will engage with the role and nature of the evolving bureaucratic processes of the European Union, including the study of the EU's civil service, of organization aspects of individual institutions such as the European Commission, the Council of Ministers, the External Action Service, the European Parliament, the European Court and the European Central Bank and of inter-institutional relations among these and other actors. The series also welcomes contributions on the growing role of EU agencies, networks of technical experts and national officials, and of the administrative dimension of multilevel governance including international organizations. Of particular interest in this respect will be the emergence of a European diplomatic service and the management of the EU's expanding commercial, foreign, development, security and defence policies, as well as the role of institutions in a range of other policy areas of the Union. Beyond this strong focus of EU administrative governance, the series will also include texts on the development and practice of administrative governance within European states. This may include contributions to the administrative history of Europe, which is not just about rules and regulations governing bureaucracies, or about formal criteria for measuring the growth of bureaucracies, but rather about the concrete workings of public administration, both in its executive functions as in its involvement in policy-making. Furthermore the series will include studies on the interaction between the national and European level, with particular attention for the impact of the EU on domestic administrative systems. The series editors welcome approaches from prospective contributors and are available to contact at tchristiansen@luiss.it and s.vanhoonacker@maastrichtuniversity.nl for proposals and feedback. All books in the series are subject to Palgrave's rigorous peer review process: https://www.palgrave.com/gb/demystifying-peer-review/792492

Adam Eick

Soft Law and National Courts in the European Union

palgrave
macmillan

Adam Eick
Geschwister-Scholl Institute for
Political Science
Ludwig-Maximilians-Universität
München
Munich, Germany

ISSN 2524-7263 ISSN 2524-7271 (electronic)
European Administrative Governance
ISBN 978-3-032-04514-0 ISBN 978-3-032-04515-7 (eBook)
https://doi.org/10.1007/978-3-032-04515-7

Cover credits: Simple Images/Getty Images

This Palgrave Macmillan imprint is published by the registered company Springer Nature Switzerland AG
The registered company address is: Gewerbestrasse 11, 6330 Cham, Switzerland

Acknowledgments This book builds on the empirical material from my Ph.D. thesis, *The Use of EU Soft Law in National Courts*, defended in December 2023 at Freie Universität Berlin. It represents a substantially reorganized and rewritten version of that dissertation. The Ph.D. research was conducted as part of the DFG/ANR-funded project *Effects of European Soft Law in the Multilevel System* (EfSoLaw; DFG project number 411037244, see https://www.efsolaw.eu), led by Prof. Miriam Hartlapp (Freie Universität Berlin), Prof. Sabine Saurugger (Sciences Po Grenoble—UGA), and Prof. Fabien Terpan (Sciences Po Grenoble—UGA). This work has also received support by the European Research Council (ERC) (grant agreement no. 101001458, CIVILSPACE). Views and opinions expressed are however those of the author only and do not necessarily reflect those of the European Union or the European Research Council. Neither the European Union nor the granting authority can be held responsible for them. Parts of the data collection for this book were carried out during my work as a research associate in this project, notably 21 expert interviews and a survey of 70 judges in France and Germany. The book is thus the outcome of a long journey with soft law and courts that has benefited from the support and encouragement of many people. I sincerely thank Miriam Hartlapp, my Ph.D. supervisor, who guided and supported this project at every stage and inspired much of my motivation and approach to research in general. I am equally grateful for the repeated input and encouragement of my co-supervisor, Oana Stefan, as well as the EfSoLaw co-investigators, Sabine Saurugger and Fabien Terpan. I have had the opportunity to share ideas and receive feedback from various audiences and colleagues, in particular at the OSIbag research seminar at Freie Universität Berlin and the Comparative Research Colloquium at LMU Munich. Finally, I am so thankful to those who encouraged and supported me throughout this process: my parents, my brother, and friends in Berlin and Munich.

Competing Interests The author has no competing interests to declare that are relevant to the content of this manuscript.

Contents

List of Figures

List of Tables

CHAPTER 1

Introduction: The Judicial Use of Soft Law

1.1 A Puzzling Phenomenon

In 2019, the French financial authority *Autorité de Contrôle Prudentiel et de Résolution* (ACPR) announced that it would follow a guideline from the European Banking Authority (EBA) on so-called product governance,[1] an area that had been largely unregulated by the European Union (EU) (Chamon, 2014, p. 290). The French Banking Federation (FBF), a national interest group, was concerned about increased regulation and sought legal action. On December 4, 2019, France's highest administrative court, the *Conseil d'État*, asked the European courts to declare the EBA guideline invalid.[2] The Court of Justice of the European Union (CJEU) took up the matter on 15 July 2021,[3] confirming that soft law is indeed subject to judicial oversight, and individuals and organizations

[1] Guidelines of the European Banking Authority of 22 March 2016 on product oversight and governance arrangements for retail banking products (EBA/GL/2015/18).

[2] *Conseil d'État*, *9ème–10ème chambres réunies*, *Décision* 415550, 04 December 2019.

[3] Judgment of the Court (Grand Chamber) of 15 July 2021. *Fédération bancaire française* (FBF) v *Autorité de contrôle prudentiel et de résolution* (ACPR). Case C-911/19.

A. Eick, *Soft Law and National Courts in the European Union*, European Administrative Governance,
https://doi.org/10.1007/978-3-032-04515-7_1

have the right to challenge such acts——even though the court upheld this particular guideline in the end and did not invalidate it.

At first glance, this merely confirms dynamics of policy-making in the EU multilevel system long identified in the Europeanization literature, such as the effects of EU regulation on national enforcement (Hartlapp, 2005) and the extension of EU regulation and enforcement into new areas of national competence (Pollack, 1994), in particular by independent agencies (Egeberg & Trondal, 2017). It is also consistent with trends identified in the law and politics literature, such as the increasing interaction between the EU and national judicial systems (Martinico & Pollicino, 2012) and the impact of private litigation on public policy (Kelemen, 2011). But if we go back to the beginning, we see a crucial difference: the guidelines at the center of this case are *soft law*, i.e. instruments that resemble law but lack binding force. This book focuses on this puzzling and understudied phenomenon: the use of EU soft law in national courts.

That courts would apply non-binding instruments is puzzling from two established literatures on EU law.[4] First, from a ***doctrinal legal perspective***, it is the binding nature of EU (hard) law that gives it exceptional power and makes it the primary medium of European Integration and the source of its far-reaching effects at the national level (Lenaerts et al., 2021, pp. 3–58). Unlike international law, which relies much more on voluntary application by national governments (Aust, 2010, pp. 2–4), EU law is fully binding and in no way inferior to national law (Craig & De Búrca, 2021, pp. 226–227). Since the European Court of Justice's landmark judgments in the 1960s, EU hard law has direct effect in the Member States and primacy over national law, and these principles have become deeply entrenched in national legal orders through a gradual process of judicial and institutional adaptation (Rasmussen, 2014). This means that national legislators must adapt their laws to comply with EU law, national authorities must enforce it directly, and national courts must apply it and can annul any conflicting national law. In addition, individuals and organizations can invoke EU law in court to enforce their rights (Eleftheriadis, 1996). Due to its lack of binding force, none of this is formally required of national actors when dealing with soft law. Thus, doctrinal legal research that focuses on the formal nature of instruments

[4] For a more in-depth discussion contrasting similar perspectives on soft law in the context of EU governance (rather than judicial usage), see Hartlapp, Saurugger, & Terpan, 2020.

considers soft law to be largely irrelevant. Thereafter, EU institutions should adopt hard law whenever they have the competence and political majorities to do so. Soft law is then viewed as a type of instrument that is adopted only as a political or symbolic measure, and that is largely ineffective. Klabbers (1998, pp. 394–385), for example, suggests that EU institutions adopt such instruments when they cannot reach consensus in the legislative process or seek to act in areas where they lack formal competences, thereby stretching the constitutional limits of EU law. In this view, soft law should especially play no role in the courts, which are the traditional domain of hard law, where binding decisions are taken on the basis of binding rules (Klabbers, 2023, p. 166). This also applies to national courts in the EU multilevel system, as their role—to ensure a harmonious interpretation and decentralized enforcement of EU law—has developed in close connection with the binding nature of EU law (Maher, 1994).

Second, the *New Modes of Governance* literature views soft law as relevant, but typically locates it outside the judiciary. It attributes to soft law unique characteristics such as informality, flexibility, and the potential to diffuse norms, which make it attractive and effective in situations where hard law adoption is impossible, too slow or too hierarchical (Caporaso & Wittenbrinck, 2006; Heritier, 2002; Zeitlin, 2005). However, this literature emphasizes cooperative tools that operate through processes of deliberation and learning within the administrative, political, and civil society arena. For example, soft law in the 'Open Method of Coordination' which encourages voluntary cooperation, benchmarking, and peer review (Borrás & Jacobsson, 2004; Regent, 2003; Tholoniat, 2010). While considering soft law to be relevant, this literature conceptualizes it as an instrument that is distinct from hard law, detached from the traditional legal order and therefore not relevant to the judiciary.

Thus, while these two established perspectives disagree on the importance of soft law in EU law and governance, neither considers it relevant in the judiciary. In contrast, the opening example was a case where soft law was clearly relevant to a national court. And we quickly find more evidence for this in landmark judgments and legal scholarship. In fact, the CJEU already ruled in 1989 in the *Grimaldi* case that not only can soft law be legally relevant, but that national courts must take it into account in their decision-making.[5] Preliminary studies also point to national cases and paint a picture in which national courts use soft law regularly and in various ways (Georgieva, 2017a; Hartlapp & Hofmann, 2020; Jiménez & de Santiago, 2020; Kovács et al., 2016).

Building on this emerging literature, this book takes the phenomenon of soft law in the courts seriously as a relevant phenomenon and sets out to study it systematically. It challenges both the traditional doctrinal view that sees soft law as deficient and the New Modes of Governance literature that sees soft law as effective but separate from the legal framework, as they fail to capture the increasing complexity of the EU legal order (Hurka et al., 2021), where soft law is closely interconnected with hard law (Trubek et al., 2005). For example, soft law often precedes hard law when it paves the way for binding legislation or follows hard law when it is adopted to interpret or support the implementation of binding rules. This interaction reflects wider trends in the transformation of law, where rules are becoming more specific, interconnected with non-legal sources, and technical knowledge is increasingly crucial to legal questions (Leszczyński, 2020).

Against this background, this book argues that soft law has become an integral part of the broader EU legal framework, which courts are increasingly unable to ignore in their legal interpretation. As part of this, the judicial use of soft law is not merely a fringe phenomenon, but a symptomatic element of the evolving nature of law and the judiciary. Studying this phenomenon reveals how EU soft law affects courts' decision-making, shapes case law, and affects broader policy outcomes. This in turn highlights the intersection between law, courts, and policy in the evolving EU multilevel system more generally. To systematically study the phenomenon, this book engages in comparative and longitudinal analysis of the judicial use of soft law along three key questions:

1. *What are the patterns of judicial usage of soft law in terms of quantity and quality?*
2. *How can the variation in the judicial usage of soft law be explained?*
3. *What are the wider effects of the judicial usage of soft law?*

[5] Judgment of the Court (Second Chamber) of 13 December 1989. *Grimaldi*. Case C-322/88.

1.2 Definitions: Soft Law and Its Usage by Courts

Before asking why and how to study the phenomenon, this section briefly clarifies definitions of 'soft law,' 'usage,' and 'judicial usage of soft law' (for details, see Chapter 2).

Soft law is a concept to describe non-binding instruments that fall somewhere in-between binding law and purely declaratory instruments. The most prominent definition of soft law in EU studies considers soft law to be "rules of conduct which, in principle, have no legally binding force but which, nevertheless, may have practical and legal effects" (Senden, 2004, p. 219; Snyder, 1994, p. 2). This minimal definition is useful in that it makes it clear that soft law instruments are neither law, as they lack binding force, nor non-legal norms, as they establish rules of conduct and have the potential to produce effects. However, it is necessary to define specific characteristics of soft law to classify concrete instruments under the concept. This book thus follows a more specific conceptualization, which will be specified in Chapter 2, as *instruments that have a certain degree of formalization and enforceability, but which are formally non-binding*. Formalization refers to the degree to which legal rules are codified, obligatory, and written in mandatory language. Enforceability refers to the potential for enforcement. This allows us to place rules on a continuum of graduated normativity, while maintaining a clear distinction between soft law and hard law. The conceptualization builds on the assumption from the 'legalization' literature that there is a continuum of norms from softer to harder forms (Abbott et al., 2000; Saurugger & Terpan, 2015). But it acknowledges that only hard law has formal legal binding force (Guzman & Meyer, 2010, p. 174).

The book studies the *usage* of EU instruments by national actors. The concept of usage was proposed by Jacquot and Woll to describe "practices and political interactions which adjust and redefine themselves by seizing the European Union as a set of opportunities, be they institutional, ideological, political or organizational" (2003, p. 4). Unlike related notions like 'compliance' with and 'transposition' of EU instruments (Treib, 2014, pp. 5–7), 'usage' highlights that we need to consider actors' agency and their motivations to understand the effects of European integration.

We can extend this concept to examine the *usage of EU soft law* by national actors. In line with the view of a continuum of legal normativity,

I follow the idea that usage can take 'softer' or 'harder' forms (Hartlapp & Hofmann, 2020, pp. 136–138). *Soft usage* is closer to politics and emphasizes deliberation, rhetoric, and the dissemination of ideas. *Medium usage*, short for 'medium-hard usage,' refers to situations in which actors attribute legal value to soft law, but do not consider it to be binding. Forms of *harder usage* are very similar or identical to the use of hard law. This may be the case when administrations formally adapt their practices, transpose soft law into national hard law or implement it in binding administrative decisions. Courts are unique actors because they are empowered to apply the law and resolve disputes in binding judgments. However, applying the law is not a purely mechanical process. Like other actors, courts have a certain degree of discretion in choosing which laws to apply and how to interpret them. This is even more the case for soft law.

To emphasize this active role of courts, I speak of the *judicial usage of soft law*. While some scholars study citations to specific instruments in judgments (e.g. Wind, 2016), they are not a suitable indicator to capture the relevance of soft law in national courts, as citations may result from litigating parties invoking soft law rather than a court engaging with it in a meaningful way. Moreover, citations may be irrelevant to the legal reasoning in a judgment and the outcome of the case. Instead, judicial usage implies that courts use tools in their legal reasoning and recognize the effects of soft law. In courts, *soft usage* refers to a situation where courts recognize or apply soft law for purely practical and extra-legal purposes. *Medium usage* describes situations where soft law is legally relevant in one dimension, but not binding. Finally, when a court recognizes or applies soft law in exactly the same way as hard law, we have *hard usage*. Of course, there is also *no usage* when courts ignore soft law altogether.

1.3 Why Study the Judicial Use of EU Soft Law?

As a basis for studying these different types of soft law use in the courts, this book aims to bridge the gap between legal scholarship on the nature of soft law, Europeanization theories on the effect of the EU at the national level, and the Judicial Politics literature on the role of courts in the policy-making process.

While the EU stands out from other international organizations in its ability to enact directly binding hard law and exercise strong judicial control over it, previous research shows that soft law is also a significant part of its legal framework and governance repertoire. At the EU level, soft law is almost as prevalent as hard law and its share has increased over time (Cappellina et al., 2022; Hofmann, 2021; von Bogdandy et al., 2004; Zhelyazkova et al., 2023) . But it is important to note that the nature and function of soft law instruments is diverse and it is adopted in a wide range of policy areas (Terpan, 2015)—ranging from Social Policy (Dura, 2024; Kröger, 2009; Zeitlin et al., 2005) to the Common Foreign and Security Policy (Saurugger & Terpan, 2015; Wessel, 2015) to emerging fields like AI regulation (Büthe et al., 2022; Schade & Flyverbom, 2023). In some areas, soft law serves as an alternative to hard law. Here, it aims at steering the behavior of its addressees (Senden, 2004, p. 119). An example is the *EU Pharmaceutical Strategy* in the area Pharmaceutical Regulation, which calls to action in areas where the EU has little competences and sets the agenda for future legislative activity by the EU.[6] In other policy areas, soft law is connected to hard law in a hybrid legal regime (Trubek et al., 2005). Soft law then interprets and clarifies the underlying hard law (Senden, 2004, p. 119). An example are guidelines in competition policy and state aid which elaborate obligations on the basis of primary law (Bouchagiar, 2017). Political science research on soft law tends to focus on instruments that stand apart from hard law and are an alternative for it in the political sphere (Copeland & ter Haar, 2013; Kröger, 2009; Radaelli, 2008; Sabel & Zeitlin, 2010; Zeitlin et al., 2005), whereas legal scholarship often examines soft law instruments that are linked to and complement hard law in the context of administrative law (Banet, 2020; Bouchagiar, 2017; Scott, 2011; Van Dam, 2017). This book considers diverse types of soft law adopted in various environments to capture the phenomenon wholistically.

But soft law can only unfold effects beyond the EU level if it is used at the *national level*. National administrations are a likely arena as they engage in problem-solving. Several studies establish that national administrations indeed make frequent use of EU soft law in diverse policy fields (Eliantonio et al., 2021; Hartlapp & Hofmann, 2020; Van Wolleghem, 2017). The theoretical and empirical approach of these studies emphasizes bottom-up processes, informality, and norm diffusion and therefore departs from traditional perspectives on the compliance with hard law

[6] European Commission. A pharmaceutical strategy for Europe. 25 November 2020. https://health.ec.europa.eu/medicinal-products/pharmaceutical-strategy-europe_en, last accessed 10 July 2025.

(Hartlapp & Korkea-Aho, 2021). Distinctive structural (Hartlapp & Hofmann, 2020) and actor-centered factors (Bérut, 2021) have been proposed as explanations for the national use of soft law. Exceptions are reactions to 'harder' forms of soft law, like guidelines in competition policy, which resemble traditional compliance with hard law, where actors adapt their actions and law to avoid sanctions (Maher, 2021).

Taken together, soft law plays a key role in the *European integration through law*. This is somewhat unexpected, given that this form of integration is traditionally associated with the expansion of binding EU law (Cappelletti et al., 1986). As described, soft law can sometimes act as a substitute for hard law. When EU institutions adopt soft law instead of binding measures, this may even hinder the extension of EU hard law into new areas of competence (Trubek & Trubek, 2005). However, in many other areas soft law rather reinforces the reach of hard law. This is the case where soft law acts as a complement to hard law and fills its gaps. In such cases, soft law enables the EU to guide Member States in their legal interpretation and technical implementation of EU law, extending the reach of EU rules into national law and policy. Moreover, soft law can evolve over time into something more binding, leading to a 'hardening' of soft law. This may occur formally, when EU institutions later adopt binding legislation based on earlier soft instruments. But more often the transformation happens more informally, when actors treat soft law as authoritative or even almost binding for practical purposes (Saurugger & Terpan, 2020). As we will see, courts can play a central role in this dynamic.

An emerging scholarship also started to examine the *use of EU soft law in courts*—the focus of this book. Korkea-aho (2018) notes that the CJEU has gradually refined the so-called Grimaldi obligation, which—based on the *Grimaldi* judgment mentioned above—initially required national courts to take soft law into account in all their decisions. However, the CJEU has now given national courts more flexibility. They only need to take into account soft law instruments that are linked to hard law, and they can disregard soft law that stands alone and is not linked to hard law. Additionally, national courts now only need to consider soft law adopted by EU institutions that have regulatory competences in the respective field of application.

For the *national judiciary*, Knauff (2018) highlights country differences influenced by legal culture, noting that while French courts are increasingly recognizing soft law as a relevant policy tool subject to judicial oversight, German courts tend to ignore the practical significance of soft law in the public administration and refuse to acknowledge its justiciability. Legal scholars have already documented various instances of the Grimaldi obligation in practice. National courts have engaged with soft law in diverse ways: they have reviewed and annulled soft law, accepted legal arguments by litigants based on soft law and used soft instruments as an aid to interpret hard law (Georgieva, 2017b; Hartlapp & Hofmann, 2020; Korkea-aho, 2015; Kovács et al., 2016; Stefan, 2012; Xanthoulis, 2021).

Initial *quantitative evidence* focused on competition policy and finds increasing citations to soft law in both EU courts (Stefan, 2013) and national courts (Georgieva, 2017b), particularly when such instruments are linked to hard law. Comparative case studies suggest more judicial usage in common law countries and technical policy fields (Eliantonio et al., 2021). Despite these important contributions, the findings remain fragmented and limited to a few policy areas, such as competition policy. This book aims to systematize these fragmented findings by mapping broader patterns of soft law usage across different countries and policy areas, while also considering various forms of the judicial usage of soft law.

To explain these patterns of the use of soft law, this book draws on the *Judicial Politics* literature. Studies on judicial behavior explain how and why judges apply the law. Legal scholars have long emphasized the role of legal constraints, while political scientists emphasize actor-centered variables, such as strategic considerations or attitudes of judges (Segal & Spaeth, 2002). While there is so far no research on the use of soft law in judicial decision-making, scholars have actively studied judicial behavior in EU and member states' courts more broadly. Dyevre (2010, p. 315) notes that in the European context, attitudes, strategy, and institutions are intertwined and different theoretical explanations may prove relevant in specific institutional contexts. Empirical studies focused on judicial dialogue between national courts and the CJEU (Belov, 2019; Claassen, 2021; Dyevre et al., 2020; Golub, 1996; Leijon, 2021; Mayoral, 2019; Pavone & Kelemen, 2019; Sweet & Brunell, 1998; Tridimas & Tridimas, 2004). In this context, scholars have put forward legal, institutional, and actor-centered explanations for judicial behavior of national judges (Alter, 1998; Golub, 1996; Leijon, 2020; Nowak et al., 2011). This literature explains what happens in the courtroom, emphasizing that judicial behavior of courts applying EU instruments is influenced by multiple interrelated factors rather than a single factor. We can adapt this literature to formulate expectations about why judges use soft law. Apart from the activity of judges, the context of judicial decisions influences judicial usage. The *mobilization of law* determines which cases end up in court and thus pre-structures constellations where soft law may be relevant in the first place (Cichowski, 2007; Kelemen, 2011). In the aftermath of judicial decisions, the effect of judgments on policy depends on *reactions to case law* by the addressees. A lively debate focuses on Member States' legislative reactions to CJEU case law. Some scholars see stronger judicial influence on legislation (Schmidt, 2018) than others (Conant, 2002; Martinsen, 2015). In contrast, we know little about the effects of the decentralized review of EU law by national courts on policy, and even less about the impact of the judicial use of soft law. To fill this gap, this book examines the entire policy process, from the legal mobilization of soft law by societal actors to its broader impact on policy outcomes.

But beyond understanding the judicial use of soft law, it is crucial to examine its broader *implications for politics and law* of the EU multilevel system. This book contributes to three broader debates. First, on the evolving *nature of the EU legislative framework*. Scholars have found that the legislative output of hard law is declining (Toshkov, 2019), while soft law is increasingly adopted (Cappellina et al., 2022). This can be interpreted as a trend towards a new form of governance that relies on soft tools in the political arena rather than hard law. However, if soft law 'hits hard' through judicial review in the Member States, this part of the EU's legal output may also be more binding in practice than previously thought. The judicial use of soft law may actually strengthen the binding force of the legal framework, which would imply that a decrease in hard law does not necessarily lead to less legal coercion. In turn, a formal 'softening' of the legal framework would then not necessarily imply a decline of hierarchical governance.

Second, this book contributes to debates on the *role of national courts*. As societies and legal systems become increasingly differentiated, the role of courts is also evolving—and soft law may play a part in this transformation. This raises the question of the conditions under which courts function as agents of 'traditional hierarchical' governance or those under which they adopt new 'deliberative forms' of adjudication (Scott & Sturm, 2007, p. 7). Soft law can be enforced like hard law, or it can be discussed in judgments in a more informative way, leading to learning, sharing of best practice, and exchange of views. There are two related visions of the role of national courts in the EU legal order. In one, national courts are a subordinate extension of the CJEU in a *system of European courts* that have the task of maintaining the harmonious interpretation of EU law (Jaeger, 2013). In the competing vision of *interpretative pluralism*, national courts deliberate and exchange over competing interpretations of EU law (Davies, 2018). National courts' use of soft law can increase or minimize divergence between European and national jurisprudence, depending on whether and which soft instruments they take seriously.

Third, this book contributes to debates on the democratic *legitimacy of EU policy-making*. Soft law has little or no input legitimacy (Dawson, 2009; Petropoulou Ionescu & Eliantonio, 2020; Senden, 2004, p. 68). While the process of adopting soft law sometimes involves consultation of stakeholders or inter-institutional exchanges, it does not involve formal voting rights associated with legislative process leading to the adoption of legislative acts. Therefore, some scholars suggest that soft law can be a symptom of democratically deficient modes of policy-making, such as technocratic (van't Klooster, 2022, p. 774) or crisis politics (Eliantonio & Stefan, 2021), which displaces deliberation and legislative processes. The use of soft law by courts may further widen this accountability gap—at least in cases where courts use soft law in 'harder' ways, as they can increase the effects of soft law or open up the possibility of judicial review of such instruments in the future. Moreover, courts are non-majoritarian institutions with weak democratic legitimacy to shape public policy. When courts use soft law adopted outside formal legislative procedures, democratic decision-making therefore risks being bypassed both during the formulation and the judicial application of such instruments. However, one could also make the counter-argument that the involvement of courts increases democratic accountability because the judiciary is a forum accessible to non-state actors who are usually excluded from policy-making, and that the judiciary is better suited to protecting individual rights and dealing with complexity than legislative processes (Cichowski & Sweet, 2003, pp. 30–31).

1.4 How to Study the Judicial Use of EU Soft Law?

Studying the judicial use of soft law is challenging, as it is an elusive phenomenon that involves informal practices and often concerns highly technical legal and policy issues. Moreover, jurisprudence is not uniform but depends on legal issues and the facts of the case. Finally, judges often decide in non-transparent procedures without publicly documenting the decision-making process. To meet these challenges, this book takes a systematic comparative approach to study the phenomenon across time, countries, and policy areas. Its main focus is on two representative and relevant countries and two policy fields. The main period of observation is 2002 to 2022. The findings on these countries and policy areas are extrapolated through an exploration of wider practices of the 28 EU Member States, including the UK, from 1975 to 2019. Specifically, the book adopts a mixed method approach to pursue three aims (Fig. 1.1). First, it systematically maps *patterns* of the judicial usage of EU soft law using two original datasets of judgments and an original survey of 70 judges from German and French courts. Second, it investigates the *reasons* behind judicial usage of soft law by testing institutional and actor-centered factors with the help of the judgment and survey data. Third, it traces the *mechanisms* that drive judicial usage of soft law and explores its broader *effects* on law and policy based on interviews and detailed analysis of judgment texts.

To pursue these aims, the book is structured as follows. Chapter 2 defines key concepts, conceptualizes the judicial use of soft law as a dependent variable and formulates theoretically derived expectations. It first argues for a fine-grained conceptualization of the phenomenon, distinguishing 'softer' from 'harder' forms of soft law use. It then proposes to conceive of courts as rational actors embedded in distinct institutions. From this perspective, actor-centered and institutional factors are proposed to explain the judicial use of soft law.

Fig. 1.1 Three aims of the book

Chapter 3 outlines the empirical approach. Germany and France are selected as the main country cases, alongside the policy areas of state aid and pharmaceutical regulation. These cases were chosen as soft law usage is likely in each, yet they differ in relevant comparative dimensions. The chapter then outlines the book's mixed-methods approach, which consists of three steps: mapping patterns, explaining variation, and uncovering mechanisms and effects. It also introduces the data sources underpinning the analysis: two original judgment databases, survey data, and expert interviews.

Chapter 4, the first of three empirical chapters, maps patterns of the judicial use of soft law based on manually coded judgment data and survey data. It finds that national courts use EU soft law infrequently but increasingly. When they do, soft law is often relevant to the judgment, serving as an interpretation aid or as a supplementary standard of review with legal effects or even indirect binding force. Finally, the chapter points to country and policy variation.

Chapter 5 tests the theoretically derived explanations on the basis of the judgment and survey data. The analysis relies on descriptive statistics to map co-variation between the use of soft law by courts and various factors (e.g., policy area, court type, judges' attitudes), supported by qualitative insights. It finds that institutional factors predict more frequent and 'harder' forms of courts' use of soft law, in particular a country's legal style and the characteristics of the administrative judiciary. Actor-centered factors are not irrelevant but have less explanatory power.

Chapter 6 presents four case studies focusing on typical strings of judgments in German courts. These case studies trace the use of soft law in state aid and pharmaceutical regulation and reveal mechanisms and effects that complement the quantitative findings of previous chapters. In the area of state aid, the EU's exclusive regulatory competence influences the courts' use of soft law. In the area of pharmaceutical regulation, however, the entanglement between the national and EU administrations ('composite administration') affects courts' approach to soft law. The case studies also highlight the significant wider effects of this phenomenon on the role of the state in economic policy and the level of risk regulation in pharmaceutical regulation.

The *conclusion* summarizes the findings and characterizes the judicial use of soft law as a relatively rare but increasingly relevant phenomenon for the judiciary and the wider administrative space. In practice, soft law is not so soft after all. The chapter goes on to emphasize the book's contributions to the recognition of courts' use of soft law as an important aspect of the growing complexity of EU law. It demonstrates the important role of national courts at all levels and in all judicial branches in EU integration, beyond the well-researched preliminary ruling procedure. Finally, it highlights the interaction between judicial decision-making and governance structures. The chapter suggests that the judicial use of soft law is part of a wider transformation of law and the role of the judiciary and is therefore likely there to stay.

References

Abbott, K. O. W., Keohane, R., Moravcsik, A., Slaughter, A.-M., & Snidal, D. (2000). The concept of legalization. *International Organization, 54*(3), 401–419.

Alter, K. (1998). *Explaining National Court acceptance of European Court Jurisprudendence: A critical evaluation of theories of legal integration* (pp. 225–250).

Aust, A. (2010). *Handbook of international law*. Cambridge University Press.

Banet, C. (2020). Legal status and legal effects of the commission's state aid guidelines: The case of the guidelines on state aid for Environmental Protection and Energy (EEAG) (2014–2020). *European State Aid Law Quarterly, 172*.

Belov, M. (2019). *Judicial dialogue*. Eleven International Publishing.

Bérut, C. (2021). The European Union as an opportunity: Structures and uses of European soft law in French, Austrian and Irish eHealth policies. *West European Politics, 44*(1), 155–175.

Borrás, S., & Jacobsson, K. (2004). The open method of co-ordination and new governance patterns in the EU. *Journal of European Public Policy, 11*(2), 185–208.

Bouchagiar, A. (2017). The binding effects of guidelines on the compatibility of state aid: How hard is the commission's soft law? *Journal of European Competition Law & Practice, 8*(3), 157–166.

Büthe, T., Djeffal, C., Lütge, C., Maasen, S., & Ingersleben-Seip, N. v. (2022). Governing AI–attempting to herd cats? Introduction to the special issue on the Governance of Artificial Intelligence. *Journal of European Public Policy, 29*(11), 1721–1752.

Caporaso, J. A., & Wittenbrinck, J. (2006). The new modes of governance and political authority in Europe. *Journal of European Public Policy, 13*(4), 471–480.

Cappelletti, M., Seccombe, M., & Weiler, J. H. (1986). *Integration through law, Volume 1: Methods, tools and institutions, Book 1: A political, legal and economic overview*. De Gruyter.

Cappellina, B., Ausfelder, A., Eick, A., Mespoulet, R., Hartlapp, M., Saurugger, S., & Terpan, F. (2022). Ever more soft law? A dataset to compare binding and non-binding EU law across policy areas and over time (2004–2019). *European Union Politics, 23*(4), 741–757.

Chamon, M. (2014). The empowerment of agencies under the Meroni doctrine and article 114 Tfeu: Comment on United Kingdom v. Parliament and Council (short-selling) and the proposed single resolution mechanism. *European Law Review, 39*(3), 380–403.

Cichowski, R. (2007). *The European court and civil society: Litigation, mobilization and governance*. Cambridge University Press.

Cichowski, R., & Sweet, A. S. (2003). Participation, representative democracy, and the courts. In R. J. D. Bruce, E. Cain, & S. E. Scarrow (Eds.), *Democracy transformed? Expanding political opportunities in advanced industrial democracies, comparative politics*. Oxford Academic.

Claassen, J. (2021). Assessing the strategic use of the EU preliminary ruling procedure by national courts. In B. Baade, T. Kleinlein, A. Zimmermann, & A. L. Paulus (Eds.), *Cynical international law?* (Beiträge zum ausländischen öffentlichen Recht und Völkerrecht, Vol. 296, pp. 241–262). Springer.

Conant, L. (2002). *Justice contained: Law and politics in the European Union*. Cornell University Press.

Copeland, P., & ter Haar, B. (2013). A toothless bite? The effectiveness of the European Employment Strategy as a governance tool. *Journal of European Social Policy, 23*(1), 21–36.

Craig, P., & De Búrca, G. (2021). *The evolution of EU law*. Oxford University Press.

Davies, G. (2018). Does the Court of Justice own the Treaties? Interpretative pluralism as a solution to over-constitutionalisation. *European Law Journal, 24*(6), 358–375.

Dawson, M. (2009). Soft law and the rule of law in the European Union: Revision or redundancy? *EUI Working Paper RSCAS, Florence* (24).

Dura, S. (2024). The European Pillar of social rights: How strategic agency shaped the European Union's flagship social initiative. *Social Policy & Administration, 58*(4), 554–567.

Dyevre, A. (2010). Unifying the field of comparative judicial politics: Towards a general theory of judicial behaviour. *European Political Science Review, 2*(2), 297–327.

Dyevre, A., Glavina, M., & Atanasova, A. (2020). Who refers most? Institutional incentives and judicial participation in the preliminary ruling system. *Journal of European Public Policy, 27*(6), 912–930.

Egeberg, M., & Trondal, J. (2017). Researching European Union agencies: What have we learnt (and where do we go from here)? *JCMS: Journal of Common Market Studies*, *55*(4), 675–690.

Eleftheriadis, P. (1996). The direct effect of community law: Conceptual issues. *Yearbook of European Law, 16*(1), 205.

Eliantonio, M., Korkea-aho, E., & Stefan, O. (2021). *EU soft law in the member states: Theoretical findings and empirical evidence*. Bloomsbury Publishing.

Eliantonio, M., & Stefan, O. (2021). The elusive legitimacy of EU soft law: An analysis of consultation and participation in the process of adopting COVID-19 soft law in the EU. *European Journal of Risk Regulation, 12*(1), 159–175.

Georgieva, Z. (2017a). Competition soft law in French and German courts. *Maastricht Journal of European and Comparative Law, 24*(2), 175–193.

Georgieva, Z. (2017b). *Soft law in EU competition law and its reception in member states' courts* (PhD Thesis). Tilburg University.

Golub, J. (1996). The politics of judicial discretion: Rethinking the interaction between national courts and the European court of justice. *West European Politics, 19*(2), 360–385.

Guzman, A. T., & Meyer, T. L. (2010). International soft law. *Journal of Legal Analysis, 2*(1), 171–225.

Hartlapp, M. (2005). *Die Kontrolle der nationalen Rechtsdurchsetzung durch die Europäische Kommission. Politik – Verbände – Recht: Die Umsetzung europäischer Sozialpolitik, Band 3*. Campus Verlag.

Hartlapp, M., & Hofmann, A. (2020). The use of EU soft law by national courts and bureaucrats: How relation to hard law and policy maturity matter. *West European Politics*, *44*(1), 134–154.

Hartlapp, M., Saurugger, S., & Terpan, F. (2020). Conceptualising the use of soft law in the multilevel system [Conference paper]. *ECPR General Conference*.

Hartlapp, M., & Korkea-Aho, E. (2021). Whatever-law and teenage member states?: The national reception of EU Soft Law and how to study it. In M. Eliantonio, E. Korkea-aho, & O. Stefan (Eds.), *EU soft law in the member states: Theoretical findings and empirical evidence* (1st ed., pp. 57–76). Hart Publishing.

Heritier, A. (2002). *New modes of governance in Europe: Policy-making without legislating?* (IHS Working Paper 81).

Hofmann, A. (2021). Types of EU Soft Law and their national impact. In M. Eliantonio, E. Korkea-aho, & O. Stefan (Eds.), *EU Soft Law in the member states : Theoretical findings and empirical evidence* (1st ed., pp. 39–56). Hart Publishing.

Hurka, S., Haag, M., & Kaplaner, C. (2021). Policy complexity in the European Union, 1993–today: Introducing the EUPLEX dataset. *Journal of European Public Policy, 29*(9), 1–16.

Jacquot, S., & Woll, C. (2003). Usage of European integration-Europeanisation from a sociological perspective. *European integration online papers (EIoP)*, *7*(12).

Jaeger, T. (2013). *System einer Europäischen Gerichtsbarkeit für Immaterialgüterrechte: Grundlagen-Struktur-Verfahren*. Springer-Verlag.

Jiménez, L. A., & de Santiago, J. M. R. (2020). European and domestic soft law within spanish administrative law. *Cátedra Jean Monnet. Derecho Administrativo Europeo y Global, Preprints series of the Center for European Studies Luis Ortega Álvarez and the Jean Monnet Chair of European Administrative Law in Global Perspective*, *2*(20).

Kelemen, R. D. (2011). *Eurolegalism: The transformation of law and regulation in the European Union*. Harvard University Press.

Klabbers, J. (1998). The undesirability of Soft Law. *Nordic Journal of International Law*, *67*(4), 381–391.

Klabbers, J. (2023). Soft authority in global governance. In *Research handbook on Soft Law* (pp. 162–176). Edward Elgar Publishing.

Knauff, M. (2018). Soft Law vor Gericht. *juris – Die Monatszeitschrift (jM)*, 71–75.

Korkea-aho, E. (2015). *Adjudicating new governance: Deliberative democracy in the European Union*. Routledge.

Korkea-aho, E. (2018). National courts and European Soft Law: Is Grimaldi still good law? *Yearbook of European Law*, *37*, 470–495.

Kovács, A., Tóth, T., & Forgács, A. (2016). The legal effects of European Soft Law and their recognition at National Administrative courts. *ELTE LJ*, 53.

Kröger, S. (2009). The open method of coordination: Underconceptualisation, overdetermination, de-politicisation and beyond. *European Integration online Papers (EIoP), Special Issue* (1).

Leijon, K. (2020). Active or Passive: The National Judges' Expression of Opinions in the Preliminary Reference Procedure. *European Papers*, *5*(2), 871–886.

Leijon, K. (2021). National courts and preliminary references: Supporting legal integration, protecting national autonomy or balancing conflicting demands? *West European Politics*, *44*(3), 510–530.

Lenaerts, K., Van Nuffel, P., & Corthaut, T. (2021). *EU constitutional law*. Oxford University Press.

Leszczyński, L. (2020). Extra-legal values in judicial interpretation of law: A model reasoning and few examples. *International Journal for the Semiotics of Law-Revue internationale de Sémiotique Juridique*, *33*(4), 1073–1087.

Maher, I. (1994). National courts as European Community courts. *Legal Studies*, *14*, 226.

Maher, I. (2021). Revisiting Soft Law : Governance, regulation and networks. In M. Eliantonio, E. Korkea-aho, & O. Stefan (Eds.), *EU Soft Law in the member states : Theoretical findings and empirical evidence* (1st ed., pp. 21–38). Hart Publishing.

Martinico, G., & Pollicino, O. (2012). *The interaction between Europe's legal systems: Judicial dialogue and the creation of supranational laws*. Edward Elgar Publishing.

Martinsen, D. (2015). *An ever more powerful court? The political constraints of legal integration in the European Union*. Oxford University Press.

Mayoral, J. A. (2019). Judicial empowerment expanded: Political determinants of national courts' cooperation with the CJEU. *European Law Journal, 25*(4), 374–393.

Nowak, T., Amtenbrink, F., Hertogh, M. L. M., & Wissink, M. H. (2011). *National Judges as European Union Judges: Knowledge, experiences and attitudes of lower court judges in Germany and the Netherlands*. Eleven International Publishing.

Pavone, T., & Kelemen, R. D. (2019). The evolving judicial politics of European Integration: The European Court of Justice and national courts revisited. *European Law Journal, 25*(4), 352–373.

Petropoulou Ionescu, D., & Eliantonio, M. (2020). Democratic legitimacy and soft law in the EU legal order: A theoretical perspective. *Journal of Contemporary European Research, 17*(1), 43–65.

Pollack, M. A. (1994). Creeping competence: The expanding agenda of the European Community. *Journal of Public Policy, 14*(2), 95–145.

Radaelli, C. M. (2008). Europeanization, policy learning, and new modes of governance. *Journal of Comparative Policy Analysis, 10*(3), 239–254.

Rasmussen, M. (2014). Revolutionizing European law: A history of the Van Gend en Loos judgment. *International Journal of Constitutional Law, 12*(1), 136–163.

Regent, S. (2003). The open method of coordination: A new supranational form of governance? *European Law Journal, 9*(2), 190–214.

Sabel, C. F., & Zeitlin, J. (2010). *Experimentalist governance in the European Union: Towards a new architecture*. Oxford University Press.

Saurugger, S., & Terpan, F. (2015). Studying resistance to EU norms in foreign and security policy. *European Foreign Affairs Review, 2*(1), 1–20.

Saurugger, S., & Terpan, F. (2020). Normative transformations in the European Union: On hardening and softening law. *West European Politics*, 1–20.

Schade, F., & Flyverbom, M. (2023). Soft law governance in the field of AI: A European perspective. In *Research handbook on soft law* (pp. 423–437). Edward Elgar Publishing.

Schmidt, S. K. (2018). *The European Court of justice and the Policy Process: The Shadow of Case Law*. Oxford University Press.

Scott, J. (2011). In legal limbo: Post-legislative guidance as a challenge for European administrative law. *Common Market Law Review*, 329–355.

Scott, J., & Sturm, S. (2007). Courts as catalysts: Rethinking the judicial role in new governance. *Columbia Journal of European Law, 13,* 565–594.

Segal, J. A., & Spaeth, H. J. (2002). *The Supreme Court and the attitudinal model revisited* (1. publ. ed.). Cambridge University Press.

Senden, L. A. J. (2004). *Soft law in European Community law*. Hart Publishing.

Snyder, F. (1994). Soft Law and institutional practice in the European Community. In S. Martin (Ed.), *The construction of Europe: Essays in honour of Emile Noël* (pp. 197–225). Kluwer Academic Publishers.

Stefan, O. (2012). European Union soft law: New developments concerning the divide between legally binding force and legal effects. *Modern Law Review, 75*(5), 879–893.

Stefan, O. (2013). *Soft Law in court: competition law, state aid and the court of justice of the European Union*. Kluwer Law International.

Sweet, A. S., & Brunell, T. L. (1998). The European Court and the national courts: A statistical analysis of preliminary references, 1961–95. *Journal of European Public Policy, 5*(1), 66–97.

Terpan, F. (2015). Soft Law in the European Union—The changing nature of EU Law. *European Law Journal, 21*(1), 68–96.

Tholoniat, L. (2010). The career of the open method of coordination: Lessons from a 'soft' EU instrument. *West European Politics, 33*(1), 93–117.

Toshkov, D. (2019). *Data on EU legislative acts extracted from EUR-Lex, 2004–2019.*

Treib, O. (2014). Implementing and complying with EU governance outputs. *Living Reviews in European Governance, 9*(1).

Tridimas, G., & Tridimas, T. (2004). National courts and the European Court of Justice: A public choice analysis of the preliminary reference procedure. *International Review of Law and Economics, 24*(2), 125–145.

Trubek, D. M., Cottrell, M. P., & Nance, M. (2005). *'Soft Law', 'Hard Law,' and European Integration: Toward a theory of hybridity*. University of Wisconsin Legal Studies Research Paper (1002).

Trubek, D. M., & Trubek, L. G. (2005). The open method of coordination and the debate over "hard" and "soft" law. In J. Zeitlin, P. Pochet, & L. Magnusson (Eds.), *The open method of co-ordination in action. The European employment and social inclusion strategies* (pp. 83–103). Peter Lang.

Van Dam, C. (2017). Guidance documents of the European Commission: A typology to trace the effects in the national legal order. *Review of European Administrative Law, 10*(2), 75–91.

Van Wolleghem, P. G. (2017). Why implement without a Tangible threat? The effect of a soft instrument on National Migrant Integration Policies. *JCMS: Journal of Common Market Studies*, *55*(5), 1127–1143.

VAN'T Klooster, J. (2022). Technocratic Keynesianism: A paradigm shift without legislative change. *New Political Economy*, *27*(5), 771–787.

von Bogdandy, A., Arndt, F., & Bast, J. (2004). Legal Instruments in European Union Law and their reform: A systematic approach on an empirical basis. *Yearbook of European Law, 23*(1), 91–136.
Wessel, R. A. (2015). Resisting legal facts: Are CFSP norms as soft as they seem? *European Foreign Affairs Review, 20*, 123–145.
Wind, M. (2016). Do Scandinavians care about international law? A study of Scandinavian judges' citation practice to international law and courts. *Nordic Journal of International Law, 85*(4), 281–302.
Xanthoulis, N. (2021). Legal effects and reviewability of EU acts: between institutional intentions and perceptions of concerned parties. In *EU Soft Law in the member states: Theoretical findings and empirical evidence*. Hart Publishing.
Zeitlin, J. (2005). Conclusion: The open method of co-ordination in action: Theoretical promise, empirical realities, reform strategy. In J. Zeitlin & P. Pochet (Eds.), *The open method of co-ordination in action: The European employment and social inclusion strategies* (Work & society, No. 49, pp. 447–503). Peter Lang.
Zeitlin, J., Pochet, P., & Magnusson, L. (Eds.). (2005). *The open method of co-ordination in action*. Peter Lang.
Zhelyazkova, A., Haverland, M., & Joosen, R. (2023). Legislating softly: The effect of preference heterogeneity on the share of EU soft-law instruments over time. *European Union Politics, 24*(3), 447–469.

CHAPTER 2

The Analytical Framework: Understanding Soft Law and National Courts

In its most basic form, the *concept of soft law* is simple: it refers to instruments that lack legal binding force and are therefore not hard law. Yet, they are not merely political documents entirely disconnected from the legal order. However, this minimal definition raises further questions: What justifies the concept of soft law as an intermediate category between law and non-law? What specific characteristics must an instrument have to be considered soft law? Similarly, the *judicial use of soft law* is easy to conceptualize in its most basic form. Courts can consult or refer to soft law in their actions, for example, as background information when preparing a judgment or in the reasoning of a judgment when presenting an argument. But how does this differ from instances in which courts invoke hard law or purely non-legal documents? Furthermore, what types of soft law usage are possible?

In order to address these questions, we need more nuanced concepts. This chapter introduces an analytical framework that is guided by the book's main objectives and is designed to systematically study the judicial use of EU soft law. The first objective is to describe how courts use soft law, which necessitates conceptualizing the behavior of courts and their environment. The second objective treats the judicial use of soft law as a dependent variable and examines competing explanations, which requires explanations guided by theory. The third objective shifts the focus to the

A. Eick, *Soft Law and National Courts in the European Union*, European Administrative Governance,
https://doi.org/10.1007/978-3-032-04515-7_2

judicial use of soft law as an independent variable in order to assess its broader effects on law and policy, which requires conceptualizing such effects. The next section of the chapter outlines the fundamental perspective of the book: the judicial use of soft law is viewed as part of a broader EU multilevel governance process. Within this process, courts are conceptualized as collective actors operating within specific institutional contexts. The chapter then proceeds to define soft law and its judicial usage, as well as the different types thereof. Finally, drawing on literature on Europeanization and Judicial Politics, the chapter proposes factors that explain judicial use of soft law.

2.1 Analytical Framework

2.1.1 *The Judicial Usage of Soft Law in EU Multilevel Governance*

The judicial usage of EU soft law in national courts can be understood as part of a broader process of EU multilevel governance. At the EU level, soft law is adopted by various actors through diverse processes. Once adopted, national actors in the administrative, political, and civil society arena may pick up these instruments. If conflicts arise, courts can become involved and may use soft law in their judgments, which can have wider legal and policy effects in some cases. This book focuses primarily on the judicial stage, examining how national courts use soft law. However, this stage cannot be analyzed in isolation, as it is influenced by earlier adoption and uptake of soft law by national actors and has consequences for subsequent legal and policy developments.

We can describe the process of soft law usage in three stages (Hartlapp et al., 2020): First, at the EU level, soft law is adopted by diverse actors, including the European Commission (Cini, 2001), EU agencies (Chiti, 2013), the Council (De Witte, 2018), the European Parliament (Webb & Kreppel, 2021) or networks involving national authorities or private actors (Eberlein, 2003). Thus, EU soft law can originate from multiple 'branches' of the EU system. This includes instruments from the legislative branch, such as European Parliament (EP) resolutions, and those shaped in intergovernmental processes involving Member State representatives in the Council or in transnational networks of national actors. Nonetheless, most EU soft law is produced by actors of the executive, particularly the Commission, but also EU agencies (Cappellina et al., 2022, p. 13). Relatedly, processes of soft law adoption can vary widely, from informal procedures involving a few actors to more formalized procedures involving multiple actors through inter-institutional coordination and consultation (Eliantonio & Stefan, 2021; Petropoulou Ionescu & Eliantonio, 2021). Commission *Staff Working Documents*[1] are an example of the former, as they are often informally drafted and adopted by one or a few services of the European Commission. Guidelines in competition policy are an example of the latter, as they are drafted by the Directorate-General (DG) for Competition in consultation with other DGs and then circulated to Member States and stakeholders for several formalized rounds of consultation and revision before a final version is published.[2] But even in the latter case, soft law adoption processes fundamentally differ from hard law adoption. Hard law is typically adopted in highly formalized and binding legislative procedures, leading in most cases to more democratic and inclusive decision-making processes. While not uniform, legislative processes involve deliberation and clear voting rights leading to participation and veto points. This is best exemplified by the Ordinary Legislative Procedure (OLP), which is the standard EU legislative procedure. To strongly simplify, the OLP involves drafting, parliamentary debate, consultation with committees and third parties and—most importantly—formal voting in the Council and EP. In this process, actors have clear formalized powers, which define specific veto powers: Typically, the Commission can propose legislation, while the EP and Council vote under Qualified Majority Voting (QMV) rules (Dionigi & Rasmussen, 2019). In contrast, soft law is usually adopted through processes that are less formalized, less inclusive, and do not involve formal voting. Although the adoption of soft law in some areas may involve a certain degree of formalization with structured inter-institutional coordination and consultations, it never rises to the level of legislative procedures (Eliantonio & Stefan, 2021; Gribnau, 2007; Ionescu, 2021; Stefan, 2020). Thus, EU soft law is created by diverse actors through various procedures, but adoption by the executive and less formal procedures dominates. These procedures typically lack the

[1] Staff Working Documents are considered soft law only when they are openly published and at least partially intended to address third parties. When such documents are purely internal to the European Commission for internal coordination, they do not qualify as soft law.

[2] See European Commission. Competition Policy. Public Consultations. https //competition-policy.ec.europa.eu/public-consultations_en, last accessed 10 July 2025.

legitimacy of legislative acts. How soft law is adopted at EU level thus influences nature of the instrument, which may become relevant later in national courts.

Second, at the *national level*, actors from the state and society may ignore soft law or use it in various ways, for example, by incorporating it into their rhetoric, by transposing it into national soft or hard law, or by adapting administrative practices (Falkner et al., 2005; Hartlapp & Korkea-Aho, 2021; López-Santana, 2006). How soft law is used at the national level is essential for understanding its effect on the ground—whether in administrative practice, policy-making and ultimately policy outcomes. This, in turn, is important to assess its legitimacy. Soft law's lack of input legitimacy becomes only meaningful if the soft law actually has effects on the ground, and it is less of a problem if national actors ignore or reject soft law. Moreover, how national actors use EU soft law also determines whether it is effective at delivering public goods and solving problems at the national level, i.e. its output legitimacy. However, output legitimacy cannot replace input legitimacy as they operate at different levels. While output legitimacy concerns the effectiveness and quality of policy outcomes, input legitimacy relates to democratic processes, participation, and representation in political decision-making (Scharpf, 1999, p. 11). But if soft law solves problems at the national level and thus has strong output legitimacy, national actors may still perceive it in a positive light, even if it's adoption was not transparent. Finally, conflicts can arise if national administrations use EU soft law in their practices and decisions. These conflicts can then turn into judicial cases involving EU soft law, which brings us to the national judiciary.

Third, the *national judiciary* is a partially distinct part of the national policy process. National courts share some similarities with other actors, as they are embedded in the same institutions and have some discretion in how and which instruments they apply. Moreover, courts are not fully removed from politicization and political decision-making (for an overview, see Dyevre, 2010). However, courts differ in important ways from other actors: they are independent in their decision-making and only bound by the law. And they are also passive actors—dependent on societal actors to initiate cases and on public authorities to enforce their rulings (Volcansek, 2019, p. 72). Because of these characteristics, the way in which soft law makes its way into national courts differs to other actors' use of soft law. EU soft law can either reach national courts directly from the EU level, when courts themselves invoke soft law in ongoing cases.

Alternatively, national actors from the administration or wider society may invoke soft law in court when they are parties to a case. However, this results only in judicial use if the court engages with these arguments and incorporates them into its reasoning or judgment. Similarly, the way in which courts can use soft law is partly different from administrations. They may use soft law informally in their deliberations without explicitly citing it in the judgment, or they may refer to it directly in their judgment. Once a judgment has been issued, it is binding. One might argue that, in some instances, when a court incorporates a soft law instrument into a binding ruling, the instrument itself effectively becomes binding (Snyder, 1994, p. 22). This would constitute a 'hardening' of soft law (Saurugger & Terpan, 2020). As argued in Chapter 1, such cases can raise questions about legitimacy and institutional balance. However, these cases are likely exceptional. Courts can use soft law in less intrusive ways, often together with binding legal sources (Stefan, 2013, pp. 152–155). For example, when a court uses soft law merely to support an argument based on hard law, this highlights its value as a useful interpretative aid, but it does not make it legally binding.

Finally, the effects of judgments involving soft law are then felt by the parties to the case in the concrete dispute, but they may also have wider effects on certain types of actors who are in a similar position to the parties to the case, on policy, when judgments influence administrative behavior or policy programs, or on law, when judgments contribute to doctrine and the established interpretation of the law. Thus, this book situates the judicial use of EU soft law within a wider sequence of EU multilevel governance that spans multiple levels. Courts do not operate in isolation but interact with other actors at the EU- and national level. But how do courts come to their decisions? The next section clarifies the book's perspective on courts as actors and their institutional context.

2.1.2 *The Importance of Actors and Institutions*

The book views courts as actors that interact with other actors within a set of institutional constraints. Doctrinal legal studies often take the constraints of law on courts very seriously but are less interested in extra-legal issues (Hutchinson & Duncan, 2012). In contrast, Empirical Legal Studies and the Judicial Politics literature often emphasize interactions of courts with other actors, informal institutions, and the agency of courts (Davies, 2020; Volcansek, 2019). The following framework brings these elements together. To do so, it draws on *Actor-Centered Institutionalism (ACI)* (Mayntz & Scharpf, 1995; Scharpf, 2000), which emphasizes the role of actors and their surrounding institutions. Following this approach, we can conceive of courts as 'corporate actors' which, despite internal differences, have a high capacity for collective and cohesive action (Scharpf, 2000, pp. 105–107). While individual judges can have their own preferences and intra-court conflict is in principle possible, judges share a common education and role and courts have effective internal coordination mechanisms, as they typically decide together as a chamber or senate (Ramos, 2002, pp. 10–11). This perspective differs from those studies of judicial behavior that focus on the decisions of individual judges (Segal & Spaeth, 2002).

Moreover, ACI leads us to expect that actors act strategically to maximize their utility. However, this is not to say that their actions will always be individualistic, and preferences are not limited to institutional self-interest. Sometimes social roles, identity, and orientations towards other actors come into play. Moreover, rationality is bounded and depends on the actor's perception of reality and knowledge (Scharpf, 2000, pp. 107–120). Courts then act in part strategically and cannot always be considered as purely neutral arbiters of the law. Specifically, they may seek institutional empowerment (Alter, 1998) or policy (Segal & Spaeth, 2002). But they are different from other actors as their social rules and modes of interaction are geared towards upholding the rule of law and delivering justice (Gillman, 2001). Courts are therefore more likely to adhere to formal legal rules and weigh the benefits and costs for other actors, rather than purely pursuing institutional or strategic self-interest through their judgments.

When a problem involves several actors, ACI emphasizes their *interaction* and lines of conflict (Scharpf, 2000, pp. 123–160). Social conflicts that originate in society and politics become relevant in the judiciary. On the one hand, judicial decision-making is mostly a hierarchical relationship, where a court gives a judgment to others, and it has the full competence to do so. On the other hand, courts depend on other actors to bring cases and to comply with their decisions and may therefore be to some extent responsive to their arguments and preferences (Garrett et al., 1998). Finally, ACI argues that actors are integrated into *institutions* that enable or constrain their actions (Scharpf, 2000, pp. 229–247). Courts are particularly affected by formal institutions, such as legal systems or rules of access to justice, but also by informal institutions, such as the norms of a particular legal culture and legal style. Taken together, this book views courts as corporate actors that are embedded in informal and formal institutions and that interact with national actors from the state and wider society.

We can also view courts' use of soft law through this lens. Typically, studies of policy-making and judicial decision-making study hard law processes (for an overview, see Treib, 2015, pp. 291–297). But actors, interactions and institutions may slightly differ due to the non-binding nature of soft law. In terms of *actor preferences*, some actors in the administration and wider society may expect benefits from soft law. It may offer opportunities for deliberation, or it may simply reduce the costs of non-compliance compared to hard law (Sabel & Zeitlin, 2010). In contrast, other actors may prefer hard law if they think soft law offers too little legal certainty and predictability (Terpan, 2015, p. 92). The benefits and costs of soft law for courts are less obvious. Drawing on soft law may enable courts to go into more detail in their legal argumentation and demonstrate the persuasiveness of their legal arguments (Scott & Sturm, 2007). Or, on the contrary, courts may have an interest in only applying hard law and ignoring soft law to ensure a harmonious interpretation of EU legislation or to defend the core of national constitutions against encroachment by EU law (Bobek, 2008). However, these are just general examples. The benefits and costs of soft law for courts depend very much on the specific case.

The *constellation of actors* involved in soft law processes may differ from those in hard law regulation. Some actors push for regulation through hard law but oppose or disregard soft law as they deem it as too weak or inconsequential. Others may engage only in soft law processes, for example, in soft governance frameworks like the *Open Method of Coordination*. For the judiciary, this means that certain social conflicts are less likely to reach the courts when they revolve around soft law rather than hard law. At the same time, soft law may give rise to a distinct set of disputes, for example if soft law establishes an administrative practice or suggests a certain legal interpretation that is not wholly apparent from hard law.

The *institutional context* for soft law also differs in some respects from that for hard law. At the EU level, soft law is adopted through more informal procedures, bypassing the formal decision-making rules that apply to hard law (Eliantonio & Stefan, 2021). At the national level, there are no or fewer formal obligations. Sometimes, national actors are required to report on their use of soft law or must 'comply or explain,' i.e. justify if they have disregarded soft law (Cappellina et al., 2022, pp. 9–12). However, these requirements are much weaker than the implementation and compliance duties associated with hard law. Finally, the binding nature of hard law itself is a powerful institution that constrains and enables actors. Hard law structures judicial decisions and lends authority to rulings. By contrast, soft law lacks these characteristics or has them to a lesser degree, shaping judicial behavior differently. These differences mean that conceptualizations and explanations associated with hard law must be adapted to reflect the distinct actor constellations and institutional context of soft law.

2.2 Key Concepts

2.2.1 Conceptualizing Soft Law

Now that the book's basic perspective on courts and their institutional context has been clarified, we can turn to the key concepts. First, the object of study—soft law. Then, the dependent variables—the usage of soft law and in particular its judicial use. This is followed by a conceptualization of the independent variables—factors that may explain when and why courts use soft law.

Perspectives on the Law. This book adopts a binary distinction between hard law and all other instruments—soft law and non-law—in line with the general approach of courts. At the same time, it treats variation within the soft law category as a continuum ranging from 'softer' to 'harder' forms. Before elaborating on this two-step approach, the section first clarifies the basic perspectives from which the phenomenon can be approached in the literature. Drawing on an often-cited distinction by H.L.A. Hart, we can distinguish between two broad analytical perspectives on the law: the internal and the external perspectives (Hart, 2012 [1961]; Goldmann, 2012). The *internal perspective* accepts norms as adopted and describes their content and systematic position within the legal system (Shapiro, 2006). Doctrinal legal analysis, for example, adopts this perspective, as it involves the systematic examination and interpretation of legal texts. This perspective also aligns with the traditional role of courts, which primarily approach the law from this standpoint, although they can go beyond it in their reasoning. Specifically, courts must identify the applicable binding legal norms and act in accordance with the law.

The German *Grundgesetz* states in Article 20 Paragraph 3 that "courts are bound by law and legislation." As this book examines how courts use soft law, the internal perspective is a suitable starting point for defining hard law and how it differs from soft law.

In contrast, an *external perspective* views the law from the outside. For example, sociological theories of the law consider actors' perceptions of legal instruments and their practical effects. A less practice-oriented version of this approach analyzes legal texts in terms of their intended or likely effects, rather than studying effects on the ground. In particular, the regulation literature and empirical legal studies often anticipate effects of instruments based on their content (Goldmann, 2012, p. 351). Such an approach can also become relevant in the argumentation of courts in a second or supplementary step, for example when examining the legislative intent of a law. As this book is also concerned with the anticipated effects of soft law, an external perspective is useful to inform a more nuanced concept that can capture differences within the variety of soft law. The following conceptualization thus draws from both the internal and external perspectives.

Demarcating Hard Law. The term 'soft law' already presupposes that such instruments can be meaningfully distinguished from 'hard law'—which is normally just called 'law.' So, what is hard law? One may argue that an external view of the law could suggest all kinds of ambiguities and complexities to this question. Thereafter, law is not a natural given, and legal theory has long debated the underpinnings of law—whether it is grounded in morality, political power, or socially constructed norms (Potacs, 2019, pp. 29–48). Sociological perspectives may find vastly different effects of instruments depending on their use on the ground. But, as argued above, this is not how courts approach hard law on a basic level, so we can set aside these debates at this point. Instead, an internal perspective is more pertinent for the research questions of this book to demarcate hard law in line with the general approach of courts. This perspective suggests a clear, binary criterion: hard law is defined by its formal *legal binding force*, which is codified within national or supranational legal orders (Guzman & Meyer, 2010, p. 174). Constitutions (or other fundamental sources of law) determine which instruments have formal binding force. They typically list the main components of a legal order, establish them as legally binding and place them in a legal hierarchy of laws, both nationally (Mayer-Maly & Mayer-Maly, 1993) and internationally (Shelton, 2006). In the EU, the Member States have established a legal hierarchy of binding legal acts in the Treaties, which has been further clarified by the CJEU. Thereafter, the Treaties are the primary sources of EU law (Article 1(2) TFEU). Over the course of European integration, the Treaties have assumed 'quasi-constitutional' status, meaning they are functionally equivalent to constitutional provisions and recognized by all Member States as sources of the European legal order (Weiler, 1991). They define Regulations, Directives and Decisions as binding secondary law (Article 288 TFEU). Further, Delegated and Implementing Acts are non-legislative acts with a more limited scope, but also with legal binding force (Articles 290–291 TFEU). According to Article 19(1) of the Treaty on European Union (TEU), the CJEU is responsible for safeguarding and enforcing binding EU law (Bobek, 2015), and national courts are required to apply such law based on Article 4(3) TEU and CJEU case law (Prechal, 2006, p. 429). Following this systematic framework, EU hard law refers to instruments that are formally recognized as legally binding within the legal order. For example, when the legislator selects a Directive as the legal form of an act, it can be assumed that the legislator intended to make the instrument binding (Láncos & Jiménez, 2023, p. 4).

Justifying the Concept of 'Soft Law'. Why do we even need a separate category of soft law? In contrast to hard law, soft law is an academic and fully artificial concept to capture norms that are neither non-law nor hard law. Courts themselves often don't use the term when referring to such instruments. Some legal positivists reject the term soft law altogether, insisting that acts are either law or not law, and an in-between category is superfluous (Klabbers, 1998, pp. 385–387; Weil, 1983, p. 424). In their view, legal normativity cannot be gradual. If there is any ambiguity, the courts could step in and declare an act to be either hard law or no law (Klabbers, 1998, p. 382). Other authors propose alternative concepts to soft law. Some use wider concepts like 'soft governance' (Lawn, 2006), 'informal governance' or 'alternative instruments' (Goldmann, 2015), while others use narrower ones to capture a narrow set of instruments, like 'tertiary law' (Sydow, 2012, pp. 150–160) or 'post-legislative guidance' (Scott, 2011). But against these criticisms and alternatives, this book sees soft law as a meaningful analytical category due to the distinct role of such instruments in the legal system: they can be conceptualized as having qualities in-between law and non-law. Of those authors who write about soft law, some emphasize its 'law-like' qualities—characteristics of hard law but in weaker form (Abbott & Snidal, 2000, pp. 422–423). Others stress its unique non-legal qualities that stipulate learning, discourses and policy experimentation (Börzel et al., 2005, p. 6; Zeitlin, 2005). But for all of them, soft law exceeds purely declaratory or symbolic instruments in terms of its normative relevance, but it does not rise up to that of hard law (Guzman & Meyer, 2010, pp. 171–175; Terpan, 2015, pp. 70–72). This 'in-between status' makes the concept relevant to study how courts approach this particular set of instruments, as it connects to the central puzzle—why and how do courts use instruments that are not disconnected from the legal order, but also not hard law.

Perspectives on Soft Law. Recognizing that soft law is in-between non-law and law still requires one to define it in positive terms. There is no single, universally accepted definition of soft law and conceptualizations strongly depend on the general view on the law (Goldmann, 2012; Terpan, 2023). Rather than developing a general theory, the following develops a working definition that is specifically tailored to the EU legal order and the book's research questions. It draws on both the *internal* and *external* perspectives on law, and strands of the soft law literature that align with these perspectives, respectively.

For the internal perspective, as mentioned above, the decisive criterion to demarcate hard law is the instrument's formal legal binding force. Below hard law, soft law is then described as encompassing those non-binding instruments that have the potential for certain normative effects. This binary approach is also dominant in EU law, where Francis Snyder defines soft law as "rules of conduct which are not in principle legally binding, but which may nevertheless have practical and legal effects" (Senden, 2004, p. 219; Snyder, 1994, p. 2). Thereafter, instruments such as Regulations and Directives can never be classified as soft law, because they have formal binding status. This has the advantage of making it analytically clear to identify hard law—which is what this book draws from this approach. The drawback is that it captures little variation within the diversity of non-binding acts and says little about the qualities inherent in soft law. To capture this variation, we can incorporate insights from the external perspective.

Because external views of the law consider how instruments (potentially) operate in practice (Goldmann, 2012, p. 532), they place less value on legal binding force as a single decisive criterion to categorize law, and rather examine multiple dimensions of norms, and they often see legal normativity not as a binary, but as something more fluid. Most notable in this regard is the *legalization* literature, which conceptualized law as a continuum ranging from non-law to hard law. These approaches define norms in terms of multiple dimensions, which can take softer and harder forms. Abbott et al. (2000) identify three dimensions of this continuum: obligation (actors are bound by a rule), precision (rules clearly specify required or prohibited conduct), and delegation (authority granted to third parties to interpret, implement, and enforce rules, and possibly make new ones). Terpan simplifies this conceptualization and considers the "existence of an obligation," and "the way the obligation is enforced" (2015, p. 73). This allows one to conceptualize differences between non-law and soft law, and a more nuanced description of the qualities of soft law. It assumes that there are softer and harder forms of soft law. But as Goldmann (2012, p. 353) notes, this risks blurring the core legal distinction between what is binding and what is not—a central distinction for courts. Thus, this book takes from the internal perspective the clear demarcation of hard law based on legal binding force but adopts from the external view the idea of multiple dimensions that describe the nature of different types of soft law.

Definition of Soft Law. Based on these discussions, this book takes a two-step approach to defining soft law. First, *hard law* is distinguished from other instruments based on the *formal legal binding force*. It encompasses formally binding instruments as defined by the Treaties and CJEU case law. Instruments falling outside this category are either soft law or non-law.

Second, to distinguish soft law from non-law and to capture the variation within soft law instruments positively, I draw on and slightly adapt the dimensions suggested by Hartlapp and Hofmann (2020), Terpan (2023) and Ausfelder et al. (2024), who identify formalization and enforceability as central characteristics of hard law that can also appear, to a lesser degree, in non-binding instruments.

Formalization refers to the degree to which legal rules are codified, obligatory, and written in mandatory language. But outside of hard law, formalization can never include formal legal binding force. This dimension essentially captures how much instruments 'look like law' in some way.

Enforceability refers to the mechanisms that ensure compliance (Terpan, 2015, p. 76). The term is used in a broad sense refers not only to legal enforcement by courts or enforcement authorities, but also to reporting mechanisms, 'comply-or-explain' duties, or 'naming-and-shaming' practices that can be found in non-binding instruments (Ausfelder et al., 2024). Mapping instruments onto those two dimensions allows us to place them on a continuum of graduated normativity while maintaining a clear distinction between soft law and hard law. Soft law can take softer and harder forms without overlapping with hard law.

To identify the lower border between non-law and soft law, we need clear indicators for formalization and enforceability, which can take softer and harder forms. Table 2.1 provides an overview. Indicators for formalization refer to the content (clear list of rules, precision), wording (language), and form (place of publication). Indicators for enforceability are enforcement mechanisms, such as comply-or-explain duties, reporting duties, or a threat of sanctions. Instruments can also establish enforcement capacities, for example, when a responsible enforcement authority is designated. Taken together, this book defines soft law as instruments which are *formalized and enforceable, but not formally binding*.

Table 2.2 further details the possible combinations of the dimensions, sorted from non-law to hard law. Instruments with *no formalization* and *no enforceability* are merely non-law. For example, a purely political speech, such as the EU State of the Union address by the President of the European Commission may set expectations or provide direction, but it has neither a law-like form nor any concrete mechanism of follow-up and is therefore classified as non-law. Similarly, instruments with some degree of (soft) *enforceability* but *no formalization* are non-law. For example, Eurostat frequently requests Member States to provide data on certain issues. But these requests are not formalized in a codified and publicly accessible format. They are thus typically rather informal means of information requests rather than formalized instruments. Non-law can also be *formalized* but have *no enforceability*. Many Commission Staff Working

Table 2.1 Dimensions and indicators of soft law

Formalization	*Enforceability*
• Clear list of rules • Precision of rules • Obligations or prescriptions—either in voluntary or imperative language • Publication (e.g. in the Official Journal)	• Specification of enforcement mechanism • Specification of enforcement capacities

Table 2.2 Combinations of formalization, enforceability, and legal binding force

Formalization	*Enforceability*	*Binding Force*	*Type of instrument*
None	None	None	Non-law
None	Yes	None	Non-law
Yes	None	None	Non-law
Yes	Yes	None	Soft law
None	Yes	Binding	Hard law
Yes	None	Binding	Hard law
Yes	Yes	Binding	Hard law

Documents (SWD) accompany initiatives by the Commission, such as legislative proposals. They typically follow a clear structure and include detailed technical information and recommendations. But they are non-law, as they typically do not contain any enforcement mechanisms—even of a soft variant.

Soft law, as argued above, refers to instruments that are *formalized and enforceable, but not formally binding*. They are often called Guidelines, Recommendations, Communications, Notices, Conclusions, Declarations, Opinions, and Resolutions.[3] Such instruments are to some degree formalized—using voluntary or even mandatory language and being published in law-like formats, while also relying on, at least soft, enforcement mechanisms such as reporting duties or 'comply-or-explain' mechanisms. They are thereby likely to produce practical and even legal effects (Láncos & Jiménez, 2023). Within the soft law category, they can take 'softer' and 'harder' forms, depending on their degree of formalization and enforceability. A softer example, close to non-law, is Commission Communications in the field of eHealth in the 2000s, which called on Member States to prepare national eHealth roadmaps and introduced only minimal reporting duties (Bérut, 2021, pp. 161–162). A harder example, close to hard law, is the *2022 Strengthened Code of Practice on Disinformation* which regulates how online platforms must counter the spread of disinformation. Although formally non-binding, it contains precise and mandatory obligations, includes monitoring and

[3] These are typical labels of soft law instruments. But classifying an instrument as soft law requires case-by-case analysis.

comply-or-explain duties and is linked to binding provisions of the Digital Services Act so that non-compliance can, in some cases, indirectly lead to fines or even service suspension (Panahi & de Bittencourt Siqueira, 2024).

Finally, hard law is defined by its *formal binding force*. The normal form of hard law is instruments with legal binding force that are fully formalized and enforceable by courts. As mentioned, these are Regulations, Directives, Decisions, and Delegated or Implementing Acts.

There are exceptions, where norms have formal legal binding force, but do not fully fulfill the other dimensions. These are still hard law, as they are recognized in a formal legal sense as such. *General Principles of EU law* have been recognized as being legally binding and enforceable by the CJEU, despite them not being codified (no full formalization). Moreover, there are formally binding provisions that are not always enforced in practice. Terpan (2015) mentions joint actions in the Common Foreign and Security Policy (CFSP) that, although formally binding, are not under review by the CJEU in practice. Falkner et al. (2005), on the other hand, study individual provisions phrased in voluntary language within social policy Directives. But as these instruments still have formal binding force, which courts recognize, they are still classified as *hard law* due to their formal binding status.[4]

For the remainder of this book, this classification allows us to define the population of soft law instruments considered in the empirical analysis and to distinguish softer from harder forms of soft law.

2.2.2 Judicial Usage of Soft Law

In the introduction, I argued that studying citations to soft law in judgments is insufficient, as they reveal little about how courts engage with soft law or its relevance to a case. Following Hartlapp and Hofmann (2020), I therefore instead conceptualize the *usage* of soft law. The concept of usage is drawn from Jacquot and Woll and "emphasizes the role of actors in the concrete translation of these effects [of European

[4] Note that Terpan (2015, 2023) and Falkner et al. (2005) classify such provisions as soft law due to their soft practical effects. The working definition in this book, however, does not follow this rationale, as its analytical focus is on the approach of courts. This does not dispute that a classification as soft law can be meaningful in broader perspectives and effects-based classifications.

Integration] and the motives of action that can be identified" (2003, p. 2). Based on this broad concept, I propose a modified and narrower framework tailored to courts.

I argue that the *judicial usage of soft law* has two dimensions that capture the central elements of the phenomenon: *application* relates to the empirical manifestation in judgments and *recognition* to the subjective evaluations and of judges or the communication of such evaluations. The terms are borrowed from the literature on hard law. Legal scholars and practitioners often speak of the *application of EU hard law*. Weber's dictionary of law emphasizes that application is about the transfer of legal acts to an individual case, that is, to the given facts of the case (Werner, 2022). In EU law, the term is also common. In *Freiburger Kommunalbauten*,[5] the CJEU states that a duty of national courts is the "application of these general criteria [of EU hard law] to a particular term, which must be considered in the light of the particular circumstances of the case" (para. 22). Beyond that, the CJEU formulated several further ways in which national courts must apply EU law (Bobek, 2008). The term is also salient in debates about the rule of law and democratic backsliding, when talking about the non-application or wrongful application of EU law (Lazowski, 2011). Schmidt-Räntsch (2006, pp. 705–706) summarizes that the application of EU (hard) law in national courts pertains to whether a law fits the individual case, how the individual case can be subsumed under the law, and whether the requirements of the individual case are met.

EU legal scholars speak of the *recognition of EU hard law* to describe the acceptance of the status and effects of EU law. Court can recognize or ignore effects of the law. Historical debates revolved especially around the recognition of supreme and direct effect of EU hard law (Kumm & Comella, 2005, pp. 483–491; Thym, 2009, p. 1807). I extend these terms to EU soft law and operationalize them based on a systematic reading of the secondary literature on soft law in EU courts (Georgieva, 2017; Knauff, 2018; Snyder, 1994; Stefan, 2012; Xanthoulis, 2021). The dimensions and indicators of judicial usage are constructed with the aim of describing relevant characteristics and capturing the largest possible variation of judicial usage (Collier et al., 2012, p. 218). They

[5] Judgment of the Court (Fifth Chamber) of 1 April 2004. *Freiburger Kommunalbauten*. Case 237/02 [2004] ECR I-3403. Para 22.

are nevertheless not exhaustive but left open for later empirical-guided refinement.

Judicial usage can then be defined as the decisions made by courts to engage with soft law, recognize its legal effects, and apply those instruments (Table 2.3). Similar categories but with a slightly different focus and terminology were proposed by Xanthoulis (2021). First, we can assess the frequency of usage by counting instances of both usage and non-usage. Second, we can differentiate between types of usage. I conceptualize the judicial usage of soft law in two dimensions, application and recognition, each ranging from softer to harder forms. These dimensions were defined theoretically and further refined through empirical analysis.

The first dimension of usage captures ways in which judges *apply* soft law, which refers to the function of soft law in the legal argument and the role of soft law within the judgment at large. In other words, to what purpose courts codify soft law in a judgment. Judges can apply soft law as a source of extra-legal knowledge, if they, for example, draw technical facts from it or when soft law is relevant as a fact to a case. They can also use it as an aid to interpret EU or national hard law. This is the case when courts cite soft law to justify a certain legal interpretation or if they discuss legal interpretations that are suggested by soft law in their reasoning. Courts can also use soft law as a supplementary standard of review alongside hard law. This occurs when courts apply criteria from soft law to evaluate the facts of a case or the lawfulness of an action. In theory, soft law could serve as the primary standard of review, where the main criteria applied by the court to assess facts or determine the lawfulness of an action are those

Table 2.3 Dimensions of the judicial usage of soft law

Dimensions	*Recognition of soft law by judges*	*Application of soft law in judgments*
Soft	Practical effects	Extra-legal information
Medium	Non-binding legal effects	Aid to interpret hard law; Supplementary standard of review (*obiter dictum*)
Hard	Indirect binding force; Direct binding force	Main standard of review (*ratio decidendi*); Object of a proceeding (judicial review)

laid down in a soft law instrument. Finally, if a court reviews the legality of a soft law instrument, it becomes the main object of a proceeding.

The second dimension of usage is the degree to which judges *recognize* soft law as a legitimate instrument of governance or act of law. We can assess their recognition by the extent to which they recognize practical and legal effects of such instruments. Judges can disregard effects of soft law if they ignore it or explicitly reject the possibility of any effects. Courts may also recognize practical effects for the administration when they mention that soft law affects actors on the ground but does not derive legal implications from it. Further, courts may recognize non-binding legal effects of soft law, for example if they argue that soft law provides an authoritative but non-binding interpretation of hard law. Courts can also recognize an indirect binding force of soft law, when they argue that soft law is de facto binding on certain actors and in certain situations due to its close association to hard law. Finally, although it is unlikely in practice, courts may recognize a direct binding force of soft law in the same way as they do for hard law.

The resulting variable, *judicial usage of soft law* can take softer and harder forms for both the recognition and application dimensions, i.e. courts recognize or apply soft law in ways that range from resembling hard law to being more like non-law. *Soft usage* refers to instances where courts recognize or apply soft law purely for practical or extra-legal purposes. *Medium usage* (or 'medium hard') occurs when soft law is legally relevant in one dimension but remains non-binding. Finally, *hard usage* describes situations where soft law is recognized or applied almost or exactly like hard law. This includes cases where courts treat soft law as 'de facto' binding in combination with hard law, even if they acknowledge that soft law is not formally binding on its own and independent of hard law. Hard usage also encompasses cases where courts treat soft law exactly like hard law, granting it direct binding force. However, due to the non-binding nature of soft law, such cases expected to be rare or non-existent. Of course, *no usage* is also possible if courts disregard soft law altogether. It is important to note that the dimensions represent ideal types, as courts do not always explicitly or clearly reveal how they recognize or apply soft law. Therefore, when analyzing judicial usage of soft law, one sometimes needs to infer the recognition and application of soft law indirectly based on the courts' legal reasoning and the context of the judgment.

The differences between types of judicial soft law usage are best illustrated through concrete examples. First, in the area of pharmaceutical regulation by the German apex administrative court *Bundesverwaltungsgericht* from 08 December 2016 exemplifies *soft usage*.[6] The court reviewed a decision by a national medicines agency concerning the authorization of a medicine and refers to the EU soft law instrument *Notice to Applicants* as source of information. However, it dismisses a legal relevance of the instrument and states that "the Notice to Applicants, as practical application notes, cannot prevail against EU law, which the Senate considers to be clear." This constitutes soft recognition, as the court acknowledges the instrument only as having practical effects, but no legal relevance.

Second, ***medium usage*** is illustrated by judgment of 31 January 2018 by the German higher administrative court *OVG Nordrhein-Westfalen*.[7] This is a dispute between a medicines manufacturer and the national pharmaceutical authority over when the so-called document protection for a certain medicine expires. The legal question is which authorization procedure applies for this specific medicine. The court draws a conclusion by interpreting EU hard law. But it cites EU soft law to reinforce its interpretation, arguing that the soft law shares the same interpretation of hard law as the court. This constitutes medium application, where soft law is used as an aid to interpret binding law. The court also engages in medium recognition by stating that the soft law instrument in question is "legally non-binding," but has "interpretative legal relevance" (para. 42).

Third, a judgment by the French *Conseil d'État* from 26 July 2018 in a state aid case illustrates ***hard recognition*** of soft law. The court reviews whether the European Commission properly applied its own soft law criteria in an enforcement decision concerning French energy subsidies.

The court finds that "the European Commission, contrary to what the applicants maintain, examined compliance with the transparency obligations imposed on the Member States by points 104 to 106 of its guidelines." It concludes that "(...) this scheme (...) was compatible with the internal market, the European Commission did not infringe point 127 of the Guidelines on State aid for environmental protection and energy for the period 2014–2020, (...)."[8] In the concrete case, the soft law

[6] BVerwG, 3 C 9/16 (3 C 18/14), 08 December 2016, para. 7.

[7] Oberverwaltungsgericht Nordrhein-Westfalen, judgment of 31 January 2018–13 B 1092/17, para 42.

[8] Conseil d'État, N° 411919, 26 July 2018, para. 7.

was applied only to support the argumentation in one of several legal questions (medium application). But the court recognizes an indirect binding force of the Guidelines (hard recognition) by stating that national schemes must comply with them, that the Commission enforces them, and that the Commission must apply the guidelines correctly during its binding enforcement.

2.3 Independent Variables: Factors for the Judicial Usage of Soft Law

2.3.1 Institutional Factors

What factors explain how and why courts use soft law? Legal scholars and literature on EU Judicial Politics discuss the reasons why courts use certain instruments, such as the reasons why national judges refer to EU law (Alter, 2000; De Witte et al., 2016). However, the non-binding nature of soft law requires adapting these theoretical explanations and expectations. Based on the above general framework, which emphasizes the importance of actors and their institutional context, I draw on various strands of literature to define how institutional factors, such as legal and bureaucratic constraints, as well as the characteristics of judges and courts, may affect the use of soft law.

Courts cannot decide in a vacuum. Their behavior is likely to be affected by formal and informal institutions. Depending on the underlying mechanism, they can either affect the frequency or type of usage, or both. Doctrinal legal studies and 'legalist' explanations in the Judicial Politics literature emphasizes the impact of *the law* on the decisions of judges. Law can constrain and enable action. Either in the form of individual instruments, precedential case law, and the wider setup of the legal order (e.g. Gillman, 2001). At the level of *instruments*, actors may perceive certain soft law instruments as particularly authoritative due to their nature. Legal scholars highlight the status of EU hard law (Dougan, 2007). It is directly applicable and can thus create enforceable rights and obligations for third parties, it holds primacy over national law, and it must be observed by national courts when interpreting national law (Claes, 2006). National courts must apply and enforce EU hard law. Soft law is of course non-binding, but the CJEU has ascribed to it a more and more authoritative status over the years. The CJEU also developed a doctrine for the judicial use of EU soft law, but a more modest one whereby a national court should take soft law into account (Korkea-aho, 2018). But this formulation is vague, and the practical implications depend on whether judges perceive EU soft law as a legal constraint. If they do, they should attribute to soft law *legal authority* and derive obligations from it. For example, an obligation to discuss a legal interpretation that is laid down in soft law or to take notice of it. On the other hand, if they don't think soft law is legally authoritative, they will ignore it.

We can also modify this hypothesis and focus on the *legal authority of the author of soft law*. In the EU legal system, Member States have delegated certain legislative and enforcement powers to EU institutions. The European Commission, for instance, is deemed to be the main formal 'agenda-setter' (Pollack, 1997) and the 'guardian of the treaties' (Börzel, 2003). One can imagine that courts use soft law because they attribute to the author of soft law an authoritative legal position. Thereafter, national courts use EU soft law because the author of EU soft law has legal authority.

Moreover, the wider *legal environment* of soft law may be relevant. Soft law is often not adopted in isolation, but rather as post-legislative guidance to explain the content, implementation process, or practical implications of hard law (Scott, 2011). If soft law is connected to hard law, the authority of hard law may spill over onto soft law. Thereby, soft law may be integrated into the formal legal order, creating a hybrid legal regime (Trubek et al., 2005). I thus expect that national courts use EU soft law if it is connected to EU hard law. This means that courts are more likely to use certain types of soft law. Senden (2004) proposes three such types, which have no relationship or a closer relationship to hard law. First, *steering instruments*, like Council Conclusions, are "measures of an encouraging nature" that "steer or guide action" (ibid. 156). They are typically not connected to hard law (ibid.). Thus, judicial usage should be less likely and softer for steering instruments. In contrast, interpretative and decisional instruments follow up on hard law and are closely tied to them. *Interpretative instruments*, such as Commission communications, are "supporting and supplementing (…) [EU] law, in particular to ensuring the proper interpretation and—uniform—application thereof" (Senden, 2004, pp. 138–147). *Decisional instruments*, like competition and state aid guidelines, are similar to interpretative instruments, but they perform a slightly different function in that they "indicate in what way a [EU] institution will apply [EU] law provisions in individual cases when it has implementing and discretionary powers" (ibid. 119). Because they are to specify enforcement competences of the EU they can "impose concrete obligations on the Member State." (ibid. 431). Therefore, I expect that usage is even harder for decisional than for interpretative instruments.

Further, institutions may influence the usage of soft law at the level of specific *policy areas*. In areas of higher EU competence, the EU holds regulatory and enforcement powers. This means that EU institutions can increase the costs of non-compliance. They can in some cases indirectly enforce soft law if it is connected to hard law. Moreover, they can adopt hard law when regulation by soft law fails. This may cast a 'shadow of the hierarchy' over non-binding instruments (Héritier & Lehmkuhl, 2008, p. 2). Additionally, the CJEU has the last word on jurisdiction in areas with more EU competences. Thus, national courts can be expected to use EU soft law more frequently and harder in areas of high EU competence. Following Börzel (2005), I define the level of EU competence by the extent of EU rule-making powers (level of EU authority) and the number of substantive issues in a policy area covered by EU law (scope of EU authority). Note that this conceptualization of competences incorporates but goes beyond the formal legal allocation of EU competences (exclusive, shared, and supporting competences), as it also takes into account the scope of EU law.

The literature on the compliance with EU hard law has identified considerable *country* variation (Falkner et al., 2005) and scholars of comparative law describe stark contrasts between the laws and courts of EU Member States (Zweigert & Kötz, 1996). *Legal cultures* influence the decisions of courts. For example, Marlene Wind (2010) identifies a reluctance to apply EU law in the courts of the Nordic EU Member States. She argues that this has to do with a particular national understanding of the legal system in a democracy and of the relationship between the government and the judiciary (ibid. 1045–1047). With regards to soft law, the legal culture towards such instruments may play a role. French highest courts are more open to legal reflection on the status of soft law than German courts (Benezech, 2020; Knauff, 2018; Rubio & Stefan, 2021). For example, the *Conseil d'État* has deliberated on the status of soft law in its annual study of 2013 (Conseil d'État, 2013) and tackled the issue head-on in several judgments, deciding that certain national soft law instruments are justiciable (Benezech, 2020). We should expect that usage is more likely in countries with a legal culture that is receptive to soft law.

Another potentially relevant factor is the *legal style* of a judiciary in a country. French judgments are typically short and leave little room to apply soft law (Rubio & Stefan, 2021, p. 137; Steiner, 2018, p. 139). German judgments, on the other hand, contain extensive legal reasoning and are much longer (Weber, 2019, pp. 2–3), leaving more room to develop arguments that draw on diverse sources including non-binding instruments. Harder uses of soft law should also be more common, as they require a substantive engagement with soft law. In contrast to the expectation based on legal culture, an argument focusing on the legal style of judgments expects German courts to use EU soft law more and in harder ways than French courts.

Moreover, factors related to the *judiciary* may affect the judicial usage of soft law. At the national level, soft law and the idea of a gradual normativity is especially prevalent in the *administrative judicial branch*. In Germany there are uncountable *Rechtsverordnungen* and in France *circulaires*, which are national instruments similar to soft law (Schmidt-Aßmann & Dagron, 2007, p. 401). We can thus expect that administrative courts are used to soft law. Due to socialization effects, they should thus more likely use EU soft law. Further, EU soft law often addresses matters of administrative procedures and the conduct of public authorities (Jiménez & de Santiago, 2020). Thus, such instruments may be especially relevant in areas where wider societal actors make claims against public institutions over actions or decisions of administrations.

The *judiciary* may also have its unique institutions. Several empirical studies find that the national judges are affected by *bureaucratic constraints* when applying EU law (Jaremba, 2012, p. 220). In particular, Pavone (2022, p. 76) describes judges' "burdensome attempts to maintain some semblance of control over their workload." He argues that particularly in lower courts "workload pressures incentivize a short-term instrumental rationality" so that EU law is applied as superficially as possible. With regard to soft law, the direction of expectations is not entirely clear. On the one hand, EU soft law often adds to the complexity of EU law. It can raise new questions and create new obligations. Judges with a heavy workload may then ignore such instruments to reduce complexity. This would lead to the expectation that courts with a heavy workload are less likely to use EU soft law. Workload pressures are also more likely in the *lower courts*, where the majority of cases end up. The first judicial instance may not have the time and space to identify and follow the detailed rules set out in EU soft law instruments.

2.3.2 *Actor-Centered Factors*

However, courts may not always act as uniform actors. Thus, another set of factors relates to the characteristics of courts as corporate actors and judges as individual decision-makers, and can be described as actor-centered factors because they focus on the agency of individual actors.

Several factors profile of *judges* could matter: their policy preferences, knowledge, and career. The argument that judges' attitudes determine judicial decisions is prominent in the Anglo-American context. Regarding national courts in the EU, Nowak and Glavina (2020) argue that national judges are more or less receptive of EU law depending on, among other things, their personal *attitude towards the European Union*. Soft law usually serves to further European integration, if only in very minor ways. It pushes for action where no hard law exists, or it aims at fostering a harmonized application of hard law throughout the Union. If judges follow their preference, those with stronger 'pro-EU integration' attitudes may be more receptive to more frequently and harder uses of soft law. Those in favor of 'national subsidiarity' and national law may be less receptive to soft law. This argument leads to the expectation that judges with more positive attitudes towards the EU are more likely to use EU soft law.

Similarly, it has been argued that often EU law does not feature strongly in the curricula of law schools and that it is burdensome process for national judges to acquire the complex knowledge required to apply EU law (Nowak et al., 2011). This may be particularly true for soft law which is often specialized in substance and not uniformly published in the Official Journal. I hypothesize that judges with better *knowledge of EU law* are more likely to use EU soft law. Further, Hartlapp and Hofmann (2020) argue that national actors use EU soft law when they routinely apply EU law. This suggests a *seniority* effect. Judges who have been in the judiciary longer are more likely to have applied soft law in the past and to have gained experience with such instruments. Thus, as Table 2.4 summarizes, we have institutional and actor-centered explanations, which raise different expectations. Not each factor can be tested against each type of data. The empirical chapters specify which factors apply and how they are operationalized in that chapter.

Table 2.4 Overview of explanatory factors

Institutional factors	
Factor type:	*Specific factor:*
Law	**Instrument characteristics** • *Perception of instrument as legally authoritative* **Author characteristics** • *Perception of author as legally authoritative* **Legal environment** • *Connection to hard law. "Spill-over" of legal effect* • *Harder usage least likely for steering soft law and most likely for decisional soft law*
Policy	**Level of EU Competence** • *shadow of hierarchy in areas of high EU competence*
Country	**Legal culture** • *'Openness' towards soft law* **Legal style** • *Length of judgments*
Judiciary	**Court instance** • *Lower courts have higher workload than other instances* • *Higher courts have more time and discretion to reach decisions* **Judicial branch** • *Administrative courts are used to soft law (socialization)*
Actor-centered factors	
Judges	**Attitudes** • *Preference for more European integration* **Knowledge** • *Knowledge to identify and apply relevant soft law* **Seniority** • *Socialization into the EU system of courts*

References

Abbott, K. O. W., Keohane, R., Moravcsik, A., Slaughter, A.-M., & Snidal, D. (2000). The concept of legalization. *International Organization, 54*(3), 401–419.

Abbott, K. W., & Snidal, D. (2000). Hard and soft law in international governance. *International Organization, 54*(3), 421–456.

Alter, K. (1998). *Explaining National Court Acceptance of European Court Jurisprudence: A critical evaluation of theories of legal integration* (pp. 225–250).

Alter, K. (2000). The European Union's legal system and domestic policy: Spillover or backlash? *International Organization, 54*(3), 489.

Ausfelder, A., Eick, A., Hartlapp, M., Mespoulet, R., Saurugger, S., Terpan, F., & Cappellina, B. (2024). EU soft-law: Non-binding but enforceable. *European Law Journal, 30*(4), 668–684.

Benezech, L. (2020). L'affermissement de la justiciabilité des actes de droit souple devant le Conseil d'État. *Droit administratif* (2), p. 33.

Bérut, C. (2021). The European Union as an opportunity: Structures and uses of European soft law in French, Austrian and Irish eHealth policies. *West European Politics, 44*(1), 155–175.

Bobek, M. (2008). On the application of European Law in (not only) the courts of the new member states: 'Don't do as i say'? *Cambridge Yearbook of European Legal Studies, 10*, 1–34.

Bobek, M. (2015). The court of justice of the European union. In A. A. Damian Chalmers (Ed.), *The Oxford Handbook of EU Law* (pp. 153–177). Oxford University Press.

Börzel, T. (2003). Guarding the treaty: The compliance strategies of the European Commission. In R. C. Tanja Börzel (Ed.), *The state of the European Union* (Vol. 6, pp. 197–220).

Börzel, T. (2005). Mind the gap! European integration between level and scope. *Journal of European Public Policy, 12*(2), 217–236.

Börzel, T., Guttenbrunner, S., & Seper, S. (2005). Conceptualizing new modes of governance in EU enlargement. *New modes of governance project*.

Cappellina, B., Ausfelder, A., Eick, A., Mespoulet, R., Hartlapp, M., Saurugger, S., & Terpan, F. (2022). Ever more soft law? A dataset to compare binding and non-binding EU law across policy areas and over time (2004–2019). *European Union Politics, 23*(4), 741–757.

Chiti, E. (2013). European Agencies' rulemaking: Powers, procedures and assessment. *European Law Journal, 19*(1), 93–110.

Cini, M. (2001). The soft law approach: Commission rule-making in the EU's state aid regime. *Journal of European Public Policy, 8*(2), 192–207.

Claes, M. (2006). *The national courts' mandate in the European Constitution*. Bloomsbury Publishing.

Collier, D., LaPorte, J., & Seawright, J. (2012). Putting typologies to work: Concept formation, measurement, and analytic Rigor. *Political Research Quarterly, 65*(1), 217–232.

Conseil d'État. (2013). *Le droit souple* (Etude Anuelle, Issue 2013). https://www.conseil-etat.fr/publications-colloques/etudes/etudes-annuelles/le-droit-souple

Davies, G. (2020). The relationship between empirical legal studies and doctrinal legal research. *Erasmus Law Review, 20*.

De Witte, B. (2018). The place of the OMC in the system of EU competences and sources of law. *European Papers—A Journal on Law and Integration, 2018*(1), 207–213.

De Witte, B., Mayoral, J. A., Jaremba, U., Wind, M., & Podstawa, K. (2016). *National courts and EU law: New issues, theories and methods*. Edward Elgar Publishing.

Dionigi, M. K., & Rasmussen, A. (2019). The ordinary legislative procedure. In *Oxford Research Encyclopedia of Politics*.

Dougan, M. (2007). When worlds collide: Competing visions of the relationship between direct effect and supremacy. *Common Market Law Review*, *44*(4) 931–963.

Dyevre, A. (2010). Unifying the field of comparative judicial politics: Towards a general theory of judicial behaviour. *European Political Science Review*, *2*(2), 297–327.

Eberlein, B. (2003). Regulating cross-border trade by soft law? The "Florence Process" in the supranational governance of electricity markets. *Journal of Network Industries*, *4*(2), 137–155.

Eliantonio, M., & Stefan, O. (2021). The elusive legitimacy of EU soft law: An analysis of consultation and participation in the process of adopting COVID-19 soft law in the EU. *European Journal of Risk Regulation*, *12*(1), 159–175.

Falkner, G., Treib, O., Hartlapp, M., & Leiber, S. (2005). *Complying with Europe: EU harmonisation and soft law in the member states*. Cambridge University Press.

Garrett, G., Kelemen, R. D., & Schulz, H. (1998). The European Court of Justice, national governments, and legal integration in the European Union. *International Organization*, *52*(1), 149–176.

Georgieva, Z. (2017). *Soft law in EU competition law and its reception in member states' courts: An empirical study on national judicial attitudes to atypical legal instruments in EU competition law* (PhD Thesis). Tilburg University.

Gillman, H. (2001). What's law got to do with it? Judicial behavioralists test the "legal model" of judicial decision making. *Law & Social Inquiry*, *26*(2), 465–504.

Goldmann, M. (2012). We need to cut off the head of the king: Past, present, and future approaches to international soft law. *Leiden Journal of International Law*, *25*(2), 335–368.

Goldmann, M. (2015). *Internationale Öffentliche Gewalt: Handlungsformen internationaler Institutionen im Zeitalter der Globalisierung* (Vol. 251). Springer-Verlag.

Gribnau, H. (2007). Improving the legitimacy of Soft law in EU Tax law. *Intertax*, *35*, 30.

Guzman, A. T., & Meyer, T. L. (2010). International Soft Law. *Journal of Legal Analysis*, *2*(1), 171–225.

Hart, H. L. A. (2012). *The concept of law* (3rd ed.). Oxford University Press.

Hartlapp, M., & Hofmann, A. (2020). The use of EU soft law by national courts and bureaucrats: How relation to hard law and policy maturity matter. *West European Politics*, *44*(1), 1–21.

Hartlapp, M., & Korkea-Aho, E. (2021). Whatever-law and teenage member states?: The National Reception of EU Soft Law and how to study it. In M. Eliantonio, E. Korkea-aho, & O. tefan (Eds.), *EU Soft Law in the Member States: Theoretical Findings and Empirical Evidence* (1st ed., pp. 57–76). Hart Publishing.

Hartlapp, M., Saurugger, S., & Terpan, F. (2020). *Conceptualising the use of soft law in the multilevel system* [Conference paper]. ECPR General Conference 2020.

Héritier, A., & Lehmkuhl, D. (2008). The shadow of hierarchy and new modes of governance. *Journal of Public Policy, 28*(1), 1–17.

Hofmann, H. C. H. (2020). *General principles of EU law and EU administrative law*. In S. Peers & C. Barnard (Eds.), European Union Law. Oxford University Press.

Hutchinson, T., & Duncan, N. (2012). Defining and describing what we do: Doctrinal legal research. *Deakin Law Review, 17*, 83.

Ionescu, D. P. (2021). Habemus legitimacy? The European Commission opens public consultation for a guidance document. *European Journal of Risk Regulation, 12*(4), 861–865.

Jacquot, S., & Woll, C. (2003). Usage of European integration-Europeanisation from a sociological perspective. *European integration online papers (EIoP), 7*(12).

Jaremba, U. (2012). *Polish civil judges as European Union law judges: Knowledge, experiences and attitudes* (PhD Thesis). Rotterdam University.

Jiménez, L. A., & de Santiago, J. M. R. (2020). European and domestic soft law within spanish administrative law. *Cátedra Jean Monnet. Derecho Administrativo Europeo y Global, Preprints series of the Center for European Studies Luis Ortega Álvarez and the Jean Monnet Chair of European Administrative Law in Global Perspective* (2), 1.

Klabbers, J. (1998). The undesirability of Soft Law. *Nordic Journal of International Law, 67*(4), 381–391.

Kleine, M. (2018). Informal governance and legitimacy in EU politics. *Journal of European Integration, 40*(7), 873–888.

Knauff, M. (2018). Soft Law vor Gericht. *juris – Die Monatszeitschrift (jM), 2018*, 71–75.

Korkea-aho, E. (2018). National Courts and European Soft Law: Is Grimaldi still good law? *Yearbook of European Law, 37*, 470–495.

Kumm, M., & Comella, V. F. (2005). The primacy clause of the constitutional treaty and the future of constitutional conflict in the European Union. *International Journal of Constitutional Law, 3*(2–3), 473–492.

Láncos, P. L., & Jiménez, L. A. (2023). Introduction to the legal effects of EU Soft Law. In *The legal effects of EU Soft Law* (pp. 1–7). Edward Elgar Publishing.

Lawn, M. (2006). Soft governance and the learning spaces of Europe. *Comparative European Politics, 4*, 272–288.

Lazowski, A. (2011). Half full and half empty glass: The application of EU law in Poland. *Common Market Law Review*, 503–553.

Lenaerts, K., & Desomer, M. (2005). Towards a hierarchy of legal acts in the European Union? Simplification of legal instruments and procedures. *European Law Journal, 11*(6), 744–765.

López-Santana, M. (2006). The domestic implications of European soft law: Framing and transmitting change in employment policy. *Journal of European Public Policy, 13*(4), 481–499.

Mayer-Maly, T., & Mayer-Maly, T. (1993). Die Rechtsquellen. *Einführung in die Rechtswissenschaft*, 10–18.

Mayntz, R., & Scharpf, F. W. (1995). der Ansatz des akteurzentrierten Institutionalismus. In *Gesellschaftliche Selbstregelung und politische Steuerung* (pp. 39–72). Campus Verlag.

Nowak, T., Amtenbrink, F., Hertogh, M. L. M., & Wissink, M. H. (2011). *National Judges as European Union Judges: Knowledge, experiences and attitudes of Lower Court Judges in Germany and the Netherlands*. Eleven International Publishing.

Nowak, T., & Glavina, M. (2020). National courts as regulatory agencies and the application of EU law. *Journal of European Integration, 43*(6), 739–753.

Panahi, T., & de Bittencourt Siqueira, A. (2024). Soft law, hardcore?: Die rechtliche Durchsetzung von Verhaltenskodizes nach dem Digital Services Act. *VerfBlog*. https://verfassungsblog.de/soft-law-dsa-ko-regulierung/.

Pavone, T. (2022). *The Ghostwriters: Lawyers and the politics behind the Judicial Construction of Europe*. Cambridge University Press.

Petropoulou Ionescu, D., & Eliantonio, M. (2021). Democratic legitimacy and soft law in the EU legal order: A theoretical perspective. *Journal of Contemporary European Research, 17*(1), 43–65.

Pollack, M. A. (1997). Delegation, agency, and agenda setting in the European Community. *International Organization, 51*(1), 99–134.

Potacs, M. (2019). *Rechtstheorie*. UTB.

Prechal, S. (2006). National courts in EU judicial structures. *Yearbook of European Law, 25*(1), 429–450.

Radaelli, C. M., & Meuwese, A. C. (2010). Hard questions, hard solutions: Proceduralisation through impact assessment in the EU. *West European Politics, 33*(1), 136–153.

Ramos, F. (2002). Judicial cooperation in the European courts: testing three models of judicial behavior. *Global Jurist Frontiers, 2*(1).

Rubio, N., & Stefan, O. (2021). No longer small enough to fall through the cracks: A French story of adaptation to the petites sources of EU Law. In M. Eliantonio, E. Korkea-aho, & O. tefan (Eds.), *EU Soft Law in the member states: Theoretical findings and empirical evidence* (1st ed., pp. 135–150). Hart Publishing.

Sabel, C. F., & Zeitlin, J. (2010). *Experimentalist governance in the European Union: Towards a new architecture*. Oxford University Press.

Saurugger, S., & Terpan, F. (2020). Normative transformations in the European Union: On hardening and softening law. *West European Politics, 44*(1), 1–20.

Scharpf, F. W. (1999). *Governing in Europe: Effective and democratic?* Oxford University Press.

Scharpf, F. W. (2000). *Interaktionsformen: akteurzentrierter Institutionalismus in der Politikforschung* (1. Auflage 2000, Unveränderter Nachdruck der 1. Auflage Juni 2006 ed.). VS Verlag für Sozialwissenschaften.

Schmidt-Aßmann, E., & Dagron, S. (2007). Deutsches und französisches Verwaltungsrecht im Vergleich ihrer Ordnungsideen. *Zeitschrift für ausländisches öffentliches Recht und Völkerrecht*(67), 395–468.

Schmidt-Räntsch, J. (2006). § 23 Die Rechtsprechung des BGH. In R. Karl (Ed.), *Europäische Methodenlehre* (pp. 552–582). De Gruyter.

Scott, J. (2011). In legal limbo: Post-legislative guidance as a challenge for European administrative law. *Common Market Law Review*, 329–355.

Scott, J., & Sturm, S. (2007). Courts as Catalysts: Rethinking the Judicial Role in New Governance. *Columbia Journal of European Law, 13*.

Segal, J. A., & Spaeth, H. J. (2002). *The Supreme Court and the attitudinal model revisited* (1. publ. ed.). Cambridge University Press.

Senden, L. A. J. (2004). *Soft law in European Community law*. Hart Publishing.

Shapiro, S. J. (2006). What is the internal point of view. *Fordham Law Review, 75*, 1157.

Shelton, D. (2006). Normative hierarchy in international law. *American Journal of International Law, 100*(2), 291–323.

Snyder, F. (1994). Soft Law and Institutional Practice in the European Community. In S. Martin (Ed.), *The construction of Europe: Essays in honour of Emile Noël* (pp. 197–225). Kluwer Academic Publishers.

Stefan, O. (2012). Hybridity before the Court: A Hard Look at Soft Law in the EU Competition and State Aid Case Law. *European Law Review, 37*(1), 49–69.

Stefan, O. (2013). *Soft Law in Court: Competition Law, State Aid and the Court of Justice of the European Union*. Kluwer Law International.

Stefan, O. (2020). COVID-19 soft law: Voluminous, effective, legitimate? A research agenda. *European Papers—A Journal on Law and Integration, 2020*(1), 663–670.

Steiner, E. (2018). *French law: A comparative approach* (2nd ed.). Oxford University Press.

Sydow, G. (2012). Europäische exekutive Rechtsetzung zwischen Kommission, Komitologieausschüssen, Parlament und Rat. *JuristenZeitung*, 157–165.

Terpan, F. (2015). Soft Law in the European Union-The Changing Nature of EU Law. *European Law Journal, 21*(1), 68–96.

Terpan, F. (2023). The definition of soft law. In *Research handbook on soft law* (pp. 43–55). Edward Elgar Publishing.

Thym, D. (2009). In the name of sovereign statehood: A critical introduction to the Lisbon judgment of the German Constitutional Court. *Common Market Law Review*, *46*(6).

Treib, O. (2015). Akteurzentrierter Institutionalismus. In *Handbuch Policy-Forschung* (pp. 277–303).

Trubek, D. M., Cottrell, M. P., & Nance, M. (2005). *'Soft Law,' 'Hard Law,' and European Integration: Toward a theory of hybridity* (University of Wisconsin Legal Studies Research Paper (1002)).

Volcansek, M. L. (2019). *Comparative judicial politics*. Rowman & Littlefield.

Webb, M., & Kreppel, A. (2021). The European Parliament's role as an informal EU agenda setter: The influence of own initiative reports. *Public Administration, 99*(2), 304–320.

Weber, R. K. (2019). *Der Begründungsstil von Conseil constitutionnel und Bundesverfassungsgericht: eine vergleichende Analyse der Spruchpraxis* (Vol. 26). Mohr Siebeck.

Weil, P. (1983). Towards relative normativity in international law? *American Journal of International Law, 77*(3), 413–442.

Weiler, J. H. (1991). The transformation of Europe. *Yale Law Journal*, 2403–2483.

Werner, R. (2022). Rechtsanerkennung. In K. Weber (Ed.), *Rechtswörterbuch* (29th ed.). C. H. Beck. Beck Online.

Wind, M. (2010). The Nordics, the EU and the reluctance towards supranational judicial review. *JCMS-Journal of Common Market Studies, 48*(4), 1039–1063.

Xanthoulis, N. (2021). Legal effects and reviewability of EU acts: between institutional intentions and perceptions of concerned parties. In *EU Soft Law in the Member States: Theoretical Findings and Empirical Evidence*. Hart Publishing.

Zeitlin, J. (2005). Conclusion: The open method of coordination in action: Theoretical promise, empirical realities, reform strategy. *The Open Method of Co-ordination in Action: The European Employment and Social Inclusion Strategies*, 447–504.

Zweigert, K., & Kötz, H. (1996). *Einführung in die Rechtsvergleichung auf dem Gebiete des Privatrechts*. Mohr.

CHAPTER 3

The Empirical Approach: Soft Law in Germany and France

3.1 Comparative Mixed-Methods Approach

Soft law is by nature informal and lacks the clear processes associated with hard law. Moreover, judicial decision-making is not directly observable beyond the formalized written judgments. Thus, studying the judicial use of EU soft law is empirically challenging. An empirical approach that draws on multiple methods and diverse data sources is thus the most suitable way to investigate this phenomenon from different angles.

Previous research on EU soft law usually adopted narrower empirical approaches. At the EU level, several studies have examined the legal status of soft law using doctrinal legal analysis (Knauff, 2010; Senden, 2004; Snyder, 1994; Láncos, Xanthoulis, & Arroyo Jiménez, 2023), while others have used quantitative methods to map its adoption at the EU level (Cappellina et al., 2022; Zhelyazkova et al., 2023). Research on national actors' use of soft law primarily relied on qualitative case studies focused on specific policy areas, countries, or instruments (Ausfelder et al., 2024; Eliantonio et al., 2021; Falkner et al., 2005; Hartlapp & Hofmann, 2020; Kollman, 2009; López-Santana, 2006). Studies on the use of EU soft law in courts have primarily relied on doctrinal legal analysis (Georgieva, 2017; Knauff, 2018; Korkea-aho, 2015, 2018; Kovács et al., 2016; Stefan, 2013). Only two studies have also incorporated a quantitative mapping of court cases involving soft law (Georgieva, 2017;

A. Eick, *Soft Law and National Courts in the European Union*, European Administrative Governance,
https://doi.org/10.1007/978-3-032-04515-7_3

Stefan, 2013). While these contributions greatly advanced our understanding of the legal status, use, and potential effects of soft law, their often-narrow empirical focus has resulted in a fragmented picture of the phenomenon. This book addresses this gap by adopting a comprehensive, mixed-method empirical approach that enables a broader and more systematic analysis of judicial usage across different countries, time periods, and policy areas.

The book focuses on two relevant and representative countries and policy fields, with a main observation period from 2002 to 2022. These findings are extrapolated through a supplementary analysis of judicial practices in 28 EU Member States, including the UK, from 1975 to 2019. The book combines quantitative mapping and descriptive statistics of judgment and survey data with qualitative analysis and in-depth case studies that trace the mechanisms of soft law usage and their broader legal and policy effects. The empirical analysis draws on several original data sources. Two original databases of court judgments that use soft law. It also draws on an original survey of national judges in France and Germany, as well as interviews with individuals involved in the administration and judiciary in both countries. These components are closely integrated: The quantitative analysis identifies patterns of judicial soft law usage and key explanatory factors. This informs the case selection and exploration of specific mechanisms in case studies. The remainder of the chapter outlines the case selection, research design, and key data sources.

3.2 Case Selection

The primary focus of this book is on the behavior of national courts in EU Member States, covering all levels of the judiciary. While apex courts hold substantial authority at both the national and European levels, examining lower courts is equally crucial, as their importance within the EU legal order has grown significantly, particularly due to the principles of direct effect and the supremacy of EU law (Alter, 2010, p. 105). The book examines the judicial use of soft law in a comparative design across two countries, two policy areas, and eight instruments. France and Germany are selected as countries and state aid and pharmaceutical regulation as policy areas. These cases are relevant and representative within the EU multilevel system, while also having variation in relevant dimensions that may explain differences in the judicial use of soft law. For in-depth case studies, typical soft law instruments in each policy area that vary in instrument type are selected. Overall, this selection of countries, policy areas, and instruments follows a general approach suggested by Seawright and Gerring, according to which the cases should "elucidate the features of a broader population" and "achieve variation on relevant dimensions" (2008, p. 301). These are cases that are relevant to the phenomenon due to certain shared characteristics, but with meaningful variation in potential explanatory dimensions.

Country Selection. *France* and *Germany* are both significant players in the EU multilevel system, holding considerable negotiation power at the EU level (Tallberg, 2002, p. 626), and they have historically had a strong influence on European integration due to their size, economic strength, and political weight (Pedersen, 1998). They are also central to EU judicial policy, with their apex courts often being cited by the Court of Justice of the European Union (CJEU) and the national courts of other Member States (Mayer et al., 2008). Due to their high level of economic activity compared to other EU countries (Eurostat, 2022, pp. 33–56), France and Germany are more likely to be involved in economic disputes, which increases the potential for the judicial application of EU law and EU soft law in such issues. Specifically, both countries have a long history of providing state aid to their economies (Cohen, 2007; Kenworthy, 1990) and are home to major pharmaceutical industries (EFPIA, 2020, pp. 7–11). Finally, both countries' legal systems belong to the civil law tradition, the most predominant legal family in Europe.

The two countries differ in terms of their judicial systems, the separation of powers, and their legal cultures (Table 3.1). In France, courts are divided into civil and administrative courts, whereas in Germany, they are divided into ordinary, administrative, specialized and constitutional courts. The French judicial system is centralized. The administrative judiciary centers on the *Conseil d'État*, while the civil branch centers on the *Cour de Cassation*. Both are responsible for setting precedent, shaping legal policy and overseeing judicial organization. While the German apex courts are also authoritative and act as a court of last resort, the lower courts are federally administered and enjoy a greater degree of autonomy (Schmidt-Aßmann & Dagron, 2007, pp. 400–404). The relationship between the judiciary and the administration also differs between the two countries. In France, judges frequently rotate into administrative roles and vice versa (Steiner, 2018, pp. 103–107).

Table 3.1 Differences between Germany and France in explanatory dimensions

Country/ Country variation	*Germany*	*France*
Organization of the judiciary	Decentralized	Centralized
Judiciary-administration relations	Independent	Interconnected
Legal culture towards soft law	No explicit engagement	Explicit engagement with the concept
Legal style	Argumentative	Concise
Number of cases involving EU law	More cases	Fewer cases

In contrast, Germany maintains a strict separation, with judges following a career judicial path and acquiring practical expertise through their work (Berlit, 1999). These differences in the judicial systems reflect broader contrasts in the political structures: France's centralized, semi-presidential system supports a strong federal bureaucracy and executive, while Germany's federal, parliamentary system emphasizes decentralization and an independent judiciary. Further, the legal cultures in France and Germany vary in how they receive EU law and EU soft law. Initially, both countries' judiciaries were slow to recognize EU law, though most observers agree that it is now strongly integrated into their judicial practices (Slaughter et al., 1998, pp. 41–132). However, more recently, the apex courts in both Germany and France have demonstrated renewed resistance to the CJEU (Vallée, 2021). But regarding soft law the French apex courts have actively engaged in discussions about its status and adopted a relatively open approach that recognizes the normative power of (national) soft law and encourages courts to review such instruments. In Germany, there has been no such explicit debate within the judiciary (Knauff, 2018). There is also a crucial difference in judicial style generally. German courts engage in extensive legal reasoning and produce long judgments, while French courts write short and authoritative judgments (Rubio & Stefan, 2021, p. 147). Finally, EU law is used less frequently in France than in Germany. Although we do not have a reliable dataset of all national judgments involving EU law, a suitable proxy is the number of preliminary rulings—requests by national courts to the CJEU for clarification on the interpretation or validity of EU law. The 'EUthority' dataset, compiled by Dyevre et al. (2019), includes all such rulings submitted to the CJEU between 1965 and 2018. During this period, German courts submitted 2,533 references, while French courts only submitted 1,039—a 59% lower number. However, this lower number of preliminary references in France also aligns with its smaller judiciary. There are significantly fewer judges, lawyers, and courts in France than in Germany (CEPEJ, 2025). Table 3.1 summarizes the variation between the countries in relevant dimensions.

Selection of Policy Areas. The policy areas of state aid and pharmaceutical regulation were selected as likely cases for judicial usage of soft law, which differ in explanatory dimensions. Previous research suggests that EU soft law is rarely used in certain policy areas (Hartlapp & Hofmann, 2020, p. 141). To ensure sufficient variation in the dependent variable, this book focuses on areas where judicial use of soft law is more likely.

The two policy areas share several characteristics that make soft law usage likely. In both, *EU law* plays a central role: state aid regulation is fully harmonized at EU level with no national regulation (Blauberger, 2009b), while pharmaceutical regulation is partially harmonized, but most medicines authorization procedures at EU and national level are subject to EU law (Permanand, 2006). Moreover, both policy areas show a *high proportion of soft law* relative to hard law. According to Cappellina et al. (2022, p. 12), 66% of EU instruments adopted between 2004 and 2019 in the field of state aid, and 77% in pharmaceutical regulation are soft law. Finally, most soft law instruments in the two policy areas are *linked to hard law*, which means that they are integrated in the existing legal framework.

What varies between the two policy areas is the *governance arrangement* between the EU and national levels, and, related to this, the configuration of actors at the national level (Table 3.2). *State aid* has a more *hierarchical* governance structure. Enforcement powers are centralized at the EU level, with national authorities and private actors as regulated parties. The Commission enforces these rules strictly, which often leads to conflict between the levels, as national macroeconomic interests can clash with European market principles (Blauberger, 2009a). This system is based on Articles 107–109 TFEU, whereby the Commission has exclusive competence and broad enforcement powers, including the ability to issue binding enforcement decisions (Art. 108 TFEU). The legislative role of the European Parliament is small, and the role of the Member States through the Council is limited, as legislative deadlock is common due to strong political divisions over national economic interests (Blauberger, 2009a). Instead, the Commission as an executive body regulates many areas of state aid policy unilaterally through soft law that concretizes the Treaties (Cini, 2001). In contrast, the governance arrangement in *pharmaceutical regulation* is more *cooperative*. Here, the EU and national authorities are co-regulators, and many regulatory processes involve intertwined decision-making steps at both the EU and national level ('composite administration'). This routine of working together and dependence fosters a more cooperative relationship between the levels and actors (Permanand, 2006). Legally, pharmaceutical governance is rooted in shared competences under Articles 114 and 168 TFEU. The former is the basis for market integration in the area, while the latter is the basis for public health protection. The standard legislative procedure is the Ordinary Legislative Procedure (OLP), which grants the Parliament and Council co-decision rights.

Moreover, the *constellation of actors* at the national level—particularly between public and private actors—typically varies in the two policy areas (Table 3.2). In *state aid*, public authorities often have a *cooperative* relationship with private actors. National authorities give subsidies to companies or other societal actors and aim at complying with EU state aid rules in the process. In contrast, in *pharmaceutical regulation*, the typical actor constellation is more *adversarial*, where public actors enforce EU and national law against private actors. This is the case when pharmaceutical companies seek marketing authorization for a medicine from medicines authorities. One should note, however, there are exceptions: in state aid, a national authority may seek reimbursement from a company

Table 3.2 Differences between state aid and pharmaceutical regulation

Dimensions with variation	*State Aid*	*Pharmaceutical regulation*
Governance in the EU system	Hierarchical, centralization of enforcement at EU level	Cooperative, EU and national enforcement
Actor constellation at national level	Cooperative relationships between public and private actors	Adversarial relationship between public and private actors

for unlawful aid—an adversarial relationship. In pharmaceutical regulation, a national authority might work in collaboration with a medicines producer to develop an innovative drug—a cooperative relationship.

Selection of Soft Law Instruments. Finally, for the judgment data and case studies, I select *soft law instruments* that are representative of the policy areas state aid and pharmaceutical regulation and cover various aspects within them. Two instruments for each policy area reflect different *subareas of the policy* and include various *types of soft law* common in that domain. These instruments are the basis of the collection of judgment data introduced below, as well as of case study research in Chapter 6. The instruments are selected to represent typical instruments in the distinct legal frameworks: EU pharmaceutical policy covers the entire policy cycles of the regulation of medicinal products, starting with the 'pre-authorization' stage, where it sets requirements for clinical trials. It also covers the 'authorization' phase, when pharmaceutical companies seek marketing authorization, and the 'post-authorization' phase, where already approved medicines are continuously monitored. The literature broadly describes *two types of EU soft law in pharmaceutical policy* (Kröll, 2017, pp. 98–99). On the one hand, instruments that interpret administrative procedures and legal terms, such as the European Medicines Agency's (EMA) 'pre-authorization procedural advice for users of the centralized procedure.'[1] Such instruments explain "the whether and how of certain claims in the market phase" of medicines (Fleischfresser, 2020, p. 21). On the other hand, instruments that set *scientific standards* that public authorities apply to assess the safety of medicine (Fleischfresser, 2020, p. 22), such as the EMA's 'scientific guidelines on the chemistry of active substances.'[2] I select two instruments from pharmaceutical regulation that represent different soft law types and distinct phases in the

[1] European Medicines Agency. Human Medicines Division. Pre-authorisation procedural advice for users of the centralised procedure. 31 July 2023. EMA/821278/2015

[2] European Medicines Agency. Committee for Medicinal Products for Human Use (CHMP). Guideline on the chemistry of active substances. 15 November 2016. EMA/454576/2016.

policy process. First, the *Notice to Applicants*,[3] a Commission instrument that mainly provides legal ***interpretations*** and ***administrative rules*** for the ***pre-authorization*** and ***authorization*** phases (Kortland, 2022, pp. para. 8–12). Second, the Commission's *Good Manufacturing Practice (GMP) Guidelines*,[4] which mostly formulate ***scientific standards*** for the ***post-authorization*** phase (Anhalt/Lützeler, 2010, p. 34).

In the area of state aid, there are two main regulatory questions that correspond to distinct types of soft law instruments (Bartosch, 2016, pp. 1–18; Hofmann et al., 2016, pp. 36–61). First, the question what is state aid? Such instruments determine the scope of state aid law. They clarify which subsidies, or similar measures fall within the scope of EU state aid rules. An example is the *Notice on the notion of state aid*.[5] In more abstract terms, such instruments have what Senden calls an ***interpretative*** function, which means they are "supporting and supplementing (…) [EU] law, in particular to ensuring the proper interpretation and uniform application thereof" (2004, pp. 138–147). The second key regulatory question in state aid is whether a given measure is "compatible with the common market." The Commission issues guidelines that outline how it will apply state aid rules in its enforcement practice. A well-known example is the *Regional Aid Guidelines*.[6] Such instruments serve, in a more abstract sense, what Senden describes as a ***decisional*** function, meaning they "indicate in what way a [EU] institution will apply [EU] law provisions in individual cases when it has implementing and discretionary powers" (2004, p. 119). As representative instruments of state aid, I thus select one soft law measure addressing the ***scope*** of state aid and another focused on its ***compatibility*** with the internal market.

[3] European Commission. EudraLex—Volume 2—Pharmaceutical legislation on notice to applicants and regulatory guidelines for medicinal products for human use. *Notice to Applicants*. https://health.ec.europa.eu/medicinal-products/eudralex/eudralex-volume-2_en, last accessed 10 July 2025.

[4] European Commission. EudraLex—Volume 4—*Good Manufacturing Practice (GMP) guidelines*. https://health.ec.europa.eu/medicinal-products/eudralex/eudralex-volume-4_en, last accessed 10 July 2025.

[5] Commission Notice on the notion of State aid as referred to in Article 107(1) of the Treaty on the Functioning of the European Union. C/2016/2946. OJ C 262, 19 July 2016, pp. 1–50.

[6] Communication from the Commission Guidelines on regional State aid. 2021/C 153/01. OJ C 153, 29.4.2021, pp. 1–46.

Based on the secondary literature, the *SGEI Communication*[7] is a key example of the former (Szyszczak, 2012), defining the *scope* of state aid with an *interpretative* function, while the *Environmental and Energy State Aid Guidelines 2014–2020 (EEAG)*[8] exemplify the latter (Banet, 2020), addressing state aid *compatibility* of state aid and fulfilling a *decisional* function.

3.3 Research Design and Data Sources

As discussed above, the judicial use of soft law is an elusive phenomenon, characterized by informal practices and untransparent procedures. Judges typically deliberate behind closed doors, and their reasoning is not always fully documented. In addition, national courts do not publish all their rulings. This makes the phenomenon difficult to study and leads to methodological challenges. To address these challenges, this book adopts a mixed-methods comparative design, consisting of both broad generalizable analysis and a detailed exploration through in-depth case studies. It follows a three-step research design, with each step employing different data sources and methods.

The first step (Chapter 4) describes the phenomenon by mapping patterns of the judicial usage of EU soft law in terms of frequency and types of soft law usage over time. This analysis draws on three main data sources, which are described in more detail further below: an original database of judgments in state aid and pharmaceutical regulation, a survey of national judges in Germany and France, and an exploratory judgment database (SLDecNat). Patterns are examined both in aggregate and broken down by policy area and country.

The second step (Chapter 5) investigates the factors that explain judicial usage of soft law. It uses the main judgment data and survey data from Chapter 4 to explore institutional explanations and actor-centered explanations for different types of usage. In addition, this step incorporates qualitative evidence from open-ended survey responses by judges.

[7] Communication from the Commission on the application of the European Union State aid rules to compensation granted for the provision of services of general economic interest Text with EEA relevance, OJ C 8, 11.1.2012, pp. 4–14.

[8] Communication from the Commission — Guidelines on State aid for environmental protection and energy 2014–2020, OJ C 200, 28.6.2014, pp. 1–55.

The third step (Chapter 6) traces the mechanisms that lead courts to use EU soft law, and assesses its broader legal and policy effects. This is done through four in-depth case studies, each focusing on a series of judgments in Germany involving a specific soft law instrument. These case studies emphasize how the institutional design of given policy area shapes judicial practice. Drawing on judgment texts and expert interviews, each case study begins by situating the soft law instrument within the broader legal framework and describing its use in national administrations and wider society. The analysis for each case study then turns to a typical and relevant series of national court cases to trace how and why soft law is used, and to evaluate its wider implications for both legal frameworks and wider policies.

As previously mentioned, the book relies on multiple *data sources*: a main judgment database, a survey of judges, exploratory judgment data (SLDecNat) as well as judgment texts and expert interviews. As summarized in Table 3.3, the main judgment and survey data form the basis for mapping and explaining patterns of soft law usage in Chapters 4 and 5. The SLDecNat dataset is used in Chapter 4 to explore broader trends across a wider set of cases. In Chapter 6, interviews together with judgment texts are used in the in-depth case studies. The following section outlines how each of these data sources was created and what information they contain.

Judgment Database. First is the main *judgment database*, which has a limited scope but comprehensively covers the entire population of judgments within its specific area. Specifically, it encompasses all cases involving six relevant and typical EU soft law instruments in France and Germany related to state aid and pharmaceutical regulation between 2002 and 2022 ($n = 111$). The sampling process involved identifying relevant judgments through systematic keyword searches in case law databases. Cases involving six soft law instruments were considered. Four instruments with an interpretative or decisional function that are linked to hard law: the *GMP Guidelines* and *Notice to Applicants* (pharmaceutical regulation), and the *SGEI Communication* and *Environmental and Energy State Aid Guidelines 2014–2020 (EEAG)* (state aid). In addition, two steering instruments were considered: the *State Aid Action Plan* and the *Pharmaceutical Strategy for Europe*. However, no cases referencing these steering instruments were identified. Accordingly, the following analysis includes only the four instruments for which relevant cases were found. These searches were carried out in official judgment databases. In France,

Table 3.3 Overview of data sources

Dataset	*Scope*	*Size (n)*	*Chapters*
Judgment Database	All court judgments citing six representative instruments in state aid and pharmaceutical regulation in France and Germany (2002–2022)	111 judgments	Chapter 4, Chapter 5
Survey of Judges	Survey of judges in German and French courts (all judicial instances, civil and administrative courts)	70 respondents	Chapter 4, Chapter 5
SLDecNat	Exploratory dataset covering judgments across all policy areas and EU Member States (1975–2019), based on third-party data from ACA-Europe (Dec.Nat)	102 judgments	Chapter 4
Interview Data	Expert interviews with actors in administrations and the judiciary in France and Germany	21 interviews	Chapter 6
Judgment texts	Judgment texts as basis for qualitative analysis	–	Chapter 6

Légifrance and the databases of the *Conseil d'État* and *Cour de Cassation*. In Germany, *Rechtsprechung im Internet*. Additional searches were performed in third-party databases: *Juris* and *Openjur* in Germany, *Dalloz* in France. All cases identified through keyword search from all court levels and judicial branches were included in the judgment database. Thereafter, duplicates and cases in which the sampled soft law instruments were not substantially used, were removed. The remaining cases were manually coded using a standardized data sheet. To ensure transparency and replicability, the judgment texts were also imported into the software MAXQDA, where the relevant paragraphs were coded directly in the judgment text. The full Codebook can be found in Appendix Section 1. Essentially, for each judgment, the dependent variable, the *judicial usage of soft law* was coded. In line with the conceptualization in Chapter 2, this involved two dimensions: application (how the court used the soft law in its reasoning or decision-making) and recognition (the extent to which the court implicitly or explicitly acknowledged the legal or practical effects of the instrument). Further, several contextual variables were coded, including the date of the judgment, the type of court, the policy area, and the type of soft law instrument involved.

Survey Data. The second data source is an original ***survey of judges*** working in German and French courts ($n = 70$),[9] which also serves to describe and explain the judicial usage of soft law. The survey was designed to complement the judgment data by capturing individual-level responses from national judges in France and Germany on the usage of EU soft law. It specifically targets civil and administrative court judges in both countries in all levels of the judiciary. Respondents are diverse in terms of seniority, legal area of specialization, and court type. Gaining access to the judges for survey or interview research is notoriously difficult (Jaremba & Mak, 2014). Thus, to contact judges in an effective way, the approach was tailored to each country. In France, where the judiciary is centralized, apex courts—the *Conseil d'État* and the *Cour de Cassation*—were approached to distribute the survey in their court and lower courts. In Germany, a more decentralized court system, all apex courts (*Bundesverwaltungsgericht*, *Bundesgerichtshof*) and all relevant higher courts, *Oberverwaltungsgerichte* and *Oberlandesgerichte,* were contacted and asked to forward it to lower courts. The survey was set up as an online questionnaire through the software *Unipark* and ran between February and July 2022. The questionnaire included both closed and open-ended questions (see Appendix Section 3 for the full questionnaire). It captured the judicial usage of soft law in terms of frequency, type of application and type of recognition. It also included several explanatory indicators, such as judges motivations, institutional context, professional attitudes, and personal profile. Finally, judges could give qualitative responses to open questions. In total, 70 judges responded to the survey. Responses skewed towards French courts, which account for 61% of the cases, and towards higher-level courts, which represent 53% of the cases. Of all respondents, 7% work in apex courts, 46% in high courts, and 43% in lower courts. The majority of them are senior in rank, with 78% holding full judge status or higher, and 63% having at least 10 years of professional experience.

SLDecNat. The third dataset, *SLDecNat* ($n = 102$), is another dataset of judgments, but of a more exploratory nature including only part

[9] The survey was conducted as part of this book's research and also the broader *EfSoLaw* project (*Effects of EU Soft Law across the Multilevel System*), led by Prof. Miriam Hartlapp (FU Berlin) and Prof. Sabine Saurugger (Sciences Po Grenoble). The project was funded by a Franco-German grant from the *Agence nationale de la recherche* (ANR) and the *Deutsche Forschungsgemeinschaft* (DFG) (grant number 411037244).

of its population of cases, that serves to extrapolate the findings to a broader population. It provides an approximation of broader usage across all policy areas and Member States from 1975 to 2019. The source of the cases in the database is the third-party 'Dec.Nat' database, which compiles national judgments from all EU Member States that involve EU law (Hübner, 2016). It is compiled by the CJEU's Research and Documentation Directorate in collaboration with ACA-Europe. Dec.Nat includes over 33,500 national decisions from 1959 to 2022 that are considered relevant to the development of EU law. Based on this data source, SLDecNat is narrowed down to focus on national judgments that explicitly use EU soft law instruments. To build the SLDecNat dataset, a systematic keyword search for all common soft law labels (e.g. *Guideline*, *Notice* or *Recommendation*) was conducted in both English and French in Dec.Nat. These soft law labels were searched in two variables of Dec.Nat: 'provisions of EU law' and 'keywords.' References to soft law in these variables were treated as proxy of relevant judicial usage of soft law in the judgment. As verification, the original judgment text or summaries of national judgments in CJEU case law were retrieved and checked for every entry. Thereafter, context variables were coded: Member State, year, instrument cited in a case (see Appendix Section 2 for the Codebook). Moreover, variables that required interpretation and background research by the coder were coded: function of the cited soft law (interpretative, decisional, or steering) and the policy area of the judgment. Overall, this dataset is less valid than the main judgment dataset and the survey data. But its wider scope allows for exploration of generalizability. Thus, it can be used to complement the other sources.

Expert Interviews. The fourth data source are *expert interviews*. We can only understand the mechanisms that lead to judicial use and the wider effects of judgments if we have a prior understanding of the use of EU soft law at national level by administrations, agencies, and society at large. The analysis draws on 21 expert interviews in Germany and France with officials from administrations, agencies, and wider societal groups. They were conducted between November 2020 and May 2022. All interviews were held via video call or phone. The interviews were transcribed and coded according to a standardized coding scheme in the software MAXQDA. Annex Sect. 4 provides an overview of the interviews and their abbreviations.

References

Alter, K. (2010). *The European Court's political power: Selected essays*. Oxford University Press.

Anhalt/Lützeler. (2010). § 8 Die Herstellung von Arzneimitteln. In Dieners/Reese (Ed.), *Handbuch des Pharmarechts* (1st ed.). C.H. Beck.

Ausfelder, A., Eick, A., Hartlapp, M., Mespoulet, R., Saurugger, S., Terpan, F., & Cappellina, B. (2024). EU soft-law: Non-binding but enforceable. *European Law Journal, 30*(4), 668–684.

Banet, C. (2020). Legal status and legal effects of the commission's state aid guidelines: The case of the guidelines on state aid for Environmental Protection and Energy (EEAG)(2014–2020). *European State Aid Law Quarterly*, 172.

Bartosch, A. (2016). *EU-Beihilfenrecht* (2. Auflage ed.) [Kommentar]. C.H.Beck.

Berlit, U. (1999). Modernisierung der Justiz, richterliche Unabhängigkeit und RichterInnenbild. *Kritische Justiz, 32*(1), 58–69.

Blauberger, M. (2009a). Compliance with rules of negative integration: European state aid control in the new member states. *Journal of European Public Policy, 16*(7), 1030–1046.

Blauberger, M. (2009b). Of 'Good' and 'Bad' subsidies: European state aid control through Soft and Hard Law. *West European Politics, 32*(4), 719–737.

Cappellina, B., Ausfelder, A., Eick, A., Mespoulet, R., Hartlapp, M., Saurugger, S., & Terpan, F. (2022). Ever more soft law? A dataset to compare binding and non-binding EU law across policy areas and over time (2004–2019). *European Union Politics, 23*(4), 741–757.

CEPEJ. (2025). *CEPEJ dynamic database of European judicial systems*. Council of Europe. https://www.coe.int/en/web/cepej/cepej-stat

Cini, M. (2001). The soft law approach: Commission rule-making in the EU's state aid regime. *Journal of European Public Policy, 8*(2), 192–207.

Cohen, E. (2007). Industrial policies in France: The old and the new. *Journal of Industry, Competition and Trade, 7*(3), 213–227.

Dyevre, A., Glavina, M., & Atanasova, A. (2019). *Codebook: Euthority project the Court of Justice of the EU and National Courts. Data set on Preliminary References in EU law, 1958–2014*. https://euthority.eu/?page_id=795

EFPIA. (2020). *The pharmaceutical industry in figures*. https://www.efpia.eu/media/554521/efpia_pharmafigures_2020_web.pdf

Eliantonio, M., Korkea-aho, E., & Stefan, O. (2021). *EU Soft Law in the member states: Theoretical findings and empirical evidence*. Bloomsbury Publishing.

Eurostat. (2022). *Key figures on Europe* (Flagship publications, Edition 2022). https://ec.europa.eu/eurostat/web/products-key-figures/-/ks-ei-22-001

Falkner, G., Treib, O., Hartlapp, M., & Leiber, S. (2005). *Complying with Europe: EU harmonisation and soft law in the member states*. Cambridge University Press.

Fleischfresser, A. (2020). § 3 Europäisierung des Arzneimittelrechts. In Fuhrmann/Klein/Fleischfresser (Ed.), *Arzneimittelrecht* (3rd ed., 2020 ed., pp. 20–38). Nomos.

Georgieva, Z. (2017). Competition soft law in French and German courts. *Maastricht Journal of European and Comparative Law, 24*(2), 175–193.

Hartlapp, M., & Hofmann, A. (2020). The use of EU soft law by national courts and bureaucrats: How relation to hard law and policy maturity matter. *West European Politics, 44*(1), 134–154.

Hofmann, H., Micheau, C., & Mihaescu-Evans, B. C. (2016). *State aid law of the European Union*. Oxford University Press.

Hübner, D. C. (2016). The 'National Decisions' database (Dec. Nat): Introducing a database on national courts' interactions with European Law. *European Union Politics, 17*(2), 324–339.

Jaremba, U., & Mak, E. (2014). Interviewing judges in the transnational context. *Journal of Law Methods, 2014*(2).

Kenworthy, L. (1990). Are industrial policy and corporatism compatible? *Journal of Public Policy, 10*(3), 233–265.

Knauff, M. (2010). *Der Regelungsverbund: Recht und Soft Law im Mehrebenensystem*. Mohr Siebeck.

Knauff, M. (2018). Soft Law vor Gericht. *juris – Die Monatszeitschrift (jM)*, 71–75.

Kollman, K. (2009). European institutions, transnational networks and national same-sex unions policy: When soft law hits harder. *Contemporary Politics, 15*(1), 37–53.

Korkea-aho, E. (2015). *Adjudicating new governance: Deliberative democracy in the European Union*. Routledge.

Korkea-aho, E. (2018). National Courts and European Soft Law: Is Grimaldi still Good Law? *Yearbook of European Law, 37*, 470–495.

Kortland, H. (2022). Vorbemerkung zu § 21 AMG. In Kügel/Müller/Hofmann (Ed.), *Arzneimittelgesetz* (3rd ed. 2022 ed.). C.H. Beck.

Kovács, A., Tóth, T., & Forgács, A. (2016). The legal effects of European Soft Law and their Recognition at National Administrative Courts. *ELTE LJ*, 53.

Kröll, R. (2017). *Das Europäische Arzneimittelrecht*. Springer.

López-Santana, M. (2006). The domestic implications of European soft law: Framing and transmitting change in employment policy. *Journal of European Public Policy, 13*(4), 481–499.

Mayer, F. C., Lenski, E., & Wendel, M. (2008). Der Vorrang des Europarechts in Frankreich–zugleich Anmerkung zur Entscheidung des französischen Conseil d'Etat vom 8. Februar 2007 (Arcelor ua)–. *Europarecht (EuR), 43*(1), 53–87.

Pedersen, T. (1998). *Germany, France, and the Integration of Europe a Realist Interpretation*. Continuum International Publishing Group.
Permanand, G. (2006). *EU pharmaceutical regulation: The politics of policy-making*. Manchester University Press.
Rubio, N., & Stefan, O. (2021). No Longer Small Enough to Fall through the Cracks: A French story of adaptation to the petites sources of EU Law. In M. Eliantonio, E. Korkea-aho, & O. tefan (Eds.), *EU Soft Law in the Member States: Theoretical findings and empirical evidence* (1st ed., pp. 135–150). Hart Publishing.
Schmidt-Aßmann, E., & Dagron, S. (2007). Deutsches und französisches Verwaltungsrecht im Vergleich ihrer Ordnungsideen. *Zeitschrift für ausländisches öffentliches Recht und Völkerrecht*(67), 395–468.
Seawright, J., & Gerring, J. (2008). Case selection techniques in case study research–A menu of qualitative and quantitative options. *Political Research Quarterly, 61*(2), 294–308.
Senden, L. A. J. (2004). *Soft law in European Community law*. Hart Publishing.
Slaughter, A. M., Sweet, A. S., & Weiler, J. (1998). *The European Court and National Courts: Doctrine & Jurisprudence: Legal Change in its Social Context*. Bloomsbury Publishing.
Snyder, F. (1994). Soft Law and institutional practice in the European Community. In S. Martin (Ed.), *The Construction of Europe: Essays in honour of Emile Noël* (pp. 197–225). Kluwer Academic Publishers.
Stefan, O. (2013). *Soft Law in Court: Competition Law, State Aid and the Court of Justice of the European Union*. Kluwer Law International.
Steiner, E. (2018). *French law: A comparative approach* (2nd ed.). Oxford University Press.
Szyszczak, E. (2012). Modernising State Aid and the Financing of SGEI. *Journal of European Competition Law & Practice, 3*(4).
Tallberg, J. (2002). Paths to compliance: Enforcement, management, and the European Union. *International Organization, 56*(3), 609–643.
Vallée, S. (2021). A securitarian solange. *Verfassungsblog: On Matters Constitutional*. https://verfassungsblog.de/a-securitarian-solange/
Láncos, P. L., Xanthoulis, N., & Arroyo Jiménez, L. (Eds.). (2023). The legal effects of EU soft law: Theory, language and sectoral insights. Edward Elgar.
Zhelyazkova, A., Haverland, M., & Joosen, R. (2023). Legislating softly: The effect of preference heterogeneity on the share of EU soft-law instruments over time. *European Union Politics, 24*(3), 447–469.

CHAPTER 4

How Courts Use Soft Law: Differences Across Countries and Policy Areas

How often and in what form do national courts use soft law? Based on judgment data and complementary survey data, this chapter maps patterns to establish the relevance of the phenomenon and describe its forms. This establishes the dependent variable of the book. The chapter finds that national courts use EU soft law rarely but increasingly. When they do, soft law is often relevant to the judgment, serving as an interpretation aid or as a supplementary standard of review with legal effects or even indirect binding force. Thus, soft law is not merely a political tool, but a phenomenon that also becomes relevant in judicial disputes and in the wider legal order. The chapter first examines the frequency of soft law usage before turning to the types in which courts use it in practice. The analysis compares both country- and sector-specific variation. As laid out in Chapter 2, the main empirical focus is on Germany and France. They have similar legal traditions (civil law) and strongly Europeanized judiciaries, but they differ in judicial organization (centralized vs. decentralized) and legal culture (concise vs. elaborate legal style).

As described in Chapter 3, the main data source is the *judgment data*. It covers 111 cases from 2002 to 2022 that involve four key soft law instruments in state aid and pharmaceutical regulation. It is complemented by *survey data*, which serves to validate the findings and generalize them across policy areas. Respondents are 70 judges from

A. Eick, *Soft Law and National Courts in the European Union*, European Administrative Governance,
https://doi.org/10.1007/978-3-032-04515-7_4

diverse German and French courts. The sample is slightly skewed towards French courts (61% of respondents) and towards high and apex courts (53% of respondents). Most respondents are full judges or head judges (78%) and have worked in the judiciary for at least 10 years (63%). Finally, the chapter explores how generalizable the results are in the broader *SLDecNat data*, which includes a subset of relevant cases involving EU soft law from 1975 to 2019 across all Member States and policy areas. Details on all data sources can be found in Chapter 3. The analysis uses descriptive statistics to present patterns of usage.

4.1 Frequency of Soft Law Usage

Before analyzing frequency in the original data, this section briefly reviews existing research on how frequent EU soft law is adopted and used in courts. Several studies found that the adoption of EU soft law has increased in diverse policy areas (Cappellina et al., 2022; von Bogdandy et al., 2004; Zhelyazkova et al., 2023). But there is only little evidence on whether this has translated into increased use of soft law in courts. Nonetheless, a few notable studies have focused on the EU courts and established the relevance of the phenomenon at EU level by identifying and discussing relevant judgments of the Court of Justice of the European Union (CJEU) (Gentile, 2020; Knauff, 2018; Korkea-aho, 2015; Snyder, 1994). They note that soft law served as an interpretative aid, but in some cases, soft law was itself subject to judicial review for compliance with EU law (Xanthoulis, 2021). The latter was only the case in preliminary ruling procedures (Gentile, 2020). But these studies do not quantify soft law usage. The exception is a landmark study by Stefan (2013), who maps soft law usage in EU competition and state aid case law in the European courts. Drawing on a dataset of 696 CJEU judgments, orders, and Advocate General Opinions from 1953 to 2011, Stefan shows that the court has actively used soft law already for decades, and the phenomenon increased over time. Moreover, EU courts typically apply soft law together with hard law and frequently justify its use by referring to general EU legal principles. But they always maintain a clear distinction between binding and non-binding instruments, and do not conflate soft law with hard law (pp. 154–155). At the national level, the only systematic quantitative mapping is by Georgieva (2017) who examines 112 judgments from France, Germany, the UK, and the Netherlands, focusing on Commission-issued soft law in competition law. In these cases, soft law is again mostly used together with hard law, while references to soft law that is not connected to hard law are rare. Unlike the EU courts, national courts do not frequently invoke general legal principles to justify their use of soft law. When comparing courts and countries, Georgieva finds a fragmented picture and no visible common approach across different types of courts and Member States (Georgieva, 2017, pp. 162–163). But we still lack a systematic cross-country and cross-sector analysis of how frequently national courts use EU soft law beyond competition policy, and of the ways in which they apply soft law exactly.

Frequency of Soft Law Usage Overall. To assess how frequently courts use soft law, the *judgment data* offers a complete overview in a limited area of application. This data captures all cases involving four selected soft law instruments—two each in the areas of state aid and pharmaceutical regulation—in France and Germany between 2002 and 2022. As noted in Chapter 3, two additional steering instruments were included in the sampling but yielded no results and are therefore excluded from the analysis. Thus, we only find cases for soft law instruments that have a connection to hard law, and no cases for steering soft law that stands alone without referencing hard law.

The final dataset includes 111 court cases, which is on average 5.3 cases per year—a relatively low, but not insignificant number. Importantly, the frequency of usage has increased over time, particularly in the past decade (Fig. 4.1). While only 32 cases occurred in the first ten years (2002–2012), the number more than doubled to 79 cases in the second decade (2013–2022). This increase can be in part attributed to the introduction of the *SGEI Communication*—one of the soft law instruments under consideration—in 2012. But the upward trend remains even when this instrument is excluded: the number of cases still rises from 32 to 61. Nevertheless, the increase is not even. Certain years, such as 2003 and 2005, have no cases at all, while in others there are peaks—15 cases in 2014 and 16 in 2018. This points to an increasing but uneven rise of EU soft law in national judicial practice.

But to interpret these numbers in a meaningful way, we need wider points of comparison. As described in Chapter 1, the CJEU's landmark *Grimaldi* judgment (case C-322/88) established that national courts must take EU soft law into account when it is relevant to a case. Thereafter, the most accurate comparison would be all cases in which soft law could have been relevant—whether or not it was actually used. However,

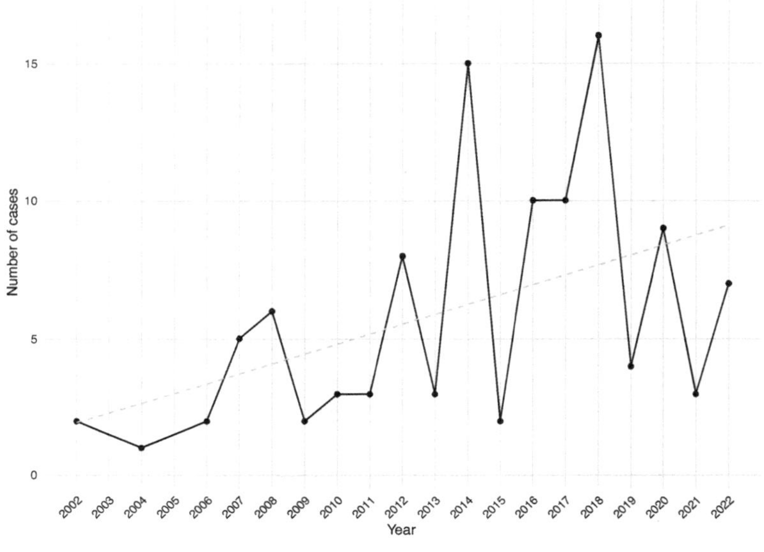

Fig. 4.1 Judgment data: Frequency of usage. Note: trendline in red; no cases in 2003 and 2005

identifying all these cases is not feasible in practice. It would require examining the substance of every judgment within a legal domain. Moreover, within the legal system, it is the judiciary's role to determine which laws and instruments are relevant to a case. Therefore, this point of comparison is not feasible nor meaningful. Instead, we can use several proxies to put the frequency of soft law use into perspective. First, in the judgment data we can look at cases where parties invoked soft law, but courts did not. In 20 of 111 cases (18%), soft law was raised by parties but not addressed by courts in their legal argumentation. This suggests that courts often use soft law when it is raised by the parties, but there is also a significant share where they ignore or reject it.

Second, we can compare EU soft law usage to EU hard law usage. We do not have systematic data for all national judgments in which EU law played a role. But in the following, I conduct an exploratory comparison that can serve as the first point of indication. Specifically, I conducted a keyword search for hard law in the national court databases described in

Chapter 3, which were also used for the creation of the soft law judgment database. The search focused on judgments that cite four key EU hard law instruments in the same two policy areas, state aid and pharmaceutical regulation. These were Article 107 TFEU and Article 108 TFEU for state aid, and Directive 2001/83/EC and Regulation 726/2004 for pharmaceutical regulation. This search led to 1,971 entries of judgments that cite one of these hard law instruments at least once. By contrast, the four soft law instruments on which the judgment database focuses were only used in 111 judgments. While this comparison is purely exploratory, it indicates that EU soft law is referenced far less frequently than EU hard law in national court decisions, likely making up only a small fraction of all judgments in these areas.

Third, we can compare patterns from the judgment data to the survey data (see Chapter 3), which contains self-reported information from judges about the frequency of soft law usage. When asked whether EU soft law had played a role in at least one of their cases, the majority of judges, 48 respondents (69.6% of respondents), answered no, while 13 (18.8%) were unsure. Only eight judges (11.6%) reported having used EU soft law. The latter reported that they had used EU soft law in between one and twenty cases, with a median of five cases. These relatively low figures align with the patterns observed in the judgment data. As the survey respondents come from diverse policy areas, they suggest that these results are generalizable beyond state aid and pharmaceutical policy.

Fourth, we can also compare these findings with national administrations. A parallel survey conducted by the EfSoLaw research project,[1] uses a very similar design but targets national administrative officials in Germany and France (63 respondents). Both surveys asked whether respondents had used EU soft law in the previous 24 months. Figure 4.2 plots the results from the administrative survey on the left and those from the judiciary on the right. It reveals strong contrasts: 92.1% of administrative officials reported using soft law during that period, compared to just 11.6% of judges. This highlights that national administrations use EU soft law much more frequently than national courts. Thus, the judicial use of

[1] Survey of staff in national authorities in Germany and France from the *ANR* and *DFG* research project "Effects of EU soft law across the multilevel system" (EfSoLaw), led by Sabine Saurugger and Miriam Hartlapp. For more information, see www.efsolaw.eu, last accessed 10 July 2025.

EU soft law remains relatively limited if we view it from a wider perspective. Courts make much more use of hard law, and soft law is primarily a tool of the national administration. Nonetheless, the use of soft law in court decisions is not negligible and occurs with some regularity.

Judgment Data: Frequency by Country, Policy Area, Court. The judgment data shows that the frequency of soft law usage in the judgment data varies significantly across countries, court branches, and litigant types. German courts account by far for most cases (95 cases or 86% of all cases). In contrast, only 16 cases (14%) come from French courts (Fig. 4.3, upper left). This contrasts with doctrinal legal debates on soft law, which describe the French judiciary as more open to soft law than its German counterpart (Knauff, 2018). Yet doctrinal receptivity does not necessarily translate into use in judgments. The divergence may reflect differences in legal style: French decisions tend to be concise and formalistic, leaving little space for elaboration and detailed discussion of soft law (Rubio & Stefan, 2021, p. 137). German judgments, by contrast, often feature detailed, structured legal reasoning (Weber, 2019, pp. 2–3),

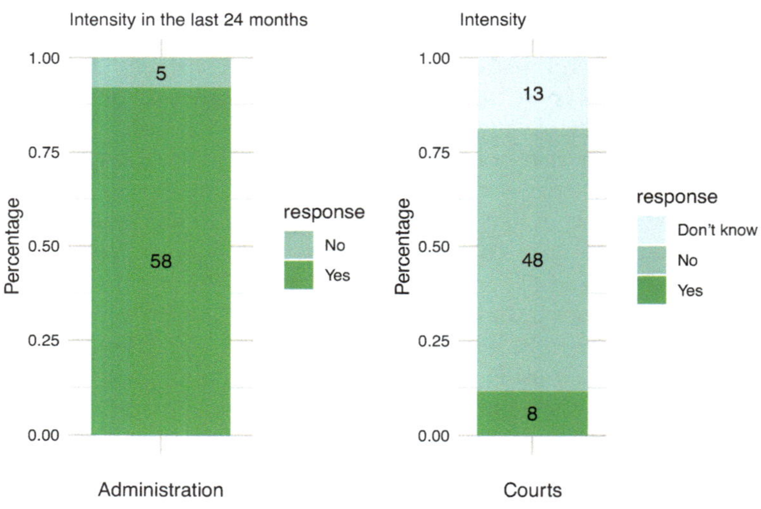

Fig. 4.2 Survey data. Usage of EU Soft Law by National Administrations ($n = 63$) and Judges ($n = 69$) in Germany and France

creating more opportunities to draw on soft law—a theme we will come back to in Chapter 5.

The data also reveal variation in the types of parties involved in cases concerning EU soft law. Most commonly, a private party brings a case against a public authority: 96% of cases are initiated by private actors, and 84% of defendants are public authorities (Fig. 4.3, bottom left and right). This likely reflects the regulatory nature of the two EU policy areas examined. At the national level, both state aid and pharmaceutical regulation primarily become relevant in relations of public authorities with private actors. Such relations are usually governed by administrative law and overseen by the administrative judiciary. This also aligns with the finding that most cases in the data are from administrative courts (Fig. 4.3, upper right). In the context of state aid, for example, a company may contest a public authority's decision to grant a subsidy to a competitor. In pharmaceutical regulation, a pharmaceutical company may contest a regulatory

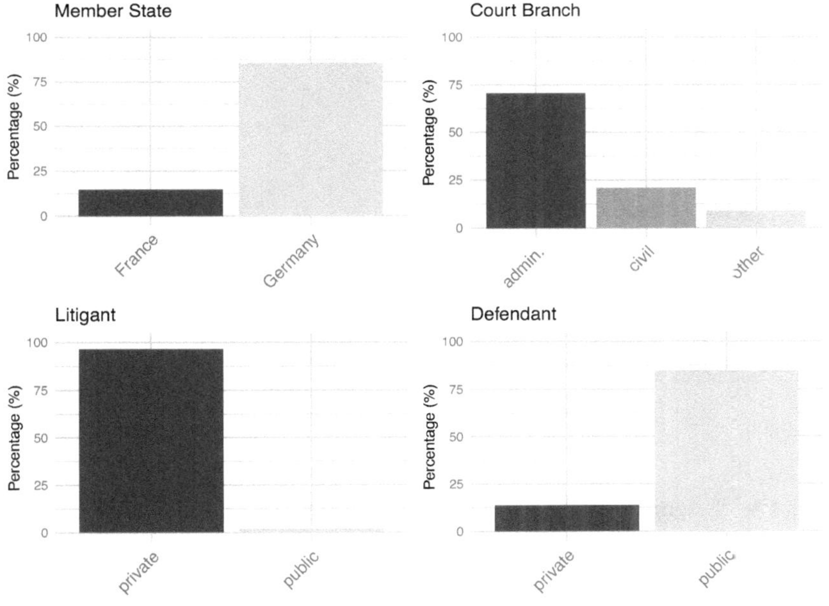

Fig. 4.3 Judgment data. Frequency of usage by country, court branch, and parties

agency's decision not to authorize a medicine. In such cases, EU soft law can be applied in judgments to support or contest how a national authority interprets EU law during enforcement.

In contrast to the variation observed by country, parties to the case and court branches, there is less variation across policy areas and judicial levels (Fig. 4.4). Cases in pharmaceutical regulation slightly outnumber those in state aid (59% versus 41%). Similarly, most cases are from lower courts (41%), followed by higher courts (33%) and apex courts (26%). While this partly reflects the greater number of judgments overall by lower courts, as only few cases reach higher courts, it is still notable that a substantial number of cases involving soft law instruments are found at a lower level. Given the time pressure and high caseloads typical for lower courts, their use of soft law suggests that the phenomenon is part of routine judicial practice, rather than a tool reserved for the typically more detailed, higher-level review.

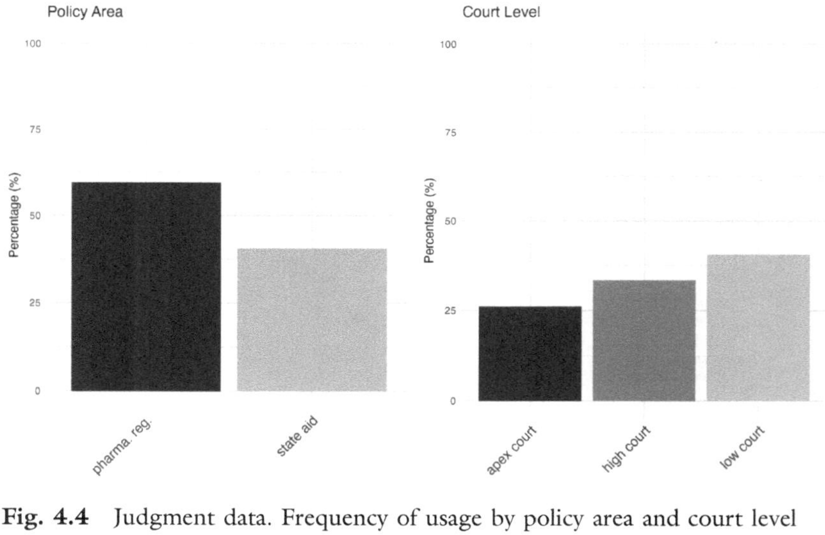

Fig. 4.4 Judgment data. Frequency of usage by policy area and court level

4.2 Type of Soft Law Usage

But frequency of usage does not equal relevance. Even a small number of cases can have significant legal or policy effects. So how do courts actually use soft law? As outlined in Chapter 2, judicial usage refers to the decision by judges to engage with soft law and to recognize or activate its legal effects. Types of usage are conceptualized along two dimensions, each of which can take soft, medium, or hard forms. The first dimension is recognition—whether judges recognize soft law as a legitimate instrument within governance or law. The second is application—how soft law is used in the court's legal reasoning within the judgment.

Figure 4.5 shows the distribution of different types of *application* in the judgment data. The most common form is the use of soft law as an *interpretative aid for hard law* (49% of cases), which is classified as a medium level of application. This is followed by its use as a *supplementary standard of review* alongside hard law (23%), which again classifies as medium application. There is also a significant share of *no application* (23%), which occurs when the court mentions that one of the parties has invoked a soft law instrument in their lawsuit or defense but does not pick it up in their own legal reasoning.

Next, Fig. 4.6 maps the types of recognition of effects of soft law in the judgment data. Courts most frequently recognize an *indirect binding force* of soft law in conjunction with hard law (38% of cases), which is surprising given the formally non-binding nature of such instruments. In such instances, soft law can then become de facto binding for at least some of its addressees or in specific situations, as long as it does not deviate from its underlying hard law. They thus classify as hard recognition. This is followed by the recognition of *non-binding legal effects* (34%), which

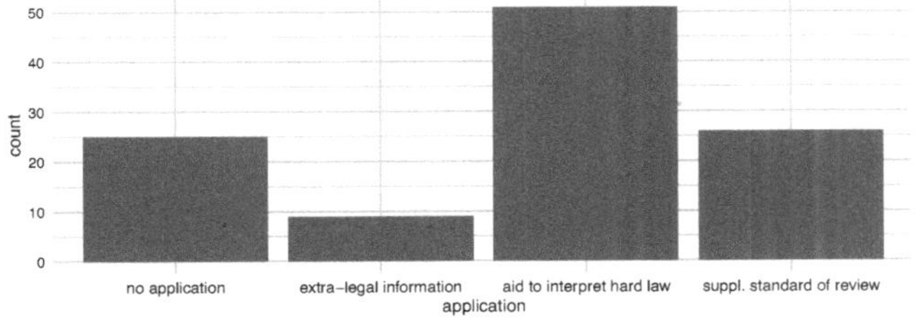

Fig. 4.5 Judgment data. Types of application in counts ($n = 111$)

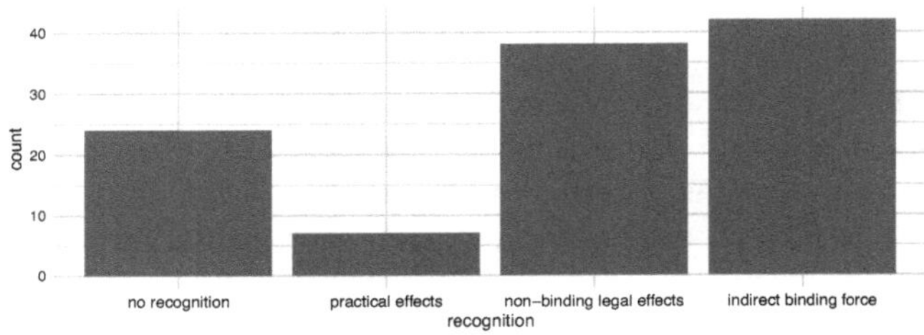

Fig. 4.6 Judgment data. Recognition of soft law in counts ($n = 111$)

classifies as medium recognition. An example is where soft law is invoked to strengthen a certain legal interpretation. This is followed by cases of ***no recognition*** (22%), where courts mention soft law in their legal reasoning, but explicitly declare it to have no effects relevant to the case. Unsurprisingly, soft law is never used exactly like hard law as main standard of review or main legal source.

We can now combine the two dimensions of application and recognition into the composite variable judicial usage of soft law—the final dependent variable. Figure 4.7 shows that hard usage of soft law is the most common in the judgment data (36% of cases). As mentioned above, this is primarily driven by hard recognition, where courts acknowledge an indirect binding force of hard law. In these cases, the effects of soft law are recognized as being almost identical to those of hard law for practical purposes. However, it should be noted that courts never treat soft law exactly the same as hard law, as they never recognize a direct binding force of soft law or apply it as the primary standard of review. The second most common type is medium usage of soft law (35%). Non-usage (18%) and soft usage (11%) are less common, but still notable.

To assess generalizability, we can turn to the ***survey data***, to which 70 German and French judges responsible for diverse legal areas responded. It suggests that similar patterns hold beyond pharmaceutical regulation and state aid. The eight judges who reported having used soft law were asked how they ***applied*** it in their rulings. Multiple responses were allowed. Judges mostly used soft law in medium and soft ways (Fig. 4.8: upper bar), with soft uses being somewhat more common than in the judgment data. However, due to the small number of responses, this result is only exploratory. To measure judges' ***recognition*** of soft law, the survey asked all respondents, whether soft law can have legal effects that

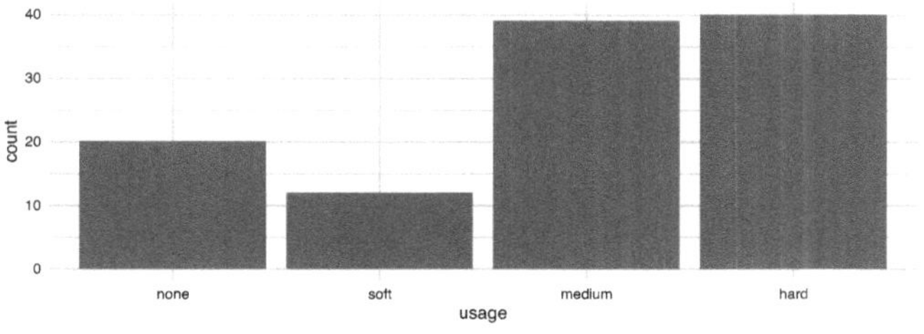

Fig. 4.7 Judgment data. Type of usage in counts ($n = 111$)

are relevant to the judiciary (Fig. 4.8: lower bar). As in the judgment data, recognition of an *indirect binding force* of soft law (hard recognition) is most common (44% of respondents). Again, soft recognition is less common, but not insignificant, as 18 respondents (38%) recognize *practical effects* of soft law. Thus, while soft law never fully takes the role of hard law, it typically serves a legal function in judgments, rather than merely a political or informational one. Such uses likely shape the court's reasoning and influence the outcome of judgments. We can therefore expect that when courts use soft law, it is often relevant to the judgment and has the potential to develop wider effects. This is reinforced by another survey question that asked all respondents whether soft law can be subject to judicial review: 34% of judges said yes, 46% under certain conditions, and only 20% said no (no figure). This is surprising given the CJEU is hesitant to allow the review of EU soft law instruments (Gentile, 2020).

4.3 Exploring Generalizability Across Countries

Exploring Frequency of Judicial Soft Law Usage Across Countries. Now that we have systematically mapped the frequency of the judicial usage of EU soft in a sample of limited countries, policy areas, and instruments, we can now explore how these findings generalize more broadly across Member States. For this purpose, the following section draws on the original *SLDecNat* dataset, which was introduced and is detailed in Chapter 3. This data builds on the third-party *Dec.Nat* database (Hübner, 2016), which includes a subset of cases from national courts that involve EU law and that were relevant to the development of EU law. SLDecNat is further narrowed down to cases in which EU soft law plays a relevant

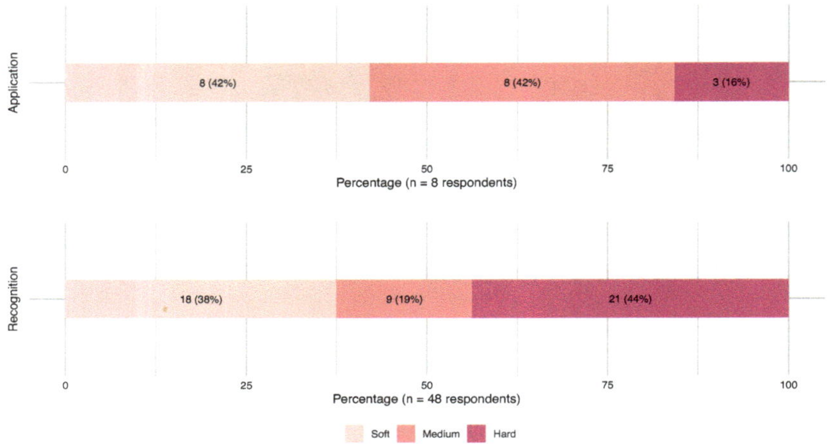

Fig. 4.8 Survey data. Types of application and recognition in percentages (*Note* Counts in bars. Percentages in brackets. Multiple responses were allowed for application. "Don't know" responses and non-responses (NAs) are excluded)

role. While the dataset does not distinguish between types of soft law usage, it provides information on its frequency and the context of judgments. The dataset covers the period 1975 to 2019 and all Member States and policy areas. Overall, we find 102 cases in which EU soft law is used in this exploratory data. This is very few, just 2.3 cases a year, as opposed to the approximately 35,000 total cases in the broader Dec.Nat database. But one should note that this data source underestimates the frequency of judicial usage, as many instances of soft law usage likely are unreported due to the selection criteria of Dec.Nat, which focuses on cases relevant to the development of EU law. But it reinforces the finding that judicial usage of EU soft law is a regular, but rather rare phenomenon.

Frequency Over Time and in Broader Context. In the SLDecNat data, soft law usage increases until 2006 and then decreases until 2019 (Fig. 4.9). However, there are also large variations between years. There is a peak of 10 cases in 2006, which is mainly due to a series of 7 related cases in the Spanish *Tribunal Superior de Justicia del País Vasco*. Controlling for this outlier, we find an increase until 2009, again followed by a decline. That we find a decrease in cases in the last third of the observation period is likely in part due to the fact that the underlying database

Dec.Nat restricted data collection from lower courts after 2003 (Hübner, 2016, p. 337), which also affects the patterns in SLDecNat.

This contrasts with the steadier increase in soft law use in the narrower judgment data described above. However, that we have a more consistent increase in the latter is not surprising, as state aid and pharmaceutical regulation were selected as likely cases for judicial usage, which are different from EU policy areas with lower levels of EU competence. To contextualize the trends in the SLDecNat, we can compare them to two wider sets of cases in which courts use EU law. The first is all cases in the original Dec. Nat dataset, i.e. cases relevant to the development of EU law. The second is the number of preliminary ruling requests from national courts, which are questions that national courts submit to the CJEU when they are uncertain about the interpretation or validity of EU law. They are thus particularly relevant cases for the interpretation of EU law. As data source on preliminary ruling requests, I use the GEOCOURT dataset by Dyevre and Lampach (2021), which reunites all such cases from 1961 to 2017. Figure 4.10 shows normalized trends over time, showing the percentage of cases per year relative to the total number of cases in each of the three datasets. While Dec.Nat cases remain stable

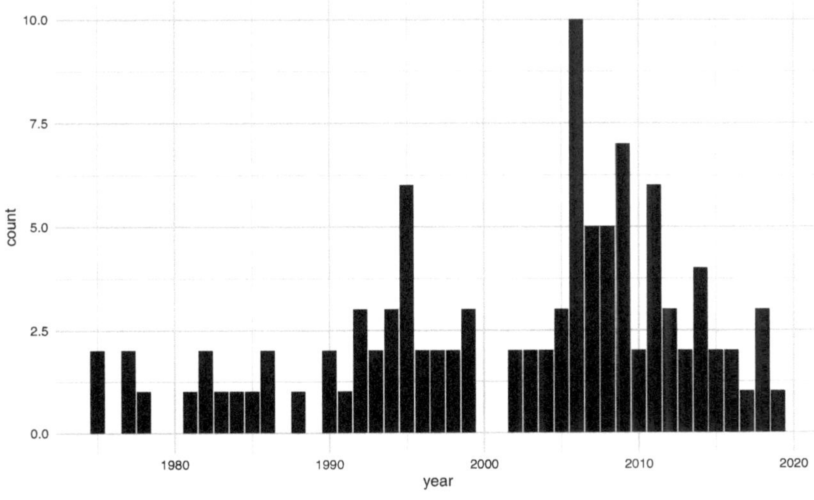

Fig. 4.9 SLDecNat. Judicial usage of soft law over time (1975–2019)

and preliminary references steadily increase, soft law cases from SLDecNat peak in 2006 and then decline. This suggests that the judicial use of soft law in SLDecNat is likely not simply driven by overall patterns of cases involving EU law. There appear to be independent drivers of the judicial usage of EU soft law in the aggregate.

Generalizing variation across countries, courts, and policy areas. Based on the narrower judgment and survey data, we have already seen variation in terms of countries and policy areas. German courts used soft law more frequently, and pharmaceutical regulation cases were slightly more frequent than state aid cases. This section maps broader variation based on the SLDecNat dataset across Member States, policy areas, court types, and legal instruments. This allows us to get an overview of the variation across Member States and policy areas, and to place the results from the narrower data sources in perspective. In terms of *country variation*, Fig. 4.11 plots the number of cases involving soft law in the SLDecNat data by country. Like in the narrower judgment and survey data, we find

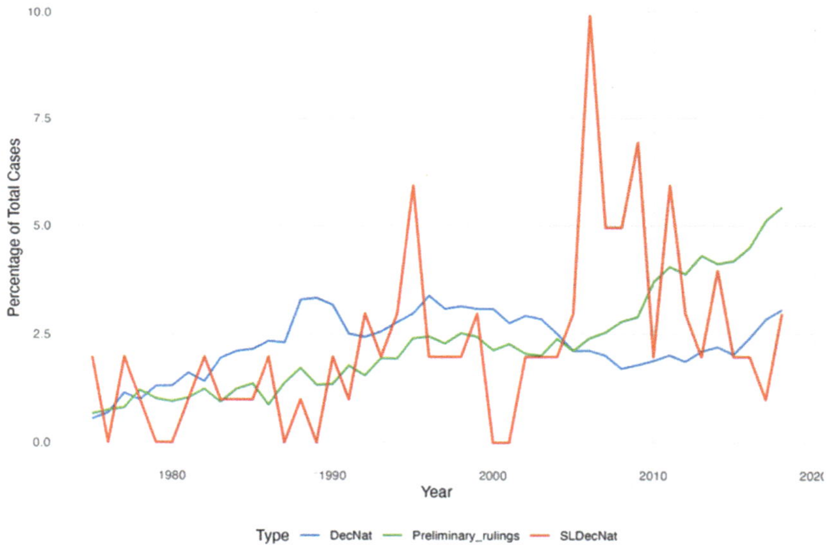

Fig. 4.10 SLDecNat. Patterns of soft law cases in comparison (*Note* Dec.Nat data (blue line), Preliminary ruling requests (green line), SLDecNat (red line))

more cases in Germany than in France. But France still ranks in the top quartile of countries. Overall, the SLDecNat data shows substantial variation across countries. Soft law is used frequently in Germany, Italy, and Spain; moderately often in France, Belgium, and the Netherlands; and only rarely in Austria, Bulgaria, the Czech Republic, Denmark, Estonia, Greece, Hungary, Ireland, Luxembourg, Poland, Romania, Slovenia, Sweden, and the United Kingdom. No cases were identified in Croatia, Cyprus, Finland, Latvia, Lithuania, Malta, or Portugal. This strong variation suggests that the judicial usage of soft law is a rather selective phenomenon that is established in various EU Member States, but not all of them.

The patterns in Fig. 4.11 also suggest that country variation seems to not always be driven by national factors that are specific to soft law. For example, the United Kingdom and Ireland are known for having a strong tradition of using national soft law (guidance documents) in the administration and courts (Dorbeck-Jung & van Amerom, 2008; Sorabji & Vaughan, 2021). One could expect that this legal culture also encourages the use of EU soft law. But we do not find many cases involving EU soft law in these countries (also not pre-Brexit in the case of the UK).

It is more likely that EU soft law usage often reflects how frequently EU law is applied more broadly in each country. Soft law usage is then a function of the Europeanization of the judiciary more generally. As a

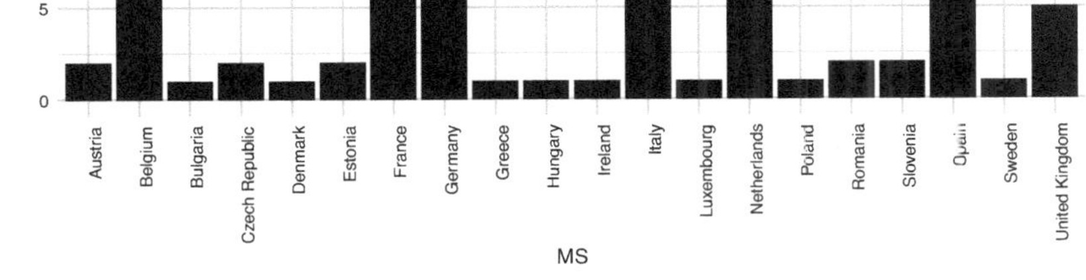

Fig. 4.11 SLDecNat. Number of cases by country

proxy for the broader engagement of the national judiciary with EU law we can again use the GEOCOURT data which includes information on the number of preliminary references of national courts to the CJEU. Figure 4.12 plots the number of soft law cases from SLDecNat against the number of preliminary ruling cases. We see that those countries with more referrals to the CJEU, such as Germany and Italy, also tend to use EU soft law more often. Countries with fewer referrals, such as Member States in Scandinavia, Eastern Europe, and the Common Law countries (Ireland, UK, Malta) have low numbers in both datasets. The only exception is Spain, where we have more use of EU soft law in relative terms than preliminary ruling requests. This suggests that country variation in the judicial use of EU soft law likely follows how often courts in a country deal with EU law in general.

It is beyond this chapter to explain the application of EU law and the Europeanization of the judiciary in national courts more generally, but scholars have pointed to various explanations which may be at play here. It has been proposed that legal cultures and court systems are resistant to EU law. Wind (2010) argues that Scandinavian courts rarely apply EU law in their judgments due to a legal culture, that emphasizes a restrained

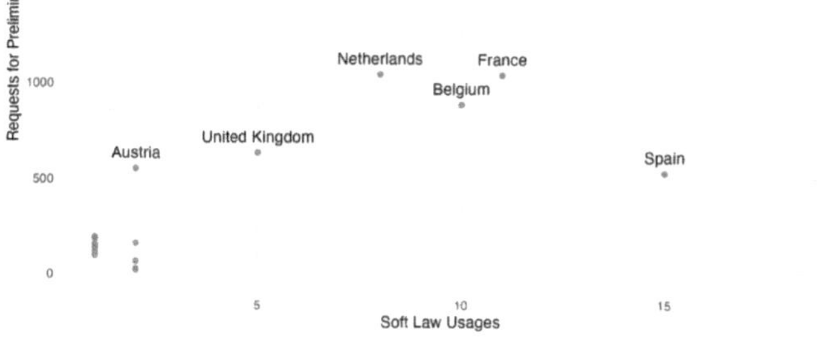

Fig. 4.12 SLDecNat. Soft law cases by number of preliminary ruling requests by country (*Note* Counts based on SLDecNat (soft law cases) and GEOCOURT (preliminary rulings) data)

judiciary. Judicial systems in Eastern Europe often had to strongly adapt to EU law since the 1990s. Today, some apex courts, such as the Polish Constitutional Tribunal, are outright hostile towards EU law (Szwed, 2022). However, several studies on the application of EU law in the wider judiciary in Eastern European countries find mixed results and no general reluctance towards EU law in the wider judiciary at lower levels in countries like Poland (Jaremba, 2012; Kuhn, 2005; Lazowski, 2011), Czechia, or Slovakia (Bobek, 2008; Kuhn, 2005). In contexts of democratic backsliding, it is more likely that specific courts, and not all courts, are reluctant to engage with EU law for political reasons.

In terms of *policy variation*, the number of cases citing soft law in the Dec.Nat. dataset varies significantly. SLDecNat includes a variable *matter* which captures the legal area of each case. Figure 4.13 plots the number of cases by legal area (see Codebook in Appendix Section 2 for the full names of legal areas). It shows that competition policy (COMP) and state aid (STAID) are clearly the most prominent. Since state aid is typically viewed as a subfield of competition law, their dominance is even more pronounced if combined. Telecommunications (CONNECT) comes in second, which reflects the widespread use of soft law instruments in this sector (Kollmann, 2023). An example of a soft law instrument cited in this area is the '1998 Commission Recommendation on interconnection in a liberalized telecommunications market.'[2] These are all areas in which the EU has significant competences and EU integration is well advanced. Moreover, they are all related to the internal market. Competition and State aid policies aim to promote market competition (Cini & McGowan, 1998), while Telecommunications policy aims to harmonize and liberalize such markets (Goodman, 2006). Next there is a group of policy areas with a few cases each: Agriculture (AGRI), Employment (EMPL), Internal Market (GROW), Taxation (TAXUD), and matters relating to the EU Treaties (TREA). These are again all policy areas with higher or medium levels of EU competence, which suggests that the judicial use of EU soft law is more common in areas where the EU is formally competent to act. We have fewer cases in areas with lower EU competence, such as Justice and Home Affairs (HOME and JUST). Finally, we have no cases in areas in which the EU only has supporting competence or no competence, such as Culture, Education, or Tourism. However, there are

[2] Commission Recommendation of 8 January 1998 on interconnection in a liberalized telecommunications market. 98/195/EC.

also exceptions. For example, there is little usage in several areas of high EU competence, such as Trade, the Customs Union, or Environmental Policy.

In terms of court level, apex courts (or peak courts), account for the largest share of cases, followed by higher courts and then lower courts (Fig. 4.14). Compared to the narrower judgment data above, lower courts have a smaller relative share. However, this likely reflects the selection criteria of the Dec.Nat database, which focuses on 'relevant judgments,' which are more likely to come from higher judicial instances. Nonetheless, the presence of a meaningful number of cases from lower courts (21% of cases) confirms that this level of the judiciary plays a relevant role in the use of EU soft law across countries and policy areas.

Further, we find variation by *type of soft law instrument*. Figure 4.15 shows that decisional soft law dominates. These are mostly competition policy and state aid guidelines. Their dominance is consistent with previous literature on the EU courts which finds extensive case law applying such competition and state aid guidelines that concretize the treaties (Stefan, 2008). Surprisingly, steering soft law comes in second. Thus, such instruments are relevant in certain areas. Examples of steering

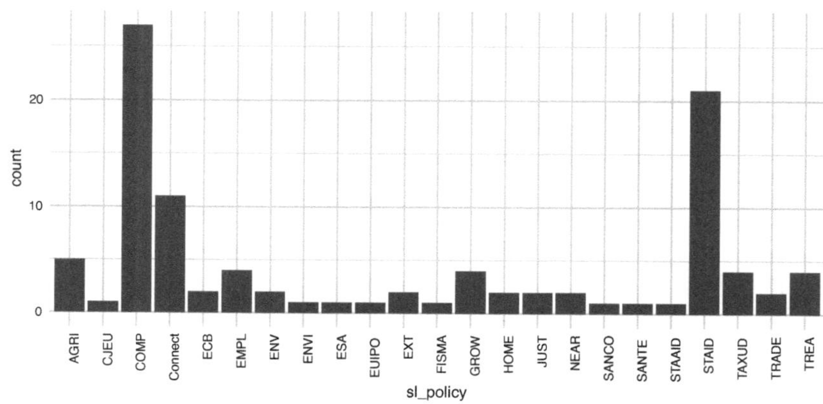

Fig. 4.13 SLDecNat. Number of soft law cases by policy area

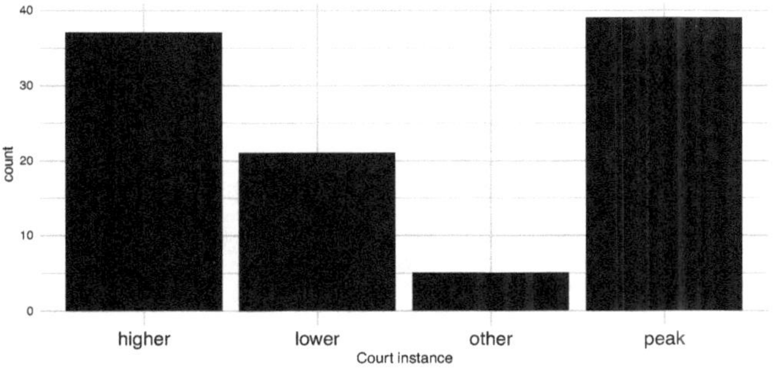

Fig. 4.14 SLDecNat. Number of soft law cases by court level

instruments used in the judgments are the 1978 *Council Resolution establishing the European Monetary System*[3] or the *Council Recommendation on the promotion of positive action for women.*[4] But as in the narrower judgment data, most instruments are linked to hard law, which is the case for the interpretative and decisional soft law. If we take these two together, they are more common than stand-alone steering soft law.

When instruments are categorized by the author of soft law, the broader SLDecNat data clearly shows the dominance of instruments issued by the European Commission (Fig. 4.16). This confirms the patterns observed in the narrower judgment data on state aid and pharmaceutical regulation. It suggests that, across policy areas and countries, courts most frequently engage with instruments issued by the executive. If this is the case, it is likely to reinforce and amplify the Commission's position and legal opinions, as well as the executive bias in soft law-making. Although Council-issued soft law plays a secondary role, it is still relevant, with 17 cases citing such instruments. An example of Council soft law that appears in the data are the *Country-Specific Recommendations* (CSRs) issued to Member States within the European Semester which provide guidance and expectations for national budgetary and structural policies

[3] Resolution of the Brussels European Council on the establishment of the EMS (Brussels, 5 December 1978).

[4] Council recommendation of 13 December 1984 on the promotion of positive action for women. 84/635/EEC.

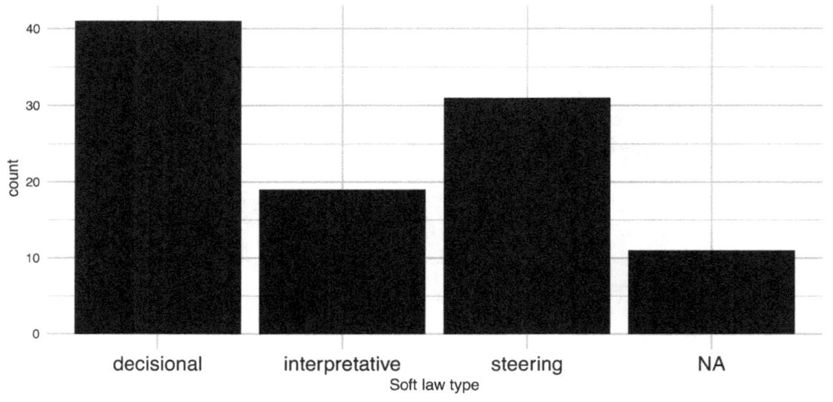

Fig. 4.15 SLDecNat. Number of soft law cases by instrument type

(Terpan, 2015, p. 78). In contrast, soft law from the European Parliament is almost entirely absent, despite the Parliament's frequent adoption of resolutions and recommendations (Kreppel & Webb, 2019).

Thus, the SLDecNat dataset suggests that central patterns observed in the narrower judgment data (focusing on two countries and policy areas) and the survey data (focusing on two countries) are generalizable across countries: The SLDecNat patterns confirm that the judicial use of soft

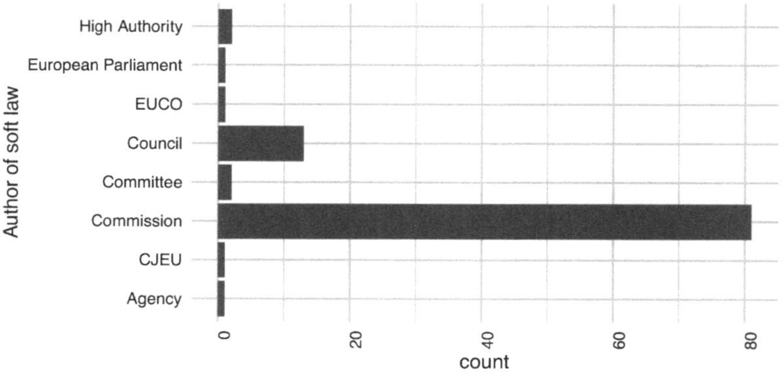

Fig. 4.16 SLDecNat. Number of soft law cases by author

law is rare, but has increased over time, even if recent years show no clear trend in the data. There are strong country differences, German, Italian, and Spanish courts are the main users of EU soft law, which aligns with their generally high engagement in a country with EU law. There are also policy differences, with a dominance of cases in areas of high EU competence which relate to the internal market: Competition, State aid, and Telecommunications. All judicial levels are relevant, and EU soft law is not a phenomenon that is only relevant in the higher courts.

However, there are some differences between the data sources. In the past decade, the SLDecNat data could not show an increase of soft law usage, which we have observed in pharmaceutical regulation and state aid in the judgment data. Moreover, in the narrower judgment data, steering soft law not linked to hard law is irrelevant. While the SLDecNat data, like the other data sources, also predominantly includes cases referencing soft law instruments that are connected to hard law, it also contains a relevant share of cases using steering soft law that stands apart from hard law. Overall, the three data sources show that while soft law appears rather rarely in courts, it does so in various countries, policy areas, and types of courts. When courts use EU soft law, it is often relevant to the judgment. It is used as an aid to interpretation or as a supplementary standard of review, and its legal effects or even indirect binding force are recognized. This suggests that soft law is not an exceptional phenomenon within the judiciary, but rather an increasingly regular instrument within the EU's multilevel legal order.

References

Bobek, M. (2008). On the Application of European Law in (Not Only) the Courts of the New Member States: 'Don't Do as I Say'? *Cambridge Yearbook of European Legal Studies, 10*, 1–34.

Cappellina, B., Ausfelder, A., Eick, A., Mespoulet, R., Hartlapp, M., Saurugger, S., & Terpan, F. (2022). Ever more soft law? A dataset to compare binding and non-binding EU law across policy areas and over time (2004–2019). *European Union Politics, 23*(4), 741–757.

Cini, M., & McGowan, L. (1998). *Competition policy in the European Union*. Springer.

Dorbeck-Jung, B. R., & van Amerom, M. (2008). The hardness of soft law in the United Kingdom: state and non-state regulatory activities related to nanotechnological development. *J. Verschuren en H. Schooten-van der Meer* (*eds.), The State Legislature and Non-State Law, Edward Elgar: Cheltenham*, 129–150.

Dyevre, A., & Lampach, N. (2021). Subnational disparities in EU law use: Exploring the GEOCOURT dataset. *Journal of European Public Policy, 28*(4), 615–631.

Gentile, G. (2020). Ensuring effective judicial review of EU soft law via the action for annulment before the EU Courts: A plea for a liberal-constitutional approach. *European Constitutional Law Review, 16*(3), 466–492.

Georgieva, Z. (2017). *Soft law in EU competition law and its reception in member states' courts* (PhD Thesis). Tilburg University.

Goodman, J. W. (2006). Telecommunications policy-making in the European Union. In *Telecommunications Policy-Making in the European Union*. Edward Elgar Publishing.

Hübner, D. C. (2016). The 'National Decisions' database (Dec. Nat): Introducing a database on national courts' interactions with European Law. *European Union Politics*, *17*(2), 324–339.

Jaremba, U. (2012). *Polish civil judges as European Union law judges: Knowledge, experiences and attitudes* (PhD Thesis). Rotterdam University.

Knauff, M. (2018). Soft Law vor Gericht. *juris – Die Monatszeitschrift (jM)*, 71–75.

Kollmann, E. (2023). Hard rules for soft law: The case of European Union telecommunications law. In *The legal effects of EU Soft Law* (pp. 213–232). Edward Elgar Publishing.

Korkea-aho, E. (2015). *Adjudicating new governance: Deliberative democracy in the European Union*. Routledge.

Kreppel, A., & Webb, M. (2019). European Parliament resolutions-effective agenda setting or whistling into the wind? *Journal of European Integration: Power Without Influence? Explaining the Impact of the European Parliament Post-Lisbon*, *41*(3), 383–404.

Kuhn, Z. (2005). European Law in the Empires of Mechanical Jurisprudence: The Judicial Application of European Law in Central European Candidate Countries. *Croatian Yearbook of European Law and Policy*, *1*(1), 1–14.

Lazowski, A. (2011). Half full and half empty glass: The application of EU law in Poland. *Common Market Law Review*, *48*(2), 503–553.

Rubio, N., & Stefan, O. (2021). No Longer Small Enough to Fall through the Cracks: A French Story of Adaptation to the Petites Sources of EU Law. In M. Eliantonio, E. Korkea-aho, & O. Stefan (Eds.), *EU Soft Law in the Member States: Theoretical Findings and Empirical Evidence* (1 ed., pp. 135–150). Hart Publishing.

Snyder, F. (1994). Soft Law and Institutional Practice in the European Community. In S. Martin (Ed.), *The Construction of Europe: Essays in honour of Emile Noël* (pp. 197–225). Kluwer Academic Publishers.

Sorabji, J., & Vaughan, S. (2021). "This Is Not A Rule": COVID-19 in England & Wales and Criminal Justice Governance via Guidance. *European Journal of Risk Regulation, 12*(1), 143–158.

Stefan, O. (2008). European Competition Soft Law in European Courts: A Matter of Hard Principles? *European Law Journal, 14*(6), 753–772.

Stefan, O. (2013). *Soft Law in Court: Competition Law, State Aid and the Court of Justice of the European Union*. Kluwer Law International.

Szwed, M. (2022). The Polish Constitutional Tribunal Crisis from the Perspective of the European Convention on Human Rights: ECtHR 7 May 2021, No. 4907/18, Xero Flor w Polsce sp. z oo v Poland. *European Constitutional Law Review, 18*(1), 132–154.

Terpan, F. (2015). Soft Law in the European Union-The Changing Nature of EU Law. *European Law Journal, 21*(1), 68–96.

von Bogdandy, A., Arndt, F., & Bast, J. (2004). Legal Instruments in European Union Law and Their Reform: A Systematic Approach on an Empirical Basis. *Yearbook of European Law, 23*(1), 91–136.

Weber, R. K. (2019). *Der Begründungsstil von Conseil constitutionnel und Bundesverfassungsgericht: eine vergleichende Analyse der Spruchpraxis* (Vol. 26). Mohr Siebeck.

Wind, M. (2010). The Nordics, the EU and the Reluctance Towards Supranational Judicial Review. *Jcms-Journal of Common Market Studies, 48*(4), 1039–1063.

Xanthoulis, N. (2021). Legal effects and reviewability of EU acts: between institutional intentions and perceptions of concerned parties. In *EU Soft Law in the Member States: Theoretical Findings and Empirical Evidence*. Hart Publishing.

Zhelyazkova, A., Haverland, M., & Joosen, R. (2023). Legislating softly: The effect of preference heterogeneity on the share of EU soft-law instruments over time. *European Union Politics, 24*(3), 447–469.

CHAPTER 5

Why Courts Use Soft Law: Evidence from Judgments and Survey Data

5.1 How to Explain Soft Law Usage

As the previous chapter demonstrated, the use of EU soft law is relatively rare, but also not uncommon. More importantly, when soft law is used, it typically informs the reasoning in a judgment. However, as discussed in Chapter 1, this phenomenon is puzzling from a traditional, formal legal perspective. The traditional role of courts is to interpret and enforce the binding law of the land, thereby upholding the rule of law. Non-binding instruments do not fit well into this role. From this perspective, one could argue that it carries the risk of undermining legal certainty and extends the formal legal framework beyond its formally defined limits (Klabbers, 1998). Why then would courts use EU soft law?

This chapter tests the theoretical expectations regarding how courts use EU soft law. The main dependent variable is the judicial usage of EU soft law, categorized in soft, medium or hard types of usage. Some explanations also address the frequency with which soft law is used. Descriptive statistics are used to map the co-variation of soft law usage with various explanatory factors. The chapter concludes that institutional factors, particularly a country's legal tradition and the characteristics of its administrative judiciary, are the strongest predictors of how courts use soft law. In contrast, actor-centered factors related to judges' personal profile play only a limited role.

A. Eick, *Soft Law and National Courts in the European Union*, European Administrative Governance,
https://doi.org/10.1007/978-3-032-04515-7_5

As in Chapter 4, the main data sources are again the main judgment data, focused on France and Germany as well as state aid and pharmaceutical regulation, and the survey data of judges from both countries. To measure soft, medium, and hard forms of usage, the judgment data captures both application and recognition of soft law (combined into a composite variable), while the survey focuses only on recognition. Application of soft law is not considered in the survey data due to the low number of respondents with experience in applying soft law. As a complement, the chapter also incorporates qualitative insights from judges' open-ended responses to the survey. Institutional explanations are examined across both judgment and survey data, whereas actor-centered explanations are explored only using the survey results as it is the only individual-level data. The chapter proceeds as follows: First, it operationalizes the explanations developed in Chapter 2. Second, it examines the co-variation between soft law usage and institutional and actor-centered factors. Third, it incorporates qualitative insights from open-ended survey responses to complement the quantitative findings.

5.2 Theoretical Explanations

Chapter 2 proposed several explanations for the judicial soft law usage based on the literatures of Judicial Politics and Europeanization. This section specifies and operationalizes these explanations for concrete testing against the judgment and survey data.

Institutional Factors. Based on the idea that courts are embedded in formal and informal institutions, Chapter 2 proposed that judicial behavior is shaped by courts' institutional context. First, it was proposed that a country's legal style matters. French judgments are usually concise with short legal argumentation, which leaves less space for courts to engage with atypical legal sources, such as soft law (Rubio & Stefan, 2021, p. 137; Steiner, 2018, p. 139). In contrast, German judgments are known for their extensive legal reasoning and length (Weber, 2019, pp. 2–3), which offers more opportunity to engage with instruments like soft law. Thus, more frequent and harder forms of soft law usage are expected in German courts than in French courts.

Second, it was proposed that characteristics of the *administrative judiciary* and administrative law could be relevant. In national administrative law, non-binding instruments that provide post-legislative guidance or give instructions to administrations are particularly common, such as *circulaires* in France and *Verwaltungsvorschriften* in Germany (König, 2007). As a result, administrative courts should be socialized into engaging with such instruments in contrast to other judicial branches where they are less common. We thus expect courts in this branch to apply EU soft law more frequently and in harder ways than other branches of the judiciary.

Third, judicial use of EU soft law was expected to vary by policy area. It was argued that high EU *competence* in a policy area encourages the usage of EU soft law. Entrenched EU enforcement powers increase the costs of non-compliance. Non-compliance with soft law may then be punished with enforcement of related hard law or followed up with hard law regulation (Héritier & Lehmkuhl, 2008, p. 2). Moreover, soft law often concretizes existing hard legal frameworks in areas of high competences. Therefore, we expect more frequent and harder forms of soft law usage in areas where the EU has high competences.

Fourth, legal factors, particularly the *type of soft law instrument* may be relevant. Soft law is often linked to hard law to specify its substance, implementation, or practical implications (Scott, 2011). In such cases, the authority of hard law can spill over onto soft law and give it more legal weight. Thus, we expected more and harder judicial usage of soft law instruments that are linked to hard law. We can add further nuance by considering the type of soft law instrument, as they vary in how closely they are connected to hard law. *Steering instruments* (e.g. Council conclusions) are typically not connected to hard law. The function of such instruments is to "steer or guide action" where the EU has less competence (Senden, 2004, p. 156). *Interpretative instruments* (e.g. Commission communications) are connected to hard law as they are "supporting and supplementing (...) EU law, in particular to ensuring the proper interpretation and—uniform—application thereof" (Senden, 2004, pp. 138–147). Finally, *decisional instruments* (e.g. competition and state aid guidelines) have an even closer link to hard law, as they indicate "in what way an EU institution will apply EU (hard) law provisions in individual cases when it has implementing and discretionary powers" (Senden, 2004, p. 119), so that they can "impose concrete obligations on the Member State" (Senden, 2004, p. 431). Soft law usage is therefore expected to be most frequent and take the hardest forms for decisional soft law, followed by interpretative soft law. Least and softer usage is expected for steering soft law.

Actor-Centered Factors. As courts are not always uniform actors, another set of proposed factors relates to the profile of judges. Fifth, we drew from the judicial behavior literature that judges' attitudes may affect judicial decisions. In the EU, national judges have been found to be more or less receptive of EU law depending on their personal *attitude towards the European Union* (Nowak & Glavina, 2020). This leads to the expectation that judges with 'pro-EU integration' attitudes are more likely to use EU soft law in harder ways.

Sixth, it has been argued that EU law requires specialized knowledge that national judges often don't acquire in law school, which hinders its application (Nowak et al., 2011). This may be particularly true for soft law which is often specialized in substance and not uniformly published in the Official Journal. Judges with more *knowledge of EU law* should be more likely to use EU soft law.

Seventh, a seniority effect was suggested, based on the idea that national actors are more likely to use EU soft law when they have more experience with EU law in general and are thus socialized into engaging with EU law and policy (Hartlapp & Hofmann, 2020). This leads to the expectation that judges with more years of experience in the judiciary are more likely to use soft law, particularly in the form of hard usage.

Eighth, bureaucratic constraints may affect judicial usage of soft law. Heavy workloads can discourage judges from engaging with complex legal materials of EU law, which is particularly the case in lower courts (Pavone, 2022, p. 76). Lower court judges were thus expected to avoid using soft law, particularly in harder forms. Table 5.1 summarizes the expectations.

5.3 Mapping Co-Variation of Usage and Explanatory Factors

We can first look at *self-reported motivations* of judges. We asked the eight judges who had applied soft law in the past about the main reason why they used it. Multiple answers were allowed. Judges primarily reported that they used EU soft law due to a 'demand for clarification of EU law' (6 out of 8 respondents), rather than because of the 'legal authority of soft law,' the 'author's status,' or 'demand for information.' Other reasons cited by respondents include 'demand for clarification of national law' and 'soft law invoked by the parties to a case.' While these responses already suggest that judges consider soft law together with the existing legal

Table 5.1 Factors explaining judicial usage of soft law

Institutional factors	
Law	**Legal environment** • *Connection to hard law: Steering, interpretative and decisional soft law*
Policy	**Level of EU Competence** • *Shadow of hierarchy in areas of high EU competence*
Country	**Legal style** • *Length of judgments and legal reasoning by courts*
Judiciary	**Judicial branch** • *Administrative courts are used to soft law (socialization)*
Actor-centered factors	
Judges	**Attitudes** • *Preference for more European integration* **Knowledge** • *Facilitates identifying and applying relevant soft law* **Seniority** • *Socialization into the EU system of courts* ***Workload*** • *Lower courts with lower capacities*

framework, they remain anecdotal due to the low number of responses. To identify reasons more systematically, the following sections map the co-variation of institutional and actor-centered factors with the type and in some cases frequency of soft law usage.

Institutional Factors

Due to countries' legal style, we expected more and harder usage in Germany. Chapter 4 already discussed that the judgment data shows significantly more usage in Germany. Figure 5.1 shows that hard usage of EU soft law is more prevalent in Germany (38% of cases) than in France (25%) in that data. In contrast, the most frequent category in France is no usage (50%), which is largely driven by cases where soft law is invoked by the parties but not picked up by the court in its own reasoning.

This trend is also evident in the survey data (Fig. 5.2), although the margin is smaller. While 39% of German respondents recognize that soft law can have hard effects in the judiciary (direct and indirect binding force), only 29% of French respondents do so. The difference persists when combining hard and medium categories (52% in Germany vs. 42%

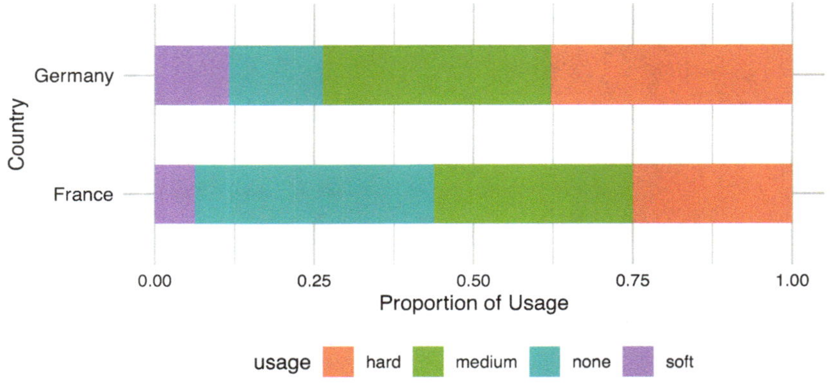

Fig. 5.1 Judgment data. Type of soft law usage by country (*Note* Proportions shown on the y-axis. Germany n = 95, France n = 16 judgments)

in France). This supports the idea that national legal styles influence judicial use of soft law. Longer judgments with extensive justification, as common in Germany, give judges more room to incorporate soft law instruments. By contrast, the French style of concise, authoritative judgments likely provides fewer opportunities to substantively engage with soft law.

Turning to *EU competences in a policy area*, we expected frequent and harder usage in policy areas where the EU has higher competences. In the judgment data, we can compare state aid, an area of high EU competence,

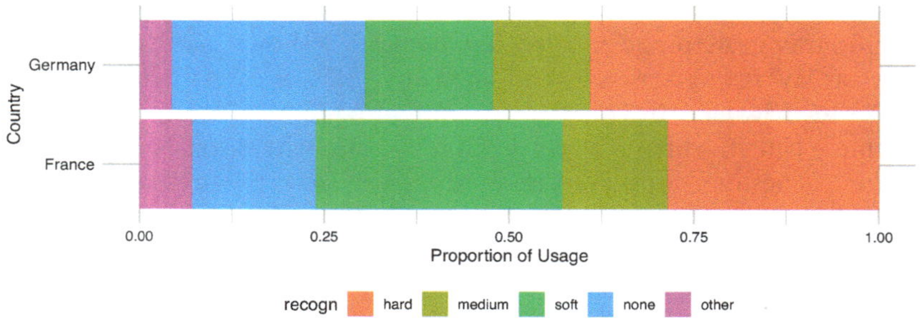

Fig. 5.2 Survey data. Recognition of soft law by country (*Note* Proportions shown on the y-axis. N = 70 respondents)

with pharmaceutical regulation, an area of medium EU competence. However, as discussed in Chapter 4, usage was slightly more frequent in pharmaceutical regulation. But the most prevalent type of usage in state aid is indeed hard usage, whereas it is medium usage in pharmaceutical regulation (Fig. 5.3). Crucially, instances of soft usage or no usage remain low across both domains, suggesting that courts in both fields regard EU soft law as normatively significant. In the survey data, we find no clear trends and the small number of respondents per area limits meaningful conclusions (no figure). Thus, policy variation seems to matter to a limited degree, but the exact mechanisms remain inconclusive. We will thus further explore them in the qualitative case studies in Chapter 6.

Further, it was expected that in terms of *court branches*, administrative courts would be particularly receptive to EU soft law. As shown in Chapter 4, soft law usage is most frequent in the administrative judiciary compared to other branches. Moreover, Fig. 5.4 shows that in the judgment data hard and medium forms of soft law usage are most prevalent in administrative courts, while civil courts exhibit the highest proportion of no usage of all branches. In contrast, we find predominantly soft usage in the 'other' courts (constitutional, labor, patent, and financial courts).

We find the same pattern in the survey data but with smaller differences: Administrative court judges more frequently recognize hard effects

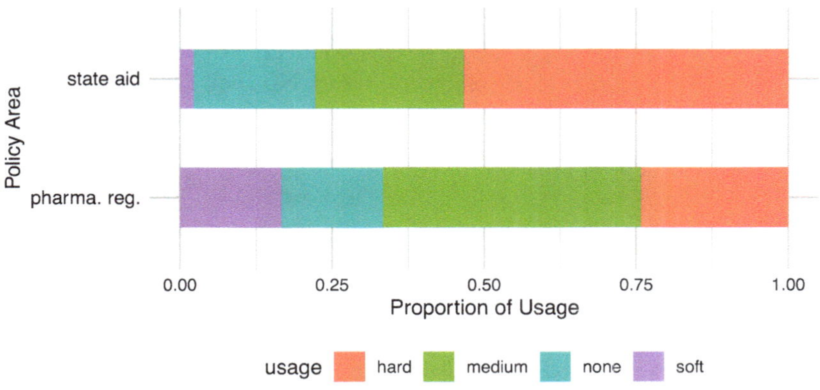

Fig. 5.3 Judgment data. Type of soft law usage by policy area (*Note* Proportions shown on the y-axis. Pharmaceutical regulation (n = 66), state aid (n = 45)

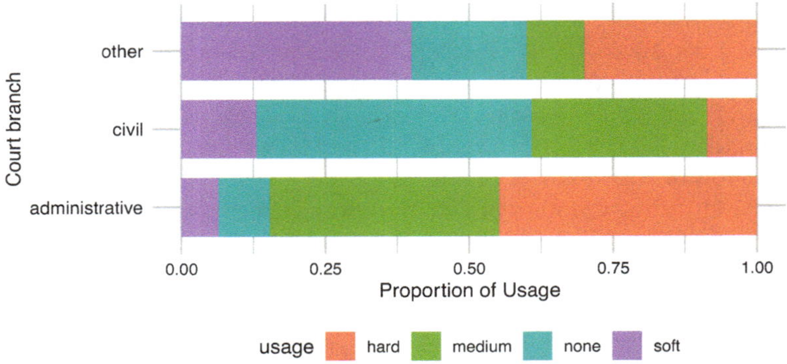

Fig. 5.4 Judgment data. Type of soft law usage by court branch (*Note* Proportions shown on the y-axis. Administrative courts (n = 78), civil courts (n = 23), other (n = 10)

of soft law than civil court judges. Additionally, judges from civil courts are more likely to state that soft law has 'no effect' (Fig. 5.5).

Turning to *legal factors*, specifically the nature of soft law instruments, it was expected that soft law instruments linked to hard law ('interpretative' and 'decisional' soft law) are used more and in harder ways than stand-alone instruments ('steering' soft law). This effect was expected to be strongest for decisional soft law, which is most closely connected to hard law. In the judgment data, there is indeed no usage of the two steering soft law instruments selected as cases. No such cases were found.

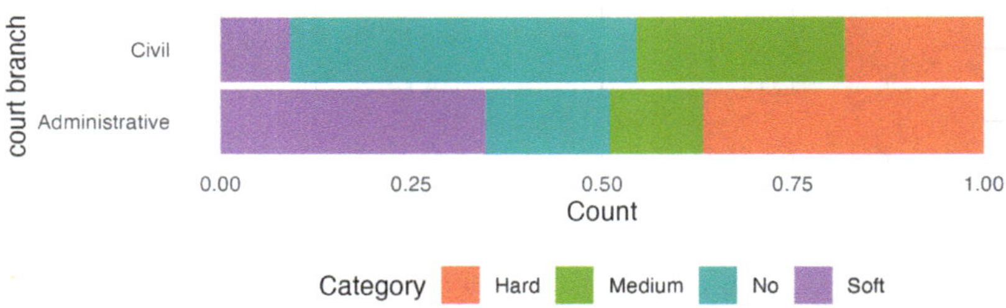

Fig. 5.5 Survey data. Recognition of soft law by court branch (*Note* Proportions shown on the y-axis. Administrative (n = 49), Civil (n = 11 respondents), other excluded)

However, there are no notable differences in the type of usage between interpretative and decisional instruments (Fig. 5.6). In the survey data, all eight judges who had previously applied soft law stated that they only used instruments linked to hard law, and never relied on stand-alone soft law without such a link (no figure). But there is again no difference between decisional and interpretative instruments.

Actor-Centered Factors. We now turn to actor-centered factors using the survey data to assess how individual judge profiles may shape soft law usage. If judges are guided by their own preferences, their attitudes towards soft law and EU integration should play a role. Respondents rated soft law on a scale from 0 ('very negative') to 10 ('very positive'), and separately rated their position on EU integration on a scale from 0 ('more national subsidiarity') to 10 ('more EU integration'). We find only a small effect of attitudes: judges with more favorable views of soft law are more likely to recognize its legal effects, while those with negative views tend to reject any effects altogether (Fig. 5.7). But attitudes towards soft law are not linked to recognizing harder types of soft law effects (no figure). We find a similar pattern for attitudes towards EU integration, but it is even weaker and not significant (Fig. 5.8).

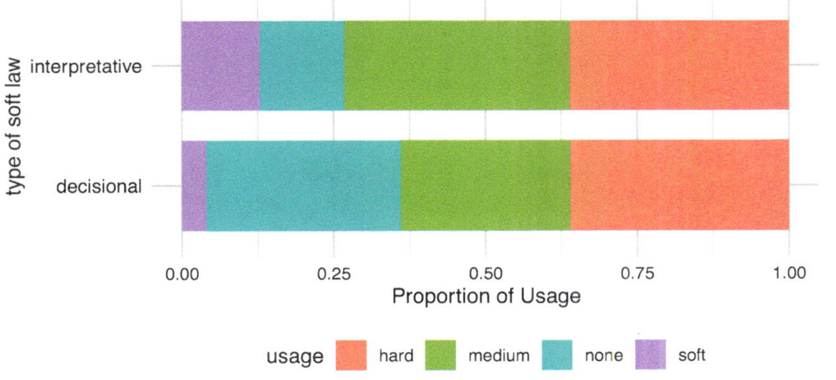

Fig. 5.6 Judgment data. Type of soft law usage by function of the instrument (*Note* Proportions shown on the y-axis. Interpretative soft law (n = 86), decisional soft law (n = 25). No cases for 'steering soft law' identified)

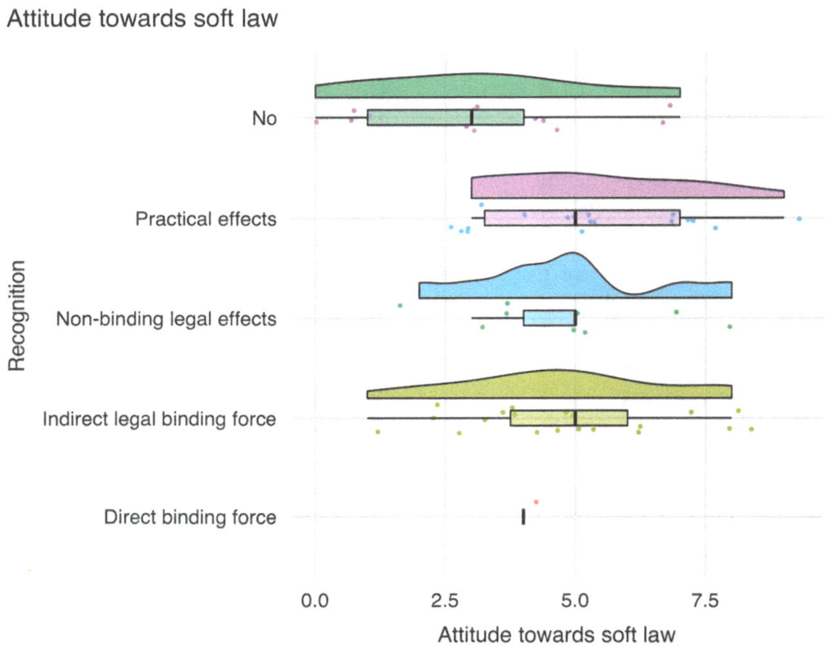

Fig. 5.7 Survey data. Recognition of soft law by attitude towards soft law (*Note* Scale from very negative (0) to very positive attitude (10). N = 70 respondents)

Moreover, judges' knowledge of EU law was expected to matter. We asked how closely respondents follow developments in EU law on a ten-point scale, expecting that more extensive knowledge would predict more frequent and harder usage. There were no significant differences in types of recognition (no figure). However, Fig. 5.9 shows the co-variation of knowledge and frequency of usage. Most judges who have applied soft law report having a good or very good knowledge of EU law, while non-users report on average lower levels of knowledge.

Finally, we hypothesized that a judge's career level might affect soft law usage, with more senior judges likely being more familiar with and socialized into using EU instruments, including soft law. Again, we do not find harder usage by more senior judges (no figure). However, Fig. 5.10 shows slightly more frequent usage among senior judges (with over 10 years of experience) compared to more junior judges (with less than 10 years of

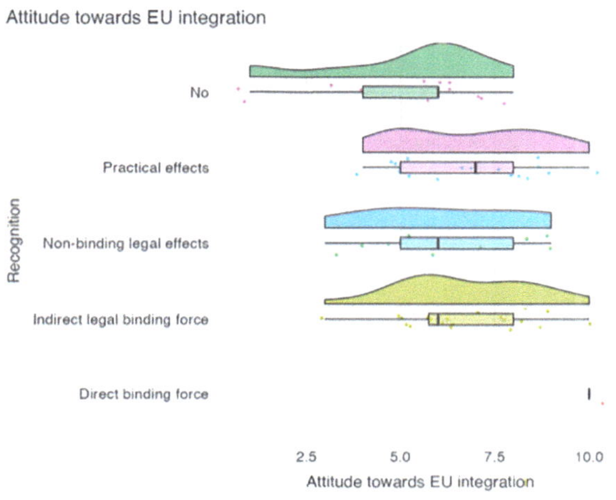

Fig. 5.8 Survey data. Recognition of soft law by attitude towards EU integration (*Note* Scale from very negative (0) to very positive (10). N = 70 respondents)

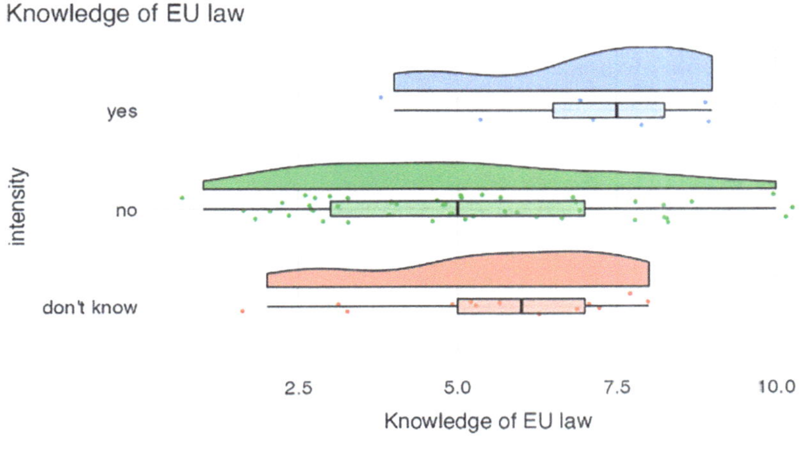

Fig. 5.9 Survey data. Frequency of soft law usage by knowledge of EU law (*Note* Scale from very little knowledge (0) to extensive knowledge (10). N = 70 respondents)

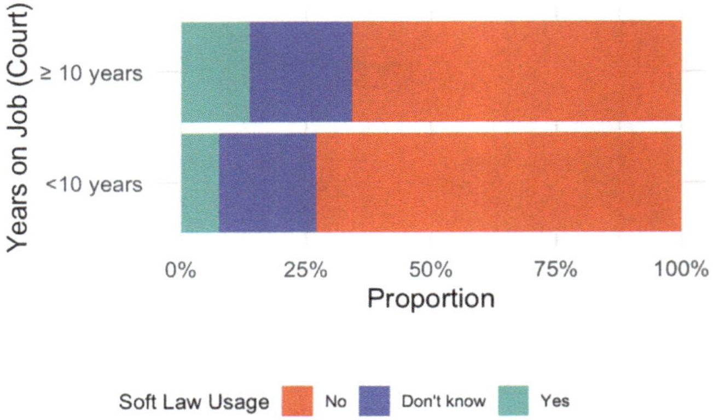

Fig. 5.10 Survey data. Frequency of usage by seniority (*Note* Proportions shown on the y-axis. Judges with 10 years' experience or more vs. those with less than 10 years)

experience), but the difference is not significant. Thus, judges' attitudes towards soft law have an effect on the way in which they use such instruments. But apart from that there are only small effects of actor-centered factors on soft law usage. This supports the idea that institutional factors are more relevant to explain the use of EU soft law in courts than the profile of individual judges.

5.4 Qualitative Evidence

To complement the quantitative survey results, this section draws on open-ended responses from 22 judges who answered the final survey question: "What other aspects of EU soft law are important to mention?" These respondents provided written answers which provide qualitative insights into the motivations to use EU soft law. This information can complement and contextualize the patterns identified in the earlier quantitative analysis. For reference, respondents are cited using abbreviations such as "SR12," indicating Survey Respondent 12 in the dataset. In the following, respondents are referred to in abbreviations such as 'SR12,' which stands for Survey Respondent with the ID variable 12 in the survey dataset.

How do Judges Use Soft Law? In terms of *how judges use soft law*, the qualitative evidence corroborates the quantitative finding that *medium-hard uses* are the most frequent. Most of the open responses that describe the type of usage fall into this category (SR24, SR25, SR28, SR96, SR132, SR49). For example, a German judge explains that "when interpreting provisions, opinions of the Commission etc. could also be taken into account within the framework of a recourse to legal materials" (SR49). Similarly, a French judge describes medium-hard effects, where soft law can "produce legal effects without binding force (sanctions)" (SR96).

A smaller number of responses point to soft usage or no usage of soft law. For example, one German judge describes soft law as something one may consider informally but which is legally irrelevant: "In the end it is irrelevant for court decisions. We take a look at it, sometimes we raise it as an issue in court decisions, but then we always point out that it is not binding. And we do not see ourselves bound by it in any way" (SR25). Another German respondent emphasizes perceived legal constraints, stating that "an influence of soft law on concrete court proceedings seems hardly conceivable in view of Art. 288 para. 5 TEU and Art. 20 para. 3 GG" (SR49). For some, soft law appears marginal in judicial practice, with one French judge admitting: "I had never heard of it before answering this questionnaire" (SR97). This qualitative evidence therefore supports the broader pattern that medium-hard usage is the most prevalent form of judicial engagement with EU soft law, while a minority of judges report only limited or no use at all.

What Judges Think of Soft Law and Why They Use It. Some of the open responses provide qualitative insight into how judges assess EU soft law and explain their use of such instruments. In line with earlier findings that interpretative uses together with hard law dominate, many judges view soft law as a helpful interpretive aid. However, the responses also highlight limitations: several judges raise concerns about soft law's legitimacy and the legal uncertainty it can create. When asked to rate their overall attitude towards soft law on a 10-point scale from very negative to very positive, the average response was slightly negative with a mean of 4.33. However, the relatively high standard deviation of 2.15 shows that views are diverse among respondents (Fig. 5.11).

We find a similar pattern when we group the qualitative responses to the open survey question into more negative and positive assessments of

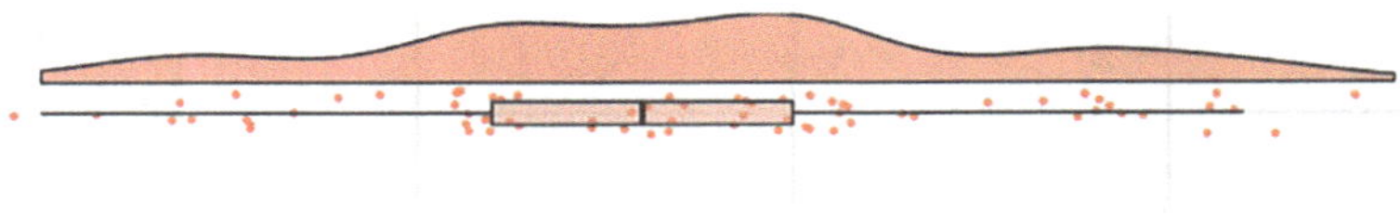

Fig. 5.11 Survey data. Distribution of attitudes towards soft law (n = 70) (*Note* Scale from very negative (0) to very positive (10). N = 70 respondents)

soft law. Twelve of the qualitative assessments of soft law are negative and only five are positive.[1]

In the *negative assessments* we find several reoccurring themes: soft law's lack of legitimacy, insufficient transparency in soft law adoption, EU overreach and increased legal uncertainty or workload. More specifically, several respondents say soft law lacks *legitimacy* or is not *transparent* (SR24, SR89, SR76, SR107). A German judge wishes that in courts "the application of soft law should be transparent and comprehensible and remain within legal standards" (SR25). A French judge says that the lack of transparency in the publication of soft law is especially problematic when courts use it in 'harder' ways. The judge specifies that "the publicity of soft law is relatively insufficient in relation to its effects, especially if soft law, as in French domestic law under the impetus of the Council of State, is to become, under certain conditions, an enforceable standard in the same way as hard law" (SR73). This refers to a series of judgments by the *Conseil d'État* that recognized national soft law as legally relevant, capable of producing legal and practical effects, and sometimes subject to judicial review (Knauff, 2018, pp. 74–75). The judge argues this could lead to courts transforming soft law into harder norms and which the judge criticizes from a rule of law perspective. This reflects a broader concern that judicial soft law usage can contribute to the *hardening* of soft law, where soft law becomes closer to hard law in practice, even if it remains formally non-binding.

Relatedly, other respondents warn that EU institutions use soft law to extend their *competences* beyond their mandate (SR76, SR89, SR107).

[1] Negative assessments of soft law were given by respondents SR24, SR28, SR49, SR73, SR116, SR76, SR89, SR107, SR108, SR115, SR138 and SR139; positive assessments by respondents SR28, SR29, SR35, SR69 and SR132.

With reference to EU soft law, one French judge says that "it would be desirable for the European Union to remain within the margins set for it and to respect the principle of subsidiarity of the Member States (...)" (SR76). Another French judge interprets the rise of soft law as "a sign that states are accepting to lose their (binding) regulatory power to the benefit of lobbyists, even though they are not elected" (SR107).

Several respondents are concerned that soft law increases *legal uncertainty* (SR28, SR89, SR138, SR108). A judge raises the concern that soft law may incorrectly explain and summarize hard law, creating "a risk that the relevant legal situation may be inaccurately captured" (SR28). Yet others say that soft law increases the *complexity* of EU law and thus contributes to legal uncertainty (SR28, SR89, SR108, SR138). A French respondent states that "soft law contributes to the inflation of regulations faced by the judge, which is not a gain in legal certainty for the public" (SR138). A German judge points to the increased workload through soft law in certain circumstances: "(...) recommendations and internal guidelines often unfortunately do not serve to provide a clear overview of the relevant law. (...) Supplementary soft references to [EU hard law], which are not legally relevant anyway and are usually more difficult to find, are therefore often rather a hindrance in the application of binding Union law. They usually increase the amount of material to be dealt with without a justifiable return in terms of finding the law" (SR28).

Yet, several respondents also expressed *positive views* of EU soft law (SR28, SR29, SR35, SR69, SR132). In line with the quantitative findings, some judges emphasize the usefulness of EU soft law in their own work as an *aid to interpreting hard law* (SR28, SR35, SR132). A French respondent finds that "soft law can help the national judge to interpret EU legal norms and certain treaty provisions (Asylum, law on foreigners, Dublin III etc.)" (SR132). A German judge agrees but qualifies this view: "[Soft law instruments] can be helpful, provided that they are very carefully limited to the secured normative status in binding interpretation by the European Court of Justice, only work towards compliance with it and otherwise make clear to what extent recommendations are only to be regarded as aids to fill in the remaining leeway in the application of the law in the Member States in an appropriate manner, without calling for strict compliance" (SR28). This aligns with the finding that courts use soft law in medium and hard ways, but never quite like hard law. Similarly, an interviewed judge from a German higher ordinary court says that soft law can help interpret the purpose, legislative history, or background of a hard law provision. But the judge emphasizes limits to this interpretative role. It can only have a meaning as a supplement to other legal sources and not on its own. If there's a serious interpretative dispute over EU law, the proper route is to refer questions to the Court of Justice of the European Union, not to simply rely on Commission opinions or other soft law (Court 1).

Further, two judges acknowledge the positive impact of soft law on the broader EU legal system, emphasizing its role in ***harmonizing EU legislation*** and its implementation across Member States (SR29, SR69). A French judge believes soft law "allows a better harmonization of administrative practices between the different Member States by avoiding differences in interpretation" (SR69).

5.5 Takeaways from the Explanations

This chapter probed institutional and actor-centered explanations for the use of EU soft law by courts based on judgment and survey data, complemented by qualitative survey responses. The results indicate that institutional factors are more relevant than actor-centered factors in explaining harder and more frequent judicial uses of EU soft law in courts. Specifically, the national legal style and characteristics of the judicial branch are relevant: German courts have more frequent and harder usage than French courts, likely due to Germany's legal style of more elaborate judicial reasoning. Similarly, administrative courts use soft law more often and in harder ways, likely reflecting the longstanding role of soft law in national administrative law into which the administrative judiciary is socialized. The level of competence in a policy area and the connection of soft law to hard law also matter for soft law usage, but to a smaller and less systematic extent.

Actor-centered factors only matter in very limited ways. For example, judges with negative views of soft law are more likely to reject its legal effects. Furthermore, judges with more extensive knowledge of EU law, as well as senior judges, are slightly more likely to have used soft law.

Finally, the qualitative survey responses reinforce the finding that judges most commonly use EU soft law to interpret hard law. Where judges view soft law positively, they do so because they consider it as a helpful tool for interpreting EU legislation and promoting harmonization of EU law. This confirms the relevance of the linkage of soft law to the existing legal framework in a hybrid legal regime where soft law and hard law coexist rather than being separate, competing phenomena.

However, some respondents also view EU soft law more negatively. They express concerns about its legitimacy and transparency, as well as its potential to exceed the EU's competences. This points to the limitations of soft law in the judiciary. Some judges are reluctant to apply EU soft law at all, and even those who embrace it are unlikely to use it in the same way as hard law. Instead, soft law is generally considered a phenomenon between non-law and hard law. This suggests that, while the judicial use of soft law can reinforce the interpretative authority of such instruments, it does not typically transform soft law into hard law. However, these findings raise further questions. While we found that institutions matter, what exactly are the mechanisms behind soft law usage? Furthermore, what are the effects of the use of EU soft law by courts? These issues will be addressed in the next chapter, which contains comparative case studies providing a more in-depth, qualitative analysis of the phenomenon.

References

Hartlapp, M., & Hofmann, A. (2020). The use of EU soft law by national courts and bureaucrats: How relation to hard law and policy maturity matter. *West European Politics, 44*(1), 134–154.

Héritier, A., & Lehmkuhl, D. (2008). The shadow of hierarchy and new modes of governance. *Journal of Public Policy, 28*(1), 1–17.

Klabbers, J. (1998). The undesirability of soft law. *Nordic Journal of International Law, 67*(4), 381–391.

Knauff, M. (2018). Soft law vor Gericht. *juris—Die Monatszeitschrift (jM)*, 71–75.

König, T., & Mader, L. (2007). *Bürokratisierung oder Politisierung? Eine Untersuchung der Umsetzungseffekte von Europäischen Richtlinien in den Mitgliedstaaten der Europäischen Union im Zeitraum von 1985–2003* (Speyerer Forschungsberichte Issue).

Nowak, T., Amtenbrink, F., Hertogh, M. L. M., & Wissink, M. H. (2011). *National judges as European Union judges: Knowledge, experiences and attitudes of lower court judges in Germany and the Netherlands*. Eleven International Publishing.

Nowak, T., & Glavina, M. (2020). National courts as regulatory agencies and the application of EU law. *Journal of European Integration, 43*(1), 1–15.

Pavone, T. (2022). *The Ghostwriters: Lawyers and the politics behind the judicial construction of Europe*. Cambridge University Press.

Rubio, N., & Stefan, O. (2021). No longer small enough to fall through the cracks: A French story of adaptation to the petites sources of EU Law. In M. Eliantonio, E. Korkea-aho, & O. Stefan (Eds.), *EU soft law in the member states: Theoretical findings and empirical evidence* (1 ed., pp. 135–150). Hart Publishing.

Scott, J. (2011). In legal limbo: Post-legislative guidance as a challenge for European administrative law. *Common Market Law Review*, *48*(2), 329–355.

Senden, L. A. J. (2004). *Soft law in European Community law*. Hart Publishing.

Steiner, E. (2018). *French law: A comparative approach* (2nd ed.). Oxford University Press.

Weber, R. K. (2019). *Der Begründungsstil von Conseil constitutionnel und Bundesverfassungsgericht: eine vergleichende Analyse der Spruchpraxis* (Vol. 26). Mohr Siebeck.

CHAPTER 6

Tracing Mechanisms and Wider Effects: Four Case Studies

6.1 Studying Soft Law Usage with Case Studies

The previous empirical chapters, based on both quantitative patterns of judgments and a survey of judges, established that EU soft law is rarely used in national courts. However, where soft law is used, it often takes legally relevant forms, where soft law informs legal interpretations and courts recognize the practical and legal effects of such instruments (Chapter 4). Institutional factors, especially those related to country and court branch, were identified as the factors that can best explain patterns of usage (Chapter 5). But these quantitative patterns cannot uncover the precise mechanisms through which such factors operate, nor can they capture the broader legal and policy effects of the use of soft law in courts. To address these gaps, this chapter conducts comparative case studies using process tracing. As detailed in Chapter 3, this empirical approach allows us to complement the previous quantitative findings in several ways. Focusing on mechanisms allows us to understand why and through what sequence soft law becomes relevant in court decisions. Tracing broader effects on legal interpretation and policy helps assess the wider relevance of soft law in courts. This in-depth knowledge also allows us to assess in a more nuanced way the normative implications of the phenomenon on the democratic quality of soft law and the evolving role of the judiciary in the EU multilevel system.

A. Eick, *Soft Law and National Courts in the European Union*, European Administrative Governance, https://doi.org/10.1007/978-3-032-04515-7_6

This chapter argues that national courts' use of EU soft law is shaped by the governance arrangements of respective policy areas. It does so by examining German court judgments in two contrasting policy areas that differ in their governance arrangements between the EU and national level. The chapter focuses on policy-specific mechanisms for several reasons. The quantitative findings in previous chapters pointed to the relevance of policy-level factors but were not fine-grained enough to trace the exact causal mechanisms. Moreover, scholarship on EU hard law leads suggests that policy variance matters: EU competences to adopt hard law developed unevenly across policy areas (Biesenbender, 2011; Börzel, 2005), and at the national level, sectoral dynamics shape implementation and application of EU law (Treib, 2014). Thus, policy variance should also matter for how EU soft law is used, as the adoption and function of soft law greatly varies between policy areas (Senden, 2004; Terpan, 2015). Another reason is that broader effects of EU soft law are linked to specific policy dynamics. Although the judicial use of soft law has an effect beyond the courtroom in both policy areas, the form and extent differ. In state aid, soft law contributes to judicial decisions that reinforce a particular view of the state's role in the economy. In pharmaceutical regulation, the use of soft law in courts contributes to the harmonization of administrative practices and the level of risk regulation in Europe.

In line with the previous chapters, *case selection* of *policy areas* focuses on state aid and pharmaceutical regulation as two contrasting yet relevant policy areas, where the judicial use of EU soft law is likely. Both policy areas are characterized by a high prevalence of EU soft law instruments and, as Chapter 4 showed, court cases involving soft law. As Chapter 5 argued, institutions of a policy area affect soft law usage. The two policy areas differ significantly in institutions related to their governance structures. On the one hand, state aid is characterized by hierarchical governance with centralized enforcement at the EU level, where the European Commission holds exclusive powers and national authorities and private actors are the regulated entities (Blauberger, 2009a). In contrast, pharmaceutical regulation follows a model of 'composite administration,' characterized by shared decision-making between national and EU authorities, involving close cooperation and involvement from national scientific experts (Permanand, 2006). Relatedly, EU competences and legal frameworks vary. State aid is a policy area of exclusive EU competence that is fully harmonized by EU law, leaving no room for national legislation (Blauberger, 2009b). Pharmaceutical regulation is an area of shared EU competence, where regulation is only partially harmonized. Some subareas, such as the authorization of medicines, are highly harmonized, others, such as the pricing of medicines, are still mostly regulated by national law (Permanand, 2006).

The same *soft law instruments* were selected as for the judgment data in Chapters 3 and 4. As a reminder, from each policy area, two soft law instruments were selected that are both relevant and representative of the sector's governance arrangement and legal framework. The case studies of *judgments* focus on German courts rather than French courts. The main reason is that, as argued in Chapter 5, German judgments have longer argumentation and have more explicit reasoning than French courts. This provides a richer empirical basis for qualitative analysis. For each instrument, a series of typical and relevant court judgments in German courts is traced. They were selected to represent the most common type of judicial usage of soft law for each instrument. Further cases are mentioned as supplementary sources to demonstrate wider generalizability. Empirically, the analysis draws on full-text judgments from all judicial instances as well as interview data. Interviewees include a judge from a German higher administrative court and several officials from national administrations and regulatory agencies.

The chapter is structured as follows: it begins with two case studies in state aid, followed by two case studies in pharmaceutical regulation. Each section opens with an overview of the governance arrangement and legal framework in the policy area. It then introduces the selected soft law instruments and judgments. Further, each case study traces the instrument's development at the EU level, its implementation in national administrative and societal practice, and its application in judicial proceedings. This is followed by an analysis of the mechanisms that drive the use of soft law in courts, as well as its broader legal and policy effects. The chapter concludes with a comparative discussion of the findings and reflects on their wider implications for law and policy.

6.2 State Aid: Hierarchical Governance and Soft Law

6.2.1 Introduction to State Aid Law and Soft Law

This first section focuses on *state aid* policy with two case studies from German courts: one involving the *SGEI Communication* and the other the *Environmental and Energy State Aid Guidelines*. The analysis argues that both national administrations and, ultimately, courts regard soft law in this area as authoritative and legally authoritative, largely due to the hierarchical nature of the governance structure in the policy area. Before going into the empirical analysis, the next section introduces the policy area's governance structure and legal framework.

Hierarchical Governance and a Hybrid Legal Framework. State aid regulation is characterized by hierarchical governance led by the European Commission, where soft law complements binding primary law and case law. State aid refers to subsidies and measures of similar effect by national authorities to private actors. The EU has competence to regulate and control them as part of competition law. EU law in principle prohibits national state aid in the economy to retain a level-playing field in the internal market, but there are many exceptions. The Commission has the sole competence to control state aid in a system of centralized and systematic enforcement: Member States must notify measures of state aid above a certain threshold to the Commission, which then takes binding decisions on their lawfulness. The Commission can prohibit planned state aid and order the recovery of illegally disbursed state aid (Hofmann et al., 2016, pp. 348–380).

The basic rules of the policy area are laid down in primary law, specifically Articles 106–108 TFEU. But these rules are vague, worded in an open-ended language, and leave a wide margin of discretion to the Commission. Soft law plays a crucial role to fill in the gaps of hard law in a hybrid legal regime. Several authors recount that this mode of regulation evolved over time due to demand by the Member States and activism by the Commission (Blauberger, 2009b, pp. 725–729; Cini, 2001; Doleys, 2013; Lavdas & Mendrinou, 1999; Smith, 1998). In the early days of European Integration, the treaty provisions stood on their own, but were largely ignored until the 1970s, when the Commission began to enforce state aid in single-case decisions. The unpredictability of enforcement on a case-by-case basis provoked a backlash from some

Member States. To gain authority and recognition as an enforcer, the Commission sought to codify the criteria of its assessment. But because of heterogeneous preferences and uneven spending capacity of governments, several early attempts by the Commission to regulate the sector through (hard) secondary law failed in the Council.[1] Instead, the Commission developed what Cini (2001) calls a 'soft law approach.' It began adopting soft law that interprets the treaties to fill in the gaps of primary law. Sinnaeve and Slot (1999, pp. 1135–1153) argue that the Commission soon found that such soft law instruments were sufficient to incrementally regulate the sector and satisfy calls for legal certainty, without running the risk of having its powers curtailed in the legislative process. Blauberger (2009b, pp. 725–726) finds that from the view of the Commission, soft law is more effective and creates less political pressure from the Member States than secondary law. But the Member States and third parties also supported the soft law approach for reasons of legal certainty, as such instruments made state aid enforcement much more predictable (Blauberger, 2009b). Since 1999, the role of secondary law has increased with the adoption of regulations on procedural rules (such as Council Regulation 2015/1589), exemptions from notification (such as Council Regulation 651/2014), and rules for narrow sectors (such as Council Regulation 2022/2586). Nevertheless, soft law remains the dominant regulatory tool in this policy area. Cappellina et al. find that between 2004 and 2019, 66% of instruments adopted in this policy area were soft law. These are the instruments that contain the most detailed interpretations and technical provisions of state aid control (2022, p. 83). Table 6.1 situates soft law in the EU wider state aid regulation by showing main types of law, their regulatory function and examples.

Thus, the *governance arrangement* in state aid can be characterized as *hierarchical* with a strong role of the Commission as enforcer and regulator acting in a supranational mode. National actors are the regulated parties, both national authorities who grant subsidies and wider societal actors, such as companies, who receive them. The legal framework is deeply entrenched in binding primary law and case law, but soft

[1] In principle, the sector could be governed by secondary law under Article 109 TFEU, which empowers the Council to adopt Regulations by qualified majority voting on a Commission proposal after consulting the European Parliament. But this legislative route has been used only rarely.

Table 6.1 Types, function and examples of state aid law

Type of law	*Notable examples*	*Regulatory function*
Primary law	• Articles 106–109 TFEU	• Legal basis of state aid control • Basic rules, procedures, competences
Secondary law	• Enabling Regulation (Council Regulation 2015/1588) • Procedural Regulation (Regulation 2015/1589) • General Block Exemption Regulation (Regulation 651/2014) • De Minimis Regulation (Regulation 1407/2013)	• Specification of primary law • Procedural rules • Exemption of certain areas from state aid reporting or control • Special sectoral rules (e.g. public passenger transport)
Soft law	• Notice on the Notion of Aid • Aviation State Aid Guidelines • Environmental- and Energy State Aid Guidelines • Code of Best Practices	• Clarification, interpretation and specification of hard law • Definition of the scope of state aid • Criteria to assess if state aid is compatible with the internal market • Practical and procedural guidance to national actors

law makes up most instruments and plays a crucial complementary role specifying the legal framework.

Role and Function of Soft Law in State Aid. As mentioned, almost all soft law instruments in the area of state aid are closely linked to and specify existing hard law. In particular, they elaborate on EU primary law, Commission enforcement decisions, and CJEU case law (Hofmann et al., 2016, pp. 25–28). The CJEU has repeatedly made clear, for example in *France v Commission*,[2] that such soft law must remain consistent with the underlying legal framework and cannot formally deviate from it. But soft law nevertheless does not only restate existing rules. It often provides detailed interpretations of vague or open-ended provisions in hard law. This can be called an 'active' interpretation, as soft law adds an additional interpretative layer to the legal framework in such cases without departing from it (Van Dam, 2017, p. 84). An example

[2] Judgment of the Court of 20 March 1997. French Republic v Commission of the European Communities. Case C-57/95, paras. 19–26.

are the *Guidelines on Regional State aid*,[3] which focus on subsidies for regional economic development. Article 107 TFEU sets out a very general framework for when state aid aimed at regional development can be compatible with the internal market. The soft law Guidelines then fill the gaps by providing precise economic indicators and thresholds that national authorities should apply when planning regional subsidies. Moreover, the guidelines introduce extensive reporting obligations not explicitly laid down in hard law. Notably, Member States must identify regions eligible for regional aid, draw up a map of those regions, and submit them to the Commission for approval (Ambroziak, 2014; Wishlade, 2003). Detailed economic indicators must be applied in this process, which requires considerable administrative capacities. Thus, the general framework comes from the Treaties, but extensive additional administrative requirements are typically detailed by soft law in the gaps of hard law.

But beyond these commonalities, state aid soft law instruments vary in function. Drawing on the Commission's legislation overview[4] and the legal literature (Bartosch, 2016, pp. 1–18; Hofmann et al., 2015, pp. 36–61), I identify three distinct types of state aid soft law instruments, each corresponding to a different stage of state aid control: First, instruments giving *practical guidance* on the application of state aid law in specific national administrative processes. Examples are 'Questions and Answers' documents[5] or the 'Code of Best Practices.'[6] They can be placed on the 'softer' side of the spectrum of legal norms (see Chapter 2): They are more informal in tone, only give suggestions rather than spelling out requirements and mostly address procedural questions. National actors perceive them as guidance that is sometimes helpful in practice, but not legally authoritative, and they often deviate from or ignore them (IG7,

[3] European Commission. Guidelines on regional State aid ('Regional Aid Guidelines'). C/2021/2594. 19 April 2021, pp. 1–46.

[4] European Commission. State Aid Legislation. Undated. https://competition-policy.ec.europa.eu/state-aid/legislation_en, last accessed 10 July 2025.

[5] E.g. European Commission. Questions and answers on the Foreign Subsidies Regulation. 9 April 2024. https://competition-policy.ec.europa.eu/foreign-subsidies-regulation/questions-and-answers_en, last accessed 10 July 2025.

[6] European Commission. Code of Best Practices for the conduct of State aid control procedures. C/2018/4412. OJ C 253. 19 July 2018, pp. 14–27.

para. 44).[7] Due to their limited effects, I will disregard them in the remaining chapter.

The second type of soft law defines the *scope* of EU state aid control—specifically, how far it extends into national policies and practices. It addresses key questions of "what qualifies as state aid" and "which forms of state aid must be notified to the European Commission." Thereby, it clarifies the definition of state aid of Article 107(1) TFEU and the related case law of the CJEU. Examples include the 'Notice on the Notion of Aid'[8] and the 'SGEI Communication.'[9] These instruments perform what Linda Senden describes as an 'interpretative' function, meaning they are "supporting and supplementing (...) [EU] law, in particular to ensuring the proper interpretation and uniform application thereof" (Senden, 2004, pp. 138–147). National actors regard them as authoritative guidance on the interpretation of hard law (Min4, para. 12; IG1, para. 20). They are commonly used during the planning of state aid measures, such as subsidies or tax incentives, to determine whether the measure falls under state aid rules and must be notified to the Commission.

When a state aid measure requires notification to the Commission, a third category of state aid soft law becomes relevant: guidelines on the *compatibility* of state aid with the internal market. These instruments clarify which forms of state aid are considered lawful under Article 107(3) TFEU and thus compatible with the internal market. Examples include instruments with horizontal aims spanning multiple sectors like the 'Guidelines on Regional Aid'[10] and the 'Environmental- and Energy State Aid Guidelines,'[11] as well as sector-specific guidelines, such

[7] In this chapter, Interviews are abbreviated in the form "IG7," "Min1," "Min2." Where applicable, a specific paragraph of the transcript is referenced. A list of interviews is provided in Appendix Section 4.

[8] Commission Notice on the notion of State aid as referred to in Article 107(1) of the Treaty on the Functioning of the European Union (Notice on the Notion of Aid). C/2016/2946. OJ C 262. 19 July 2016, pp. 1–50.

[9] Communication from the Commission on the application of the European Union State aid rules to compensation granted for the provision of services of general economic interest ("SGEI Communication"), OJ C 8, 11 January 2012, pp. 4–14.

[10] Guidelines on regional State aid for 2014–2020 (Regional Aid Guidelines). OJ C 209, 23.7.2013, pp. 1–45.

[11] Communication from the Commission. Guidelines on State aid for environmental protection and energy 2014–2020 (EEAG). OJ C 200, 28.6.2014, pp. 1–55.

as the 'Aviation Guidelines.'[12] These instruments are adopted by the Commission to summarize its past decision-making practice, harmonize enforcement procedures, and communicate to Member States and stakeholders how it intends to apply state aid rules (Hofmann et al., 2016, pp. 50–52). As such, they fulfill what Senden (2004, pp. 148–154) calls a 'decisional' function: they "indicate in what way a [EU] institution will apply [EU] law provisions in individual cases when it has implementing and discretionary powers" (ibid. 119). This decisional function is similar to an interpretative function, but the emphasis is here on providing criteria for the Commission's decision-making when applying EU law in concrete cases. Substantively, these guidelines provide legal criteria, economic assessments, and indicators used to evaluate the compatibility of national state aid measures. Blauberger (2009b, p. 726) emphasizes that state aid guidelines often indirectly formulate goals beyond competition policy, for example by encouraging certain aims of industrial policies. They are thus not only tools of 'negative integration' (Scharpf, 2008), where the EU prohibits certain actions by national actors to create a level-playing field across Member States, but they often also serve as instruments of 'positive integration,' where the EU actively shapes and coordinates national policy goals across Member States.

State aid soft law is clearly at the 'harder' end of the soft law spectrum: it resembles hard law in some respects, despite being formally non-binding. But there is a debate over state aid soft law's exact legal status (Banet, 2020). The CJEU has repeatedly confirmed, notably in *Kotnik*,[13] that the Commission must follow its own guidelines to maintain legal certainty and equal treatment among Member States. By publishing its enforcement criteria in the form of soft law, the Commission then effectively limits its own discretion. This means that if a national authority justifies a measure of state aid based on criteria from state aid guidelines, the Commission cannot use wholly different evaluation criteria during enforcement. This makes state aid guidelines indirectly binding for the Commission in practice. However, the Court emphasizes that this is formally not the same as the binding force of hard law. First, the binding force for the Commission stems not directly from the guidelines

[12] Communication from the Commission. Guidelines on State aid to airports and airlines (Aviation Guidelines). OJ C 99, 4 April 2014, pp. 3–34.

[13] Judgment of the Court (Grand Chamber) of 19 July 2016. *Kotnik*. Case C-526/14, paras. 39–45.

themselves, but indirectly from general principles of EU law and treaty provisions (Banet, 2020; Bouchagiar, 2017; Stefan, 2008). Second, in cases such as *Pfleiderer*,[14] the Court has held that the guidelines are not binding on national authorities (Hofmann et al., 2016, p. 25). In principle, Member States retain the formal legal freedom to disregard the guidelines and rely solely on primary law in justifying their measures. The Commission cannot reject a measure solely because national authorities did not invoke soft law criteria.

In practice, however, national actors experience this freedom as largely theoretical. While they are formally free to ignore soft law, doing so leads to significant legal uncertainty. The Commission, as the guardian of the Treaties, holds considerable interpretive discretion in state aid enforcement. This means that deviations from soft law increase the risk that aid measures will be challenged or rejected. As a result, even when Member States disagree with certain criteria in soft law, they often choose to rely on them because doing so ensures predictability in enforcement. Therefore, national actors perceive state aid guidelines in many situations as binding for practical purposes (Min1, para. 38; IG2, para. 15; IG7, para. 2).

State Aid: Case Selection. The case selection follows the general rationale of the book introduced in Chapter 2 and is further detailed here for each policy area. The *soft law instruments* were chosen as typical and relevant examples within their respective categories. As argued above, the most important policy-specific functions of state aid soft law the defining the 'scope' of state aid and providing criteria for the 'compatibility' of state aid. The *SGEI Communication* is selected as a case of interpretative soft law, performing a scope function by interpreting hard law on the boundaries of the state aid regime. In contrast, the *Environmental and Energy State Aid Guidelines* (EEAG) are a decisional soft law, operationalizing the Commission's discretionary powers under the Treaties and specifying the conditions under which aid is compatible with the internal market.

The *selection of relevant judgments* involving these instruments for the case studies builds on the main judgment data that was introduced in Chapter 3 and analyzed in Chapters 4 and 5. From this data, judgments were chosen based on how typically courts applied a soft law instrument

[14] Judgment of the Court (Grand Chamber) of 14 June 2011. *Pfleiderer AG v Bundeskartellamt*. Case C-360/09.

and recognized its legal effects. The SGEI Communication was used in 20 German judgments but not in any French cases, while the EEAG appeared in 20 German and 12 French judgments. The SGEI Communication was most frequently used as an *aid to interpret hard law* (in 18 of 20 cases), whereas the EEAG was mostly used as a *supplementary standard of review* (9 cases) and as *aid to interpret hard law* (5 cases). For both instruments, courts most often recognized an *indirect binding effect* of soft law (see Chapter 3). In state aid cases, the composition of actors involved in judicial disputes also varies significantly. Cases concerning the SGEI Communication consistently involved private actors challenging public authorities, whereas cases related to the EEAG included public–private disputes as well as private-private disputes, e.g. between competing companies. Two series of judgments were selected that are relevant and reflect this variation. They are relevant and typical cases that both illustrate medium-hard usage: a public–private conflict concerning hospital financing in which the SGEI Communication was used to interpret hard law (BGH, 24 March 2016, I ZR 263/14), and a private-private conflict involving renewable energy support where the EEAG was applied as both aid to interpret hard law and supplementary standard of review (BGH, 14 July 2020, XIII ZR 12/19).

6.2.2 SGEI Communication

The first case study examines the 2012 *SGEI Communication*,[15] a *scope* soft law adopted by the European Commission. It aims to clarify when EU state aid rules apply to the financing of public services, especially in the sectors of social services, education, and health care. It does so by summarizing and interpreting Commission decisions and CJEU case law, particularly the landmark *Altmark Trans* judgment (C-280/00).[16] Substantively, the SGEI Communication clarifies when compensations of public service providers constitute state aid, which would trigger the application of EU state aid rules and potentially require notification to the Commission. The underlying broader policy question is how far EU

[15] Communication from the Commission on the application of the European Union State aid rules to compensation granted for the provision of services of general economic interest Text with EEA relevance, OJ C 8, 11 January 2012, pp. 4–14.

[16] Judgment of the Court of 24 July 2003. *Altmark Trans*. Case C-280/00.

competition law extends into the realm of national public service provision, which is closely linked to wider political debates about the degree of market exposure for public services and the state's role in the economy (Bieling, 2023).

EU law distinguishes between different types of public services. Purely non-economic public services are exempt from state aid control altogether. But public services with a potential economic dimension are called *Services of General Economic Interest* (SGEIs), and they fall under state aid control, although they receive lighter regulatory treatment than other state aid measures. While SGEIs are monitored in the EU state aid regime, they typically don't require advance notification and approval by the Commission (European Commission, 2022).[17] The critical challenge for national authorities is determining whether their public service financing arrangements fall outside state aid control or qualify as SGEI. When national authorities compensate a public service provider, they need to make several assessments to make sure they comply with state aid law. First, assess whether their measure constitutes state aid at all. If a measure is not state aid, they can ignore state aid law and control. But if it does qualify as state aid, the next step is to evaluate whether the measure qualifies as SGEI. If it does not, the full state aid requirements and in many cases, notification of the measure to the Commission is required. However, if the measure is an SGEI, state aid requirements are more relaxed, and notification is generally not necessary. Thus, for national authorities, the ideal outcome is to design public service financing arrangements in a way that avoids classification as state aid altogether. The next-best scenario is for the measure to qualify as an SGEI. This is where the Commission's SGEI Communication comes in as a scope soft law by interpreting the legal definitions and criteria relevant to this evaluation based on Commission decisions and CJEU cases.

Formulation of the SGEI Communication at EU level. Before the 1990s, EU state aid enforcement did not target public services. This changed with market liberalization of the 1990s and increased Commission and CJEU activism, which expanded state aid enforcement slowly to publicly funded services (von Danwitz, 2009, p. 103). This was possible due to the open-ended definition of state aid in Article 107(1) TFEU, which does not clearly exclude public services from the scope of state

[17] European Commission. Services of general interest. Undated. https://ec.europa.eu/info/topics/single-market/services-general-interest_en, last accessed 10 July 2025.

aid enforcement. This broad definition of state aid led to ambiguity for national authorities regarding the legality of public service financing. Once the logic of state aid control was applied to this area, all types of public services which receive some kind of compensation from public authorities could potentially be affected, from public transport to waste management to welfare provision (Gerber, 1994). For national authorities, arrangements for the financing of public services were therefore long surrounded by legal uncertainty in state aid law. This was partially resolved by the CJEU's 2003 landmark judgment *Altmark Trans*,[18] which established four criteria under which such financing would not qualify as state aid. But Member States still perceived them as too vague and difficult to apply in practice.

The Commission took steps to further specify SGEI state aid under certain circumstances with the *2005 SGEI package*. This package consisted of a Decision and a Framework. However, this did not cover all situations and expired in 2011, still leaving legal uncertainty. In response, the Commission issued a further 'SGEI Package' in 2012, most notably including the SGEI Communication, which clarified legal concepts and the Commission's approach to state aid control in the sector (Géradin, 2012). The SGEI Communication was adopted for two reasons. First, Member States' demand for guidance, as they signaled a need for further clarity following the *Altmark* ruling. Second, the Commission pursued a broader strategic agenda at the time to reshape state aid policy through a 'more economic approach' characterized by market-oriented and efficiency-based analysis (Szyszczak, 2012, p. 322). The Communication operationalizes abstract criteria from Commission decisions and CJEU case law into concrete guidance involving economic benchmarking and profit assessment based on metrics of market efficiency. An example of this 'more economic approach' can be seen in how the SGEI Communication (paras. 69–77) clarifies the so-called fourth criterion from the *Altmark* judgment, which concerns the appropriate level of compensation for public services. This criterion requires that public authorities avoid overcompensation when financing public services. This can be achieved by either selecting the public service providers through public procurement, i.e. a tendering procedure, or by demonstrating that

[18] Judgment of the Court of 24 July 2003. *Altmark Trans*. 24/7/2003, C-280/00. paras. 87 ff.

the compensation does not exceed "the costs a typical, well-run undertaking would have incurred" (*Altmark* judgment, para. 93). This notion of a 'well-run undertaking' is very vague, but in line with the more economic approach, the SGEI Communication operationalizes it into detailed economic performance indicators, cost ratios and measures for return on capital. The Communication recommends national authorities to apply these methods when evaluating state aid measures in the area. This, in turn, requires from national authorities substantial economic knowledge and administrative capacities, which pushes them towards more market-efficient practices when financing public services.

The SGEI Communication in National Administrations. In *national administrations*, the SGEI Communication is widely used as *interpretive guidance* to address legal uncertainties around state aid rules for public service financing. It is particularly relevant at the subnational level, where services such as hospitals, social care, public transport, and social housing are typically financed by regional or municipal authorities. These actors, such as regional economic ministries and local governments, report that they frequently consult the Communication to assess whether a financial measure classifies as SGEI and thus state aid (Min4, para. 12; IG1, para. 18). However, consistent with its non-binding nature, the Communication is not regarded as a formal legal source, but rather as practical guidance to aid in the interpretation of binding EU law, such as the Treaties, CJEU cases, and Commission decisions (Min4, para. 12; IG1, para. 12; IG2, para. 20).

The overarching reason national authorities use the SGEI Communication is the *hierarchical governance structure* of the policy area state aid. As the Commission is both the enforcer of state aid rules and the guardian of the Treaties, its interpretations in the Communication are seen as highly authoritative. Thus, national authorities often align their funding practices with the criteria set out in the Communication and reference it in administrative decisions and contracts to demonstrate compliance with EU state aid law. However, the Communication is not always treated as definitive. When more recent CJEU judgments or Commission decisions suggest different interpretations, authorities sometimes diverge from the Communication's guidance. This has become increasingly common, particularly since the Communication has not been updated since its adoption in 2012 (IG2, para. 18–22).

In substance, national actors perceive the SGEI Communication as significantly extending the reach of state aid control into national policy, because it applies to nearly all public service arrangements involving third-party providers. This is because the Communication excludes almost no sector outright from state aid control. Diverse public services, such as social housing, public broadcasting, and welfare services can fall under state aid rules. Crucially for this case study, even hospitals, whose provision is often seen as core state power, are not automatically exempt. Moreover, the rules apply not only in cases of actual market competition but also when a market is potentially competitive. Further, this applies regardless of the provider's legal status, whether they are commercial companies, non-profits, or charities (Min4, para. 38; IG1, para. 18; IG7, para. 36). All of these points to the wide reach of EU state aid control.

The SGEI Communication in National Courts. The hierarchical governance structure of the policy area also plays a role in national courts. In a 2016 case, the *Bundesgerichtshof* (BGH) drew extensively on the SGEI Communication as an aid to interpret hard law alongside binding EU law to determine whether municipal hospital funding qualified as SGEI and thus as state aid. The court ultimately used the Communication to support the exemption of local hospitals from state aid control, reinforcing national discretion in public service provision.

Background to the Case. The first relevant case is the judgment *I ZR 263/14* of 24 March 2016 by the German ordinary apex court *Bundesgerichtshof* (BGH).[19] In this case, an association of private hospitals sought the suspension of payments for investments and operating costs made by the municipality of *Calw* to two municipal hospitals in the area. The association argued that these payments constituted unlawful state aid because they had not been notified in advance to the Commission, as required under EU state aid law (para. 1 of the judgment). The case raised two central legal questions: first, whether public funding for hospitals qualifies as state aid under EU rules. Second, if it does, whether this funding requires prior notification to the Commission or can instead be exempted due to its qualification as compensation for a Service of General Economic Interest (SGEI) (para. 13). The broader issue at stake was whether compensating public hospitals for losses falls under EU state aid rules, thereby giving the Commission the power to prohibit such funding. According to one interviewee involved in the case, it was intentionally framed as a test case aimed at challenging the legality of these widespread

[19] BGH 1. *Zivilsenat*, 24 March 2016, judgment I ZR 263/14.

funding practices and, potentially, calling them all into question (IG6, para. 6).

The case had potentially significant policy implications, as most German public hospitals do not operate at a profit and regularly receive public support from municipalities or regional authorities to cover operational costs (Malzahn & Wehner, 2010, pp. 113–117). It highlighted a potential tension between national policy of supporting healthcare services for the public good and EU competition law which aims to prevent unfair market advantages. One could even argue that the case had transnational relevance. In the absence of definitive CJEU case law, the underlying legal questions at stake were unresolved across Europe (Gallo & Mariotti, 2017). In fact, many Member States organize hospital financing according to principles of solidarity rather than a pure market logic. An extension of state aid rules could then disrupt established models of financing. While a German judgment holds no formal authority elsewhere, it could nonetheless serve as a reference point for other national courts and EU authorities.

Judgment by the Bundesgerichtshof. The case proceeded through the German court system, from the lower court *LG Tübingen*[20] to the higher court *OLG Stuttgart*[21] to the apex court *Bundesgerichtshof (BGH)*.[22] Both the LG Tübingen and OLG Stuttgart assessed the notification requirement solely on the basis of hard law, without engaging with the SGEI Communication. In contrast, the BGH made extensive use of the SGEI Communication in case *I ZR 263/14* (paras. 41, 79, 80, 99 of the judgment). The Court always used it as an aid to interpret hard law. Specifically, to interpret key legal concepts at issue. A judge of a German higher civil court confirms that this is a typical use of soft law in competition policy: "When you question EU law. What does that mean? Then it is possible to refer to such statements—white papers or something else, statements of the Commission" (Court1, para. 14).

Substantively, the BGH used the SGEI Communication in its judgment in several arguments to determine whether the municipal support

[20] LG Tübingen 5. Zivilkammer, 23 December 2013, 5 O 72/13. Available at: https://www.juris.de/r3/document/JURE140000386/part/L, last accessed 14 July 2025.

[21] OLG Stuttgart 2. Zivilsenat, 20 November 2014, 2 U 11/14. Available at: https://www.juris.de/r3/document/KORE228502014/part/L, last accessed 14 July 2025.

[22] BGH 1. Zivilsenat, 24 March 2016, I ZR 263/14. Available at: https://www.juris.de/r3/document/KORE313822016/part/L, last accessed 14 July 2025.

to hospitals qualifies as state aid and SGEI and, consequently, whether prior notification to the Commission was necessary (paras. 41, 79, 80). First, the court used the SGEI Communication to support its finding that the hospital had been entrusted with a *special task* within the healthcare system. Based on prior Commission decisions, it argued that fulfilling such a special task could justify classifying the hospital as a provider of SGEIs, thereby making it eligible for a more relaxed application of state aid rules (para. 41).

Second, the court drew on both the SGEI Communication and relevant CJEU case law to outline the criteria that public authorities must follow when calculating compensations for public hospitals in order to remain exempt from state aid notification requirements (paras. 79–80). As part of this assessment, it examined the entrustment act issued by the public authority to the hospital. Based on the criteria in the SGEI Communication, the court found that the compensation was not calculated correctly by the public authority thus agreeing with the plaintiff on this point (para. 80). This implies that the measure should potentially have been notified to the Commission for prior approval.

However, in a third step, the court examined on a more fundamental level whether the support in question constituted state aid in the first place (para. 99). It noted that financial support for purely local activities typically does not qualify as state aid since it does not affect competition within the internal market. The BGH cited the SGEI Communication to suggest that this principle might extend to municipal hospitals: "In the Commission's view, there is no effect on cross-border trade in the case of grants to local hospitals which are intended exclusively for the local population (cf. SGEI Communication para. 40)" (para. 99).

Thus, the BGH follows the interpretation provided by the Commission in the SGEI Communication to argue that state aid rules do not apply to the compensation of hospitals if the services provided are strictly local in nature and do not affect trade between Member States—at least as long as the entrustment act from the public authority is sufficiently detailed and meets all procedural and substantive criteria. In the specific case, this implies that the municipality was not required to notify the Commission. However, since the BGH had not been explicitly tasked by the lower court (OLG Stuttgart) with determining whether the payments constituted state aid, it sent the issue back to the OLG. The OLG Stuttgart subsequently adopted much of the BGH's reasoning and ultimately ruled in favor of the defendant (judgment in case 2 U 11/14, para. 26). In this way, the use of soft law as an interpretive aid for EU hard law played a central role in shaping the court's argument that compensations for losses of municipal hospitals fall outside the scope of state aid control.

Explaining Judicial Usage of Soft Law in State Aid Policy. The case study above shows that in this policy area, the *hierarchical governance* plays a central role. The Commission is both the regulator and enforcer of EU state aid rules. It has the authority to decide what counts as state aid and how the vague rules of EU law should be applied. Moreover, it is the guardian of the Treaties, which provides authoritative interpretations of EU law. National courts, unlike the CJEU, cannot review the Commission's enforcement decisions and the Commission's interpretations of hard law. Instead, national courts look to the Commission's soft law in these sectors as an authoritative guide for interpreting the hard law, even in matters that fall in their area of competence. This is exacerbated by the fragmentation and complexity of hard law in the area. The criteria to assess SGEI state aid in the Treaties are vague and specifications are fragmented across countless Commission decisions and CJEU case law. The Communication summarizes this information and derives from it legal interpretations in an accessible way that can be useful for national judges.

Wider Effects of the Case. The case study on the SGEI Communication demonstrates that the judicial use of soft law can significantly contribute to the argumentation and outcome in a judgment. The case addressed whether the funding of hospitals by municipalities falls under state aid rules. In the abstract, such cases are linked to debates about the balance between a national guarantee of public goods and the European liberalization of services in the internal market (Bieling, 2023). It is noteworthy that although the soft law instrument contains legal interpretations by the Commission, the guarantor of competition in the internal market, the application of the instrument does not seem to clearly favor an extension of state aid law through the liberalization of hospital services in this case. On the contrary, the court has used the soft law instrument to keep hospital funding outside the scope of EU state aid enforcement in certain situations, thus preserving it as a national public good.

Specifically, the BGH judgment reinforces that public funding for health services can be lawful under EU state aid rules if clearly justified and structured in a transparent way. A prerequisite is that hospitals must be explicitly entrusted with the provision of SGEIs through a formal entrustment act that conforms to the criteria of state aid law. Thus, the court specifies administrative requirements that apply in such situations. This makes the judgment relevant for the practice of national authorities who give subsidies to public service providers. Moreover, the judgment reinforces and clarifies the Commission's view that state aid for public services with only *local* impact do not fall under state aid law. The national court followed the interpretation of the SGEI Communication that purely local operations do not affect EU competition and fall outside the scope of state aid. This is especially relevant for municipal hospitals, which are often set up to meet local public health needs rather than to compete on a European market. The judgment strengthens the legal position of municipal hospital operators and provides them with legal certainty when they compensate deficits of public hospitals. More broadly, beyond hospital financing, the judgment enables local authorities to provide subsidies to public service providers that carry out purely local tasks in compliance with state aid law with more legal certainty. Finally, although the effects of national judgments, except those of constitutional courts, are formally limited to the specific case, the general nature of the reasoning in this case likely makes it relevant to similar legal questions in other areas of public service provision. Notably, the BGH judgment discussed above has since been cited by several other German courts, all of which have found that the public financing of retirement and nursing homes complies with state aid rules.[23]

6.2.3 *The Environmental- and Energy State Aid Guidelines*

This second state aid case study examines the judicial use of the *Environmental and Energy State Aid Guidelines 2014–2020* (EEAG).[24] In contrast to the previous case, where soft law was used in court to limit the reach of EU state aid rules, this case shows how soft law can shape judgments and policy in a more interventionist way, where EU soft law affects national renewable energy support. The EEAG served as a key

[23] *LG Regensburg*, judgment of 15 December 2016. 6 O 381/16. https://openjur.de/u/2293828.html, last accessed 10 July 2025; *OLG Nürnberg*, judgment of 21 November 2017. 3 U 134/17, https://openjur.de/u/974419.html, last accessed 10 July 2025; *LG Würzburg*, judgment of 26 February 2019. 1 HK O 336/19, https://openjur.de/u/2276037.html, last accessed 10 July 2025.

[24] Communication from the Commission — Guidelines on State aid for environmental protection and energy 2014–2020 (EEAG), OJ C 200, 28 June 2014, pp. 1–55.

compatibility soft law setting out criteria under which environmental and energy-related state aid is compatible with the internal market according to Article 107(3)(c) TFEU. They have now been replaced by updated successor guidelines.[25] Although formally non-binding, the guidelines can be characterized as a very 'hard' form of soft law, as they are closely linked to Treaty provisions and integrated into a system of hard enforcement. They use imperative language, whereby Member States *must*, *shall*, or *should* grant and report state aid in a certain way (EEAG, paras. 7–33 and 252–253). They are also extensive, spanning 55 pages of detailed rules. The Commission announces that it will enforce the guidelines, stating that it "will apply these guidelines to all notified aid measures" (EEAG, para. 267).

In substance, the EEAG apply broadly to national spending on environmental and energy policies. This case study focuses on support schemes for renewable energy—the most significant subarea. Here, the guidelines aimed at a shift towards market-based mechanisms of renewable energy support. Such systems vary in their exposure to market forces (Jacobs, 2016). Many Member States, including Germany and France, traditionally used *feed-in tariffs*—schemes that guarantee fixed prices to renewable energy producers and thus shield them to a certain degree from market forces. The EEAG required governments to phase out these systems and instead introduce *market premiums* and public procurement (Haas, 2017, pp. 118–126). This new model meant that instead of getting a fixed payment, renewable energy producers now had to compete for government support, with those offering the lowest price winning the aid. Governments were also required to provide technology-neutral support, treating all energy sources equally in the auction process. The guidelines thus imposed a uniform, market-based approach that reduced Member States' sovereignty in designing their energy support schemes.

Formulation at the EU level. The EU-level process leading up to the adoption of the guidelines was long, politicized, and controversial. During two public consultations in 2012 and 2013–2014, more than 5000 public authorities and third parties submitted responses to the Commission's draft of the guidelines (Szyszczak, 2014, p. 616). A central concern was that the guidelines intervene in areas of energy policy that are not within EU competence (Min1, para. 50; Min2, para. 13; Min3, para. 11). For

[25] Communication from the Commission—Guidelines on State aid for climate, environmental protection and energy 2022 (CEEAG), COJ C 80, 18.2.2022, pp. 1–89.

example, the French government criticized the guidelines' mandate for public procurement and technology neutrality. It accused the Commission of competence overreach, arguing that "it is not the role of the guidelines on State aid for the environment and energy to define the energy policy tools available to Member States to achieve the objectives set by the RE directive" (ibid. p. 7, quoted after Dezobry, 2015, p.8). Germany submitted a more moderate critique, focusing mainly on securing exemptions for energy-intensive industries. In response to the backlash, the Commission revised some of its proposals, such as easing the technology neutrality requirement, but ultimately adopted a guideline that reflected a clear shift towards stricter, market-oriented rules for renewable energy support (Haas, 2017, p. 126). In the final version, the guidelines main stated aim was to "incentivize the market integration of electricity from renewable sources" (EEAG, para. 124).

The EEAG in national administrations. In Germany, the EEAG strongly shaped the 2014 reform of the country's main renewable energy support scheme and legislation, the Renewable Energies Act 2014 (*Erneuerbare Energien Gesetz 2014, EEG 2014*). While the reform process was already underway when the EEAG were adopted, the guidelines helped steer the ongoing legislative changes towards a more market-oriented approach. Most notably, the EEAG contributed to the transition from a feed-in tariff system in Germany to a market premium system based on competitive bidding auctions. Interviewees involved in the process note that the EEAG were not the sole driver of this shift, but they emphasized the guidelines' strong influence in steering national reforms in a more market-driven direction (IG8, para. 11; IG9, para. 31).

Why did the EEAG affect the reform of national law? Like in the first case study, the hierarchical governance structure of the policy area matters. A key reason is that national authorities perceived the Commission as a credible state aid enforcer and feared a negative state aid decision declaring national renewable support schemes incompatible with the internal market (Min1, Min2, Min3). This had precedent, as Germany had a long history of conflict with the Commission over renewables support under state aid law (Soltész, 2014).

Another reason lies in the domestic political dynamics. The EEAG strengthened the arguments of national actors who had long favored a shift to market premiums by allowing them to restate their policy preference as a legal necessity in light of technical EU requirements (Min1, para. 44; Min2, para. 29). Beyond shaping the overall system change, the

EEAG also influenced several specific provisions within the 2014 EEG reform. One such example is the treatment of renewable energy during periods of negative electricity prices, which is addressed in the remainder of this case study (EEAG, points 124–125). The next section summarizes the relevant paragraphs in EU soft law and national legislation, before examining their application in German courts.

Rules on Negative Prices. In electricity markets, prices can sometimes turn 'negative.' If there is more supply than demand, electricity producers have to pay to feed electricity into the grid, rather than receiving fees. This usually happens when electricity supply suddenly increases or demand drops (Aust & Morscher, 2017).

When adopting the relevant soft law, the EEAG, the European Commission was concerned that renewable energy support in the form of market premiums could encourage renewable energy producers to keep generating electricity even during these periods, which would further lead to oversupply of electricity and make the problem of negative prices even worse. To prevent this, the EEAG stated that electricity producers should not receive renewables support during such times of negative prices (EEAG, point 124c). However, to give smaller producers more economic security, the EEAG made exceptions: installations producing renewable energy under 500 kW, and for wind energy, under 3 MW, were exempted from the rule (EEAG, point 125). This was so that they could count on a steadier income from renewables support. But in practice, these definitions were not always clear (Kahles, 2015, pp. 9–10).

Germany implemented these rules in national law through paragraph 24 of the EEG 2014, which prevents renewables support during negative price periods, and also exempts small producers. The justification of the government made explicit that this rule was introduced to comply with the EEAG.[26] Thus, national hard law was adapted to EU soft law.

But the way the exemptions were implemented in German law were even stricter than in the EU soft law due to an additional 'proximity rule:' If several small installations are located close together ('in close proximity'), their capacities are added up. This makes it more likely that they exceed the threshold above which they no longer fall under the exemption (para. 32 EEG 2014). Therefore, small producers are more

[26] Deutscher Bundestag Drucksache 18/1891, 18. Wahlperiode, Beschlussempfehlung und Bericht.

des Ausschusses für Wirtschaft und Energie (9. Ausschuss), 26 June 2014, p. 202.

likely to receive no support during negative price periods (Kahles, 2015, pp. 9–10). In essence, the German legislator thus 'overcomplied' with the rules on negative prices from EU soft law, implementing stricter rules with narrower exemptions. But these national rules were still not entirely clear. A key issue was wind parks, which often include many wind turbines located near each other. The law did not clearly define when such installations should be counted together or not. Thus, it was not entirely clear when the smaller wind parks would lose renewables support.

While it is not uncommon for EU state aid law to affect national energy law, this case is unique in that the chain of norms begins with a non-binding act, the EEAG. In court, this could interfere with traditional interpretive methods and legal hierarchy. To assess this issue, the following section traces a string of cases in the German ordinary judiciary.

The EEAG in National Courts. German ordinary courts used the EU soft law, the EEAG, as an aid to interpret provisions of national hard law (EEG 2014), in a string of cases concerning wind energy support during periods of negative electricity prices. The courts recognized that German law was designed to comply with EU state aid requirements, and therefore interpreted the national provisions in light of the EEAG. As a result, the soft law instrument had indirect legal effect by affecting the interpretation of national energy law and policy. This case study focuses on a series of rulings in 2019 by the higher court *OLG Braunschweig* and the apex court *Bundesgerichtshof* (BGH).

In this case, a wind energy producer contested a grid operator's decision to withhold payments during a period of negative prices, arguing their wind turbines should be exempt from a reduction of renewables support. The grid operator countered that the turbines were situated in 'close proximity' to each other. It argued that, when aggregated, they exceeded the 3 MW threshold, so they do not qualify as 'small installations' under the relevant exemption rules of national law. Essentially, the wind energy producer argued they are entitled to renewables support during such periods of negative prices, while the grid operator did not. In legal terms, the question was whether such wind turbines in 'close proximity' to each other must be combined for purposes of calculating exemption thresholds under para. 32 EEG 2014, which affects their eligibility for renewable energy support under para. 24 EEG 2014. While sounding technical, this is also a relevant wider policy question, as it directly affects the financial viability of many small- and medium-sized wind energy projects. In practice, wind parks often consist of multiple turbines located close to each other. If they must be aggregated for the purposes of the EEG, they lose a substantial amount of renewables support, affecting their viability. Although both courts referred to the EEAG as part of their reasoning, they arrived at opposing outcomes. The *OLG Braunschweig* interpreted the EU soft law as favoring a more permissive interpretation of national law, ruling in favor of the wind energy producer. In contrast, *Bundesgerichtshof* (BGH) sided with the grid operator. It viewed the EEAG as setting only minimum EU standards and concluded that Germany can adopt stricter national rules.

OLG Braunschweig, Judgment of 27 May 2019 (9 U 47/18). The *OLG Braunschweig*[27] ruled in favor of the wind energy producer, applying a narrow interpretation of the term 'spatial proximity' and emphasizing the EU's supportive stance towards small producers. It viewed the EEAG as guiding national law towards a more permissive interpretation.

The case originated at the *LG Braunschweig* (judgment of 13 July 2018, 4 O 1987/17),[28] which sided with the plaintiff. On appeal, the OLG upheld this ruling. The court gave several reasons for its decision on the same legal question and resorted to different legal methods of interpretation—typical for the German legal style of reasoning. It first interpreted the provisions of national law on installation combination and negative prices according to the wording and systematic of the law (Möllers, 2017, pp. 139–146). Thereby, it identified a narrow scope of the requirement for the combination of plants (para. 52) and a wide scope for the reduction of payments during negative prices (para. 53). Because the national provisions were ambiguous, the court then turned to the preparatory documents of the EEG 2014. It found that the relevant provision of national law (para. 24 EEG 2014) explicitly implemented the EU's EEAG: "(…) according to the explanatory memorandum to the Act (…), Sentence 3 of Paragraph 24 EEG 2014 (reduction of feed-in tariff in the event of negative prices) implements the temporal and material scope of application for the reduction of the value to be invested in phases of negative prices (European Guidelines on State Aid for Environmental Protection and Energy 2014–2020—C 200/01)" (para. 74).

Thus, at this point, the court applies EU soft law as an aid to interpret national hard law in a method of 'historical interpretation,' which

[27] OLG Braunschweig, judgment of 27.05.2019, case 9 U 47/18.

[28] BGH, judgment of 14/07/2020–XIII ZR 12/19, paras 1, 8.

is a common method of interpretation in German courts that draws on materials that give an indication of the aim of the law at the time of its adoption (Kötter, 2011). The court then tests whether the regulatory intent of the guidelines allows for a different interpretation of the national law but finds that this is not the case:

"Para. 124 EEAG provides that as of 1/1/2016, regulations and measures on aid must ensure that electricity producers do not have an incentive to generate electricity at negative prices. Pursuant to marginal no. 125 EEAG, wind turbines with an installed generation capacity of less than 3 MW are exempt from this requirement. Para. 32 (1) sentence 1 EEG complies with these requirements (...)" (para. 53).

Overall, the court applied the EU soft law as an *aid to interpret national law*. In doing so, the court recognizes *legal effects* of soft law, at least implicitly, by assuming that national law must conform to EU soft law and provisions of national law must be interpreted in line with the aims of EU soft law. Ultimately, the court ruled in favor of the wind energy producer, allowing their turbines to be treated as separate and exempt from payment reductions during negative price periods.

BGH, Judgment of 14 July 2020, XIII ZR 12/19. On appeal, the German Federal Court of Justice (BGH) overturned the decision of the lower courts. It adopted a broad reading of 'close proximity,' arguing that turbines that are connected with the same grid access point should be considered spatially close and thus treated as a single installation. It thus concluded that the grid operator was not obligated to pay the wind energy producer.

Like the previous judicial instance, the BGH also used EU soft law (the EEAG) in a similar manner. First, it engaged in historical interpretation and confirmed that the German legislature had introduced para. 24 EEG 2014 to comply with the EU's EEAG. As the court explains:

"As can be seen from the explanatory memorandum of the resolution recommendation and the report of the Committee on Economic Affairs and Energy (cf. BT-Drs. 18/1891, 202), the introduction of Sect. 24 I EEG 2014 was based on the requirements of the Guidelines on State Aid for Environmental Protection and Energy 2014- 2020 of the European Union (2014/C 200/01) for the promotion of electricity from renewable energy sources. These stipulated, among other things, that in the case of aid schemes and other aid measures from 1.1.2016, it must be ensured that electricity producers have no incentive to generate electricity at negative prices, although this was not to apply to wind power plants with an installed electricity generation capacity of no more than 3 MW (Guidelines 2014/C 200/01 paras. 124 f.)" (BGH judgment, para. 20).

However, the BGH departed from the OLG's more permissive interpretation of national law by emphasizing that the German legislator intentionally went beyond the minimum requirements set by the EEAG. The court argued that Germany had purposefully adopted stricter rules to prevent the abuse of benefits related to small installations. Specifically, the court stated:

"The fact that the analogous application of the provisions on the aggregation of installations in the context of the spot market price-related reduction in remuneration—which is not provided for in the Guidelines—is also intended to prevent the improper exploitation of the privileged treatment of small installations cannot be inferred from the justification of the recommendation for a resolution of the Committee on Economic Affairs and Energy from 2014. However, this intention is clear from the legislative process for the amendment of the EEG in 2016" (para. 22).

The BGH thus interpreted Germany's stricter provisions as deliberate 'overcompliance' with the minimum standards set by EU soft law. For the court, this justified a strict reading of the relevant provision of national law. Specifically, the court adopted a narrow reading of 'spatial proximity,' by linking it to shared grid infrastructure of wind turbines rather than the geographical distance between such turbines (paras. 1, 28–29). This interpretation excludes the producer from receiving renewable energy support during periods of negative prices, which ultimately benefits the grid operator. Thus, the outcome contrasts with that of the preceding legal instance, even though both courts relied on EU soft law as an aid to interpret national law.

EEAG: Mechanisms That Led to Usage and Wider Effects. This second case study shows how the Environmental and Energy State Aid Guidelines 2014–2020 (EEAG) have shaped German energy law. Overall, we can observe a process where national law is adapted in light of EU soft law, and national courts further entrench the relation of national law and EU soft law. Courts recognized that the national legislator has designed national rules to align with the EU soft law, and thus should be interpreted in light of it. Although both courts, the OLG Braunschweig and BGH relied on the EEAG, they reached opposite conclusions, which demonstrates that the use of soft law as interpretative device does not automatically lead to a certain outcome. The use of soft law in court further increases its legal relevance, as it is established as a relevant benchmark to interpret national provisions.

The broader *policy effect* of the BGH's decision extends beyond the case at hand. Wind turbines are commonly installed in clusters (wind farms), and the abstract criteria established by the BGH for determining 'spatial proximity' now make it more likely that such installations must be aggregated. Consequently, fewer wind turbines will be eligible for support during periods of negative electricity prices, limiting renewables support. A German Wind Energy Association (*Fachagentur Windenergie an Land*) expected the ruling to have "economic consequences for many wind farms commissioned from 2016 onward," since eligibility for continued remuneration often hinges on a strict reading of "immediate geographical proximity."[29] The wider effect is that this constrains the state's ability to provide support to renewable energy in certain situations, which is in line with a broader market-oriented shift in renewables support in EU and national law.

Comparing the State Aid Case Studies. If we compare the two cases from state aid, we see that both the SGEI Communication and the EEAG are used by German courts as aid to interpret hard law. This is despite their different functions, with the SGEI Communication defining the scope of state aid control in public service provision, and the EEAG providing criteria for the compatibility of state aid with the internal market in energy policy. Rather, the use of EU soft law shifts the interpretation of EU and national hard law in a particular direction, which can affect the legal reasoning of the court and the outcome of a case. But the SGEI Communication is used to justify a certain interpretation of EU law, while the EEAG is used to steer the interpretation of national law in a certain direction.

Regarding explanations of judicial usage, the case studies found that the setup of the policy area in the EU multilevel system matters. In particular, the *hierarchical governance structure* in state aid policy with high regulatory and enforcement competences of the Commission. This mechanism plays out in different ways in line with the function of the

[29] Fachagentur Windenergie an Land. 14 July 2020. E*EG, negative Strompreise, unmittelbarer räumlicher Zusammenhang BGH, Urteil vom 14. Juli 2020—XIII ZR 12/19*, p. 2, https://www.fachagentur-windenergie.de/fileadmin/files/Rechtsprechung/18._Sitzung/FA_Wind_BGH_Urt_v_14072020_XIII_ZR_12.19.pdf, last accessed 10 July 2025.

instrument. The SGEI Communication is treated in court as an *authoritative interpretation aid* by the Commission, which is competent to define the scope of state aid based on vague Treaty provisions. In turn, the EEAG deeply affect the design of national energy law, which makes them relevant once the national law is interpreted. National law is then interpreted through the lens of EU soft law. In policy terms, SGEI state aid is often associated with expanding EU competences into areas of national subsidiarity. But in the observed case, the opposite is true. The BGH used the Communication to limit the reach of EU law into national healthcare policy. The EEAG reflect the Commission's goals of energy policy. The court's use of the instrument reinforces the Commission's position by applying it to interpret national law. National law is then read more closely in light of EU energy policy. Both case studies thus point to extensive effects of the judicial usage of EU state aid soft law on the *role of the state in the economy*. However, the direction of these effects varies, and the use of EU soft law does not automatically lead either to more national subsidiarity or to greater EU involvement in national policy.

6.3 Pharmaceutical Regulation

6.3.1 *Introduction to EU Pharmaceutical Law and Soft Law*

The next two case studies examine the judicial usage of soft law in pharmaceutical regulation, beginning with an overview of the policy area and the significance of soft law in it. They trace how the governance arrangement of the policy area, a closely interlocked system of *composite administration* between the national and EU levels, translates into soft law usage in national medicines agencies and ultimately in courts.

The policy area is partly Europeanized. On the one hand, some issues relating to the core state powers of health care or national budgets remain purely national. Examples are the pricing and reimbursement of medicines (Kanavos & Mossialos, 1999). But EU law harmonizes almost all issues at the intersection of free movement, industrial policy, and public health (Permanand & Mossialos, 2005, p. 690). Most importantly, rules on the authorization of medicines.[30] Certain types of medicinal products are

[30] An exception are a few specific areas that still rely on purely national authorizations and national law, but they are rare in practice.

authorized through purely national procedures based on national legislation, and some are authorized directly by the Commission at EU level (such as the Covid-19 vaccines), but these are the exception (Kröll, 2017, pp. 153–187). By far most common are Europeanized national procedures, where national authorities apply EU law to authorize medicines for the entire single market.[31]

An extensive framework of EU hard law regulates the authorizations of medicines. In particular, Directive 2001/83 and Regulation 726/2004 lay down the basic product and process standards which apply to national enforcement authorities and market participants (Kröll, 2017, pp. 17–21). But crucially, the governance setup of the policy area is characterized by *composite administration*, which means that EU and national authorities work together closely throughout the regulatory process. Composite administrative procedures, which involve both EU and national authorities, are very common in this policy area (Röttger-Wirtz & Eliantonio, 2019). This is possible because national authorities are embedded in a strong European network (Krapohl, 2008, pp. 86–117), set up by the European Medicines Agency (EMA) and the Commission (Kröll, 2017, p. 139). The EU institutions almost have no scientific experts, but rather rely on national experts for scientific expertise and the elaboration of standards. National medicines agencies play a central role in implementing EU rules, and decisions are often based on input from expert working groups that include representatives from both levels.

Against this backdrop, soft law plays a prominent role in the legal framework, and makes up 77% of all instruments adopted in the area from 2004 to 2019 (Cappellina et al., 2022, p. 13). As in state aid, these soft law instruments mostly have an *interpretative* function and follow up on already existing hard law. However, in pharmaceutical regulation they specify complex scientific standards and detailed administrative procedures. This is because the substance of the policy area is largely based on scientific and therefore complex extra-legal knowledge (Fleischfresser, 2020, p. 20). Soft law also specifies highly complex administrative procedures, which are common in the area. According to EMA, the average

[31] They are the 'Decentralized Procedure' under Directive 2004/27/EC and the 'Mutual Recognition Procedure' under Directive 2001/83/EC. The former functions through simultaneous authorization for all Member States, the latter through mutual recognition of authorization decisions by authorities from other countries.

marketing authorization procedure for a new medicine involves 21 steps and takes one year.[32]

In line with the composite administrative structure of the policy area, soft law is formally adopted by the Commission or EMA, but is typically drafted in working groups composed of national experts from national medicines authorities. These working groups often reach decisions by unanimity. According to the EMA, such soft law instruments are intended to represent "a harmonized approach of the EU Member States and the Agency on how to interpret and apply the requirements for the demonstration of quality, safety, and efficacy set out in the Community directives."[33] Overall, soft law in pharmaceutical regulation complements hard law by concretizing and harmonizing highly complex procedures and policies. It is adopted in an environment of composite administration, with strong input from national actors.

6.3.2 Notice to Applicants

This case study focuses on the *Notice to Applicants*,[34] a soft law instrument that interprets legal terms and clarifies administrative procedures related to the marketing authorization of medicines (Kortland, 2022, pp. para. 8–12). It builds on and clarifies Regulation 726/2004 and Directive 2001/83/EC, but it also sets out new rules within the framework of hard law. While the underlying hard law only defines framework rules, it goes into much more detail with regard to the rules and their interpretations for practitioners. For example, it addresses the design of national databases, the deadlines for certain authorization steps and how applicants for marketing authorizations must prepare their dossiers. The instrument is addressed to national authorization agencies, as well as to third parties, i.e. pharmaceutical companies applying for marketing authorization. In line with the setup of the policy area (composite administration),

[32] European Medicines Agency. The evaluation Medicines, step-by-step. Undated. https://www.ema.europa.eu/en/human-regulatory/marketing-authorisation/evaluation-medicines-step-step, last accessed 10 July 2025.

[33] EMA. Scientific Guidelines. https://www.ema.europa.eu/en/human-regulatory/research-development/scientific-guidelines, last accessed 10 July 2025.

[34] Eudralex Volume 2—Notice to applicants and regulatory guidelines for medicinal products for human use. In: European Commission. The rules governing medicinal products in the European Union.

the instrument is formulated in an expert group also called 'Notice to Applicants,' chaired by the Commission, and composed of experts from national authorities who draft the instrument. It was originally published by the Commission in 1986 and is partially updated at least once a year through formalized revision procedures.

The Notice to Applicants in National Administrations. In Germany, the instrument is published and applied by the national medicines agency *Bundesinstitut für Arzneimittel* (BfArM).[35] National agencies perceive the Notice to Applicants as a common interpretation of EU law, particularly of Regulation 726/2004, which is as such almost binding in practice in national authorization procedures (AG1, para. 30). As a result, they tend to adapt their administrative procedures and requirements to the rules of the instrument (AG1, para. 16). A key reason for this is their involvement in formulating the rules at EU level, which creates a sense of joint ownership. A national expert who formerly chaired the EU level expert group reports that "the fact that we have agreed on this means that we have a uniform position, and nobody deviates from it" (AG1, para. 8). As the national regulator, the BfArM, mostly complies with the Notice, the pharmaceutical companies applying for a marketing authorisation are also strongly incentivised to comply and usually do (IG3, para. 23; IG5, para. 14). However, they also see scope to deviate in exceptional cases if they can provide a convincing explanation to the national regulator ('comply-or-justify') (IG3, para. 27; IG5, para. 40).

The Notice to Applicants in National Courts. A string of cases in the German administrative judiciary illustrates a typical judicial usage of the instrument as ***aid to interpret*** a term from hard law, 'serious risk to public health.' The dispute concerned the re-authorization of the medicine Phlogenzym, which is used in enzyme therapy to treat muscle inflammation, among other conditions. The medicine had already long been on the market, but medicines authorized before 1978 need a renewed authorization (*Nachzulassung*) under the Europeanized rules to stay on the market under the German law (*Arzneimittelgesetz*). In 2005, BfArM refused such a renewed authorization for Phlogenzym under the mutual recognition procedure. The pharmaceutical company producing this medicine then took legal action against the negative decisions of the authority.

[35] *Bundesinstitut für Arzneimittel* (BfArM). National Licensing Procedures. Undated. https://www.bfarm.de/EN/Medicinal-products/Licensing/Licensing-procedures/NLP-National-Licensing-Procedures/_artikel.html?nn=968814, last accessed 10 July 2025.

To briefly summarize the general arguments and outcome: In the first instance, the *Verwaltungsgericht Köln* (VG Köln) ruled in favor of the BfArM and against the pharmaceutical company.[36] This was overturned on appeal by the *Oberverwaltungsgericht Nordrhein-Westfalen* (OVG NRW), which ruled in favor of the company.[37] The BfArM then appealed to the *Bundesverwaltungsgericht* (BVerwG), which ultimately agreed with the first instance and ruled against the BfArM, ordering it to reopen the authorization procedure.[38]

In substance, two questions on which the parties to the case disagreed were at stake. First, whether the pharmaceutical company had sufficiently documented the efficacy and safety of the medicine. Second, whether mutual recognition rules would apply: the Austrian authority had already authorized the medicine, so Germany would need to follow suit if this were the case. At this point the Notice to Applicants becomes relevant as concretization of hard law. According to EU law (Article 29 of Directive 2004/27/EC) and its German transposition in national law (Para. 105 *Arzneimittelgesetz—AMG*), a national authorization agency can refuse the mutual recognition of a foreign authorization decision in exceptional cases, if the authority identifies a "potential serious risk to public health" resulting from the medicine. Such a case poses an exception from the European harmonization of medicines authorization. But the hard law does not specify what a potential 'serious risk to public health' is. Article 29(2) of Directive 2004/27/EC stipulates that the Commission shall draw up guidelines to specify this legal term, which the Commission did in a guideline within the Notice to Applicants.[39] The BfArM originally invoked the guideline to support its decision against the extension of the medicine of 25.05.2005 (13 A 2103/08, para. 39). The next section describes how and to what effect the instrument was used in court.

First Instance Judgment: VG Köln. In the first instance, the *VG Köln* ruled in judgment 18 K 545/06 of 30 March 2009 in favor of the public

[36] VG Köln. 30 May 2008. VG 18 K 545/06.

[37] OVG für das Land Nordrhein-Westfalen. 02 December 2010. OVG 13 A 2103/08.

[38] BVerwG, Urteil vom 15.12.2011. BVerwG 3 C 2.11.

[39] To be precise, in a guideline that forms part of the Notice to Applicants: European Commission. Notice to Applicants: Guideline on the definition of a potential serious risk to public health in the context of Article 29(1) and (2) of Directive 2001/83/EC — March 2006 (2006/C 133/05). 08 June 2006. https://eur-lex.europa.eu/LexUriServ/LexUriServ.do?uri=OJ:C:2006:133:0005:0007:EN:PDF, last accessed 10 July 2025.

authority, the BfArM, upholding its decision to deny re-authorization of the medicine.[40] The court concluded that the medicine posed a 'potential serious risk to public health' and relied on the Notice to Applicants to interpret this—relevant but rather vague—legal term (judgment VG Köln, para. 87). Specifically, the court applied the guideline to clarify what medically significant outcomes can be subsumed under the term: "According to the guideline (…) 'serious' (…) means that a hazard may be fatal or life-threatening, require hospitalization or prolongation of hospitalization, result in permanent or severe disability or incapacity, be a congenital anomaly or birth defect, or cause continuous or prolonged symptoms in exposed individuals" (para. 88).

Based on this interpretation, the court concluded that the BfArM had sufficiently demonstrated such risks for the product in question (para. 91). Thus, from the court's perspective, the soft law strengthens the authority's case, and the litigant could not prove that the medicine does not pose serious health risks under the criteria of hard and soft law.

Second Instance Judgment: OVG NRW. The case then went to the *OVG NRW*,[41] which delivered a judgment on 2 December 2019 (case 13 A 2103/08). Like the lower court, the OVG relied on the Notice to Applicants as aid to interpret the term 'serious risk to public health,' stating that: "[…] in Guideline 2006/C133/05, the Commission of the European Union explained the conditions under which a serious risk within the meaning of the European directives and (…) the national implementation (…) can be assumed to exist" (judgment OVG NRW, para. 86).

The court acknowledged the legal effects of the soft law instrument, emphasizing its legitimacy due to the inclusive, multilevel drafting process: "Even if this guideline, as an interpretative instrument of the executive, does not have any normative and thus legally binding force, it reflects the view gained by the European Commission in a procedure involving numerous institutions and is thus highly relevant for the interpretation of Directive 2004/27/EC, which was adopted with the participation of the EU Commission" (para. 86).

[40] VG Köln. 08 August 2008. 18 K 472/06, https://www.juris.de/r3/document/MWRE210016271/part/L, last accessed 10 July 2025.

[41] OVG Nordrhein-Westfalen. 02 December 2010. 13 A 2103/08, https://www.juris.de/r3/document/MWRE210016271/part/L, last accessed 10 July 2025.

But the *OVG NRW* reached the opposite conclusion to the first-instance court. After applying the criteria laid out in the soft law instrument, the court held that the BfArM had not sufficiently justified the existence of a serious public health risk (paras. 101–122). It placed the burden of proof on the national authority and found that this burden was not met. As a result, it ruled in favor of the plaintiff and ordered that the authorization procedure be reopened (para. 157). Thus, while both courts used the Notice to Applicants in a formally similar way—as a non-binding but authoritative guide for interpreting vague legal concepts—the outcome varied.

Last Instance Judgment: Bundesverwaltungsgericht. The BfArM appealed to the last instance, the *Bundesverwaltungsgericht*, which ruled on 15 December 2011 in case 3 C 2/11.[42] The court cited the soft law instrument only in its summary of the lower courts' decisions and did not use it in its own reasoning (case 3 C 2/11, para. 7). However, this may have to do with the fact that the judgment is shorter and, in particular, reviews the decision of the second instance for errors of law rather than going into the facts of the case. In substance, the court agrees with the second instance court that the exception to mutual recognition must be interpreted narrowly (paras. 22–30). Finally, the court upholds the decision of the previous instance and rules in favor of the pharmaceutical company so that the BfArM's negative decision is partly annulled, and the process must be reopened (para. 30). Thus, the court did not use soft law, but it accepted the soft law-based argumentation of the previous instance.

Reasons for Usage and Wider Effects. The three judicial instances engaged with the Notice to Applicants to varying degrees: explicitly in the first and second instances, and only implicitly in the final instance. But they all recognized its interpretative value. The Notice to Applicants is used in the context of a complex EU legal framework that concretizes legal definitions and administrative procedures in the form of soft law. German administrative courts refer to it when they interpret legal terms of hard law. They recognize it as 'common legal interpretation' of regulators at both levels of government. The main reason for judicial usage of the Notice to Applicants is therefore the cooperative governance structure in the policy area. Courts rely on the Notice to Applicants because it is developed through a multilevel process involving

[42] BVerwG, 15.12.2011–3 C 2.11, https://www.juris.de/r3/document/WBRE410018452/part/K, last accessed 10 July 2025.

the Commission, the EMA, and national authorities, giving it strong legitimacy. This reflects the broader institutional and actor relationships in a 'composite administration' setting of the policy area identified above.

The cases cited above show that the Notice to Applicants never decides a case on its own, but its legal interpretations can have a significant impact on the outcome of cases. The immediate effect of the rulings on the market is that a negative decision by the authority was overturned, and the authority had to decide again on the re-authorization of the drug. The litigating pharmaceutical company won the case against the regulatory authority. The wider effect was that the court, guided by the Notice to Applicants, interpreted the definition of the term 'serious risk to public health' in a narrow way. In more abstract terms, this legal interpretation concerns the harmonization of administrative procedures in Europe and the level of risk regulation in pharmaceutical regulation. Several other judgments follow this interpretation and cite the initial judgment on this point, which points to wider effects in the judiciary.[43]

6.3.3 EU Good Manufacturing Practices (GMP) Guidelines

The second case in pharmaceutical regulation focuses on the EU Good Manufacturing Practices Guidelines (EU GMP Guidelines).[44] This is a soft law instrument that sets minimum standards for manufacturers of medicines in their processes to guarantee product quality and medicines safety.

As part of the European pharmaceutical regulatory framework, Commission Directive 91/356/EEC, as amended by Directive 2003/94/EC and Directive 91/412/EEC, sets out general rules for the manufacture of medicinal products in Europe. The GMP guidelines set standards for practical enforcement in this area. But the guidelines do not just interpret what is already there. Instead, they provide an active interpretation of hard law, adding de facto additional obligations in the process of interpretation (Van Dam, 2017, p. 84). They set a wide variety

[43] E.g. VG Köln. Judgment of 20 October 2015. 7 K 146/06; VG Köln. Judgment of 23 October 2012. 7 K 636/06; OVG Nordrhein-Westfalen. Order of 09 July 2012. 13 A 560/09.

[44] European Commission. EudraLex—Volume 4—*Good Manufacturing Practice (GMP) guidelines*. https://health.ec.europa.eu/medicinal-products/eudralex/eudralex-volume-4_en, last accessed 10 July 2025.

of product and process standards, ranging from the manufacturer's quality assurance system to the composition of personnel.

The adoption of the instrument reflects a transnational and scientifically grounded approach to regulation. While the Commission publishes the final instrument, it is drafted by the Inspectors Working Group, a transnational forum of experts from national authorities established at the European Medicines Agency (EMA).[45] Thus, they again emerge from a context of composite administration as both EU and national actors are involved in the decision-making during their adoption.

Usage at the National Level. National hard law formalizes the legal status of the EU GMP Guidelines. In Germany, para. 3 of the *Arzneimittel- und Wirkstoffherstellungsverordnung* (AMWHV) requires that the GMP Guidelines "shall apply" when hard law provisions of good manufacturing practices are interpreted and used in practice.[46] The fact that hard law confirms that soft law should be applied binds the national authorities, but in principle third parties can deviate. In France, the EU guidelines are transposed into the national *Guide des bonnes pratiques de fabrication*.[47] It is published as an attachment to a hard *décision* by the director general of the ANSM. Their applicability is further confirmed by Article L5121-5 of the *code de la santé publique (CSP)*.

In national practice, the competent authorities apply the guidelines as a standard of review or test grid while carrying out inspections at the sites of medicines manufacturers and when they certify production facilities. National inspectors who carry out these tasks perceive the guide, for the most part, as de facto binding (AG2, para. 18; AG4, para. 18; AG5, para. 20; AG6, para. 22). While they see some room for discretion in the application of a few open-worded provisions, they apply most provisions very strictly. For example, the detailed technical requirements for cleanrooms for pharmaceutical manufacturing. The inspectors use the guidelines so strictly because they value their quality, which makes them

[45] See European Medicines Agency. GMP/GDP Inspectors Working Group. Undated. https://www.ema.europa.eu/en/human-regulatory/research-development/compliance/good-manufacturing-practice/gmp-gdp-inspectors-working-group, last accessed 10 July 2025.

[46] § 2 Nr. 3 *Arzneimittel- und Wirkstoffherstellungsverordnung*—AMWHV.

[47] *Agence nationale de sécurité du médicament et des produits de santé. Guide des bonnes pratiques de fabrication*. 19 October 2015. https://ansm.sante.fr/uploads/2020/10/20/2019-guide-bpf-mai-2019-3.pdf, last accessed 14 July 2025.

suitable to solve problems—in this case the problem of finding accurate indicators for the safe production of medicines. They are based on scientific evidence and up to speed with international and European developments in the sector. Therefore, they can provide procedural clarity and legal certainty. An interview from the German Federal Health Ministry says that "this is not for nothing the knowledge of the world, compiled by everyone on this subject, and one then simply adheres to it" (Min5, para. 32). National actors say that the quality results from their scientific background, bundling accepted and current scientific knowledge.

Moreover, national actors value that the GMP guidelines further the harmonization of rules across borders. The European internal market is based on the *mutual recognition* of authorizations by authorities of different Member States (Schmidt, 2007). This also applies to GMP certificates. But in this mode of governance, medicines safety is only guaranteed if authorization processes are harmonized. National authorities appreciate that the guidelines work in this direction (AG3, para. 3). But, manufacturers can deviate in principle from the instrument if they bring forth good arguments. As Anhalt and Lützeler write: "for citizens, the guide has only a recommendatory character." However, they have a strong incentive to comply, because "(...) as far as the citizen/entrepreneur complies with the recommendations of the guide, the authorities cannot argue against him that the requirements of good manufacturing practice are not fulfilled" (2010, p. para. 34).

Judgment by the VG Köln. We find an illustration of a typical case of judicial usage of the instrument in case 7 K 6685/15 decided by the VG Köln on 12/06/2018.[48] The dispute concerns an application for a manufacturing authorization for medicinal products under Sect 13 of the German Medicines Act (AMG).

The plaintiff is an individual who holds an academic degree in the field of pharmacy and is building up a site to produce medicines. The plaintiff established a medicines manufacturing business and is seeking authorization to manufacture a set of medicinal products (judgment VG Köln, para. 4). The defendant is the GMP inspectorate of the District Government of Cologne. It previously rejected a manufacturing authorization for the plaintiff (para. 14). One reason for the rejection is that an inspection at the intended manufacturing site revealed "deficiencies with regard to

[48] VG Köln. Judgment of 12 June 2018. 7 K 6685/15. https://openjur.de/u/2154870.html, last accessed 10 July 2025.

GMP-compliant manufacture of medicinal products, in accordance with the state of the art in science and technology, referred to in Sect. 14 (1) No. 6a AMG" (para. 22). Another reason is concerns about the expertise and qualifications required of the litigant to act as a 'qualified person' to monitor GMP compliance in the facility. Among other legal sources, the defendant cites the GMP Guidelines to argue that the plaintiff failed to comply with safety requirements, in particular to "[...] provide evidence of a documented quality assurance system as defined in the EU GMP Guide, in particular a list of all SOPs (standard operating procedures) for the planned manufacturing activities, individual specific SOPs, evidence of the qualification of contractors (contract manufacturers, test facilities) and contracts with the contract manufacturers" (para. 18).

The court argues that a manufacturing authorization can only be fully rejected if "the manufacturer is not able to ensure that the manufacture or testing is carried out in accordance with the (current) state of the art in science and technology." The court then argues that the state of the art in science and technology (*Stand der Wissenschaft und Technik*) requires from the manufacturer to "[...] comply with the principles and Guidelines of Good Manufacturing Practice (GMP) for medicinal products, cf. Art. 46(f) of Directive 2001/83/EC. The principles and guidelines of good manufacturing practice are laid down by Directive 2003/94/EC and specified in the Guide to Good Manufacturing Practice (EC GMP Guideline), which is published by the Commission and continuously revised in accordance with technical and scientific progress, Art. 47 of Directive 2001/83/EC" (para. 71).

The court affirms that the GMP Guidelines are legally relevant due to their transposition into national hard law, and they can be applied as a standard of review together with hard law. Because the soft law instrument "concretizes the concept of the state of the art in science and technology, it is therefore possible to refer to the specifications of the EC GMP Guidelines, among others" (para. 72). In particular, the court states that manufacturers of medicines must demonstrate a 'quality management system' that complies with the GMP Guidelines (para. 73). The court agrees with the authority that the litigant could not demonstrate that it has established such an appropriate system in accordance with the requirements of the soft law. Such a system requires complex and in-depth documentation that various requirements were met. This includes a 'quality manual,' procedural instructions ('SOPs'), and contracts with manufacturers, all of which must be in accordance with the Guidelines (para. 100).

However, in contrast to the public authority, the court concludes that these deficiencies do not justify a complete rejection of the manufacturing authorization. The court argues that in cases of "(...) deviations from the GMP Guidelines, if they are not significant (...), no intervention measures are foreseen as in the case of critical or serious defects, in particular no refusal of a manufacturing authorization" (para. 85).

The *VG Köln* concludes that if the "elimination of defects is possible by way of an order, the refusal of the production permit is disproportionate and thus unlawful" (para. 86). The court thus states that the authority must use a milder means of enforcement and order the remedy of the remaining deficiencies. Overall, the court partially agreed with the plaintiff, the medicine producer. The court ruled that the authority was right to find non-compliance with the GMP guidelines and hard law, but its response of refusing the medicine re-authorization was not proportionate. As a result, the court gives the plaintiff a chance to remedy certain deficiencies in a reopened authorization process. Thus, this is a case where the failure to comply with soft law that specifies hard law leads to clear legal effects for both the medicines producer and a public authority.

In summary, in terms of the judicial use of soft law, the court recognizes an *indirect binding force* of GMP guidelines in conjunction with hard law. It applies the instrument as a *supplementary standard of review*, as it systematically examines the facts of the case against the requirements of the guidelines. But it always makes sure to add that soft law requirements concretize the underlying hard law. The reason the court used the EU GMP Guideline was especially due to its scientific quality. The court treated the guidelines' requirements as de facto binding together with hard law, due to their status as widely accepted 'state of the art' scientific knowledge among both European experts and national authorities. This authority again stems from the inclusive drafting process, carried out by experts from medicines agencies across all Member States, but also from the scientifically grounded nature of the instrument, as it reflects the state of scientific and technological knowledge—similar to the role of a scientific expert report.

6.4 Comparing the Case Studies

The case studies traced typical cases of usage in the areas of state aid and pharmaceutical regulation to uncover such mechanisms. Soft law was found to play a role as *supplementary standard of review* against which the facts of the case are tested, as in the cases concerning the EU GMP Guidelines. Or it can serve as an *aid to interpret hard law* and shift the interpretation of EU and national hard law in a particular direction, as in the cases concerning the SGEI Communication and the Notice to Applicants. Thus, courts may use soft law rarely and they may not use soft law in the same way as hard law, but the judicial usage of soft law can nevertheless substantively affect the legal reasoning of the court and the outcome of a case.

Summarizing *explanations of judicial usage*, the case studies show that the *institutional set-up of policy areas* in the EU multilevel system matters for how national courts use EU soft law. In state aid, the *hierarchical governance*, characterized by high regulatory and enforcement powers at EU level, affects why and how courts use soft law. In the *Bundesgerichtshof* case involving the *SGEI Communication*, the court implicitly recognized the European Commission's role as authority in interpreting what constitutes state aid and SGEIs. In such contexts, national courts treat the Commission's soft law instruments as authoritative legal opinions for interpreting hard law. In the second state aid case, the German courts interpreted national legal provisions in light of the *Environmental- and Energy State Aid Guidelines* (EEAG). They recognized that national legislators had aligned national rules with EU soft law, thereby reinforcing the relevance of EU soft law as an interpretative framework.

In pharmaceutical regulation, the overarching institutional factor that led to the usage of soft law in court was the *cooperative governance* setup in the policy area ('composite administration'), where decision-making at national and EU level is closely entangled. German administrative courts invoked the *Notice to Applicants* to interpret legal terms of hard law, as they recognize the soft law as a harmonized and common legal interpretation of national and EU actors. Soft law then draws its authority as common position of regulators at both levels of governance. Moreover, a German administrative court uses the *GMP guidelines* as a supplementary standard of review. In this case, national courts consider its requirements to be de facto binding because of their status as *accepted scientific knowledge* across European experts and national authorities. Again, this is linked to the inclusive formulation of the instrument by experts from medicines authorities from all Member States, but here the scientific method in the creation of soft law plays an especially relevant role. Finally, the case studies show that the judicial use of soft law can contribute to the wider policy effects, but their direction is not uniform. The case studies in state aid pointed to effects on the role of the state in the economy. The SGEI case probed the lawfulness of national subsidies for public hospitals. This ties into debates about the balancing of public goods against the European liberalization of services in the internal market. But the instrument does not systematically favor an extension of state aid law into areas of national competence. On the contrary, the court applied the SGEI Communication to justify an exemption of the financing of hospitals from the scope of State aid enforcement. The second state aid case concerning the EEAG reinforced the relevance of EU energy policy for the design of national renewables support schemes.

In the pharmaceutical policy cases, the German administrative judiciary invoked the Notice to Applicants to interpret Europeanized national law on the authorization of medicines. In policy terms, the case concerns scope of national exceptions from the harmonization of medicines authorizations. Similarly, the EU GMP Guidelines case concerns the level of EU harmonization—in this case, of enforcement criteria in medicines authorization. Again, it became clear that the soft law instrument clearly affects the balancing between purely national practices and Europeanized administrative procedures. Thus, the judicial usage of EU soft law can substantively restrict the behavior of public and private actors and alter the policy at the national level. However, the use of soft law does not always result in a stronger role of EU law vis-à-vis national law, nor in the systematic strengthening of a certain type of actor, such as public authorities or private litigants. It is rather dependent on the case at hand and the reasoning of the court.

References

Ambroziak, A. A. (2014). The legal framework for regional state aid in the European Union in 2014–2020 and its impact on the attractiveness of Poland's regions to investors. In *New cohesion policy of the European Union in Poland: How it will influence the investment attractiveness of regions in 2014–2020* (pp. 63–76). Springer.

Anhalt/Lützeler. (2010). § 8 Die Herstellung von Arzneimitteln. In Dieners/Reese (Ed.), *Handbuch des Pharmarechts* (1st ed.). C.H. Beck.

Aust, B., & Morscher, C. (2017). Negative Strompreise in Deutschland. *Wirtschaftsdienst, 97*(4), 304–306.

Banet, C. (2020). Legal status and legal effects of the commission's state aid guidelines: The case of the guidelines on state aid for Environmental Protection and Energy (EEAG)(2014–2020). *European State Aid Law Quarterly, 20*(2), 172–184.

Bartosch, A. (2016). *EU-Beihilfenrecht: Kommentar* (2nd edn, 2016 edn). C.H. Beck.

Bieling, H.-J. (2023). Gewährleistungsstaatlichkeit in der Europäischen Union. Die regulative Strukturierung sozialer Infrastrukturen durch die europäische Handlungsarena. *GROEG-Arbeitspapier Nr. 5.*

Biesenbender, J. (2011). The dynamics of treaty change: Measuring the distribution of power in the European Union? *European Integration Online Papers (EIoP), 15*(5).

Blauberger, M. (2009a). Compliance with rules of negative integration: European state aid control in the new member states. *Journal of European Public Policy, 16*(7), 1030–1046.

Blauberger, M. (2009b). Of 'Good' and 'Bad' subsidies: European state aid control through soft and hard law. *West European Politics, 32*(4), 719–737.

Börzel, T. (2005). Mind the gap! European integration between level and scope. *Journal of European Public Policy, 12*(2), 217–236.

Bouchagiar, A. (2017). The binding effects of guidelines on the compatibility of state aid: How hard is the commission's soft law? *Journal of European Competition Law & Practice, 8*(3), 157–166.

Cappellina, B., Ausfelder, A., Eick, A., Mespoulet, R., Hartlapp, M., Saurugger, S., & Terpan, F. (2022). Ever more soft law? A dataset to compare binding and non-binding EU law across policy areas and over time (2004–2019). *European Union Politics, 23*(4), 741–757.

Cini, M. (2001). The soft law approach: Commission rule-making in the EU's state aid regime. *Journal of European Public Policy, 8*(2), 192–207.

Dezobry, G. (2015). *Les lignes directrices concernant les aides d'État à la protection de l'environnement et à l'énergie pour la période 2014–2020* (CEEM Working Paper No. 2015-12). Université Paris-Dauphine.

Doleys, T. J. (2013). Managing the dilemma of discretion: The European Commission and the development of EU state aid policy. *Journal of Industry, Competition and Trade, 13*(1), 23–38.

Fleischfresser, A. (2020). § 3 Europäisierung des Arzneimittelrechts. In Fuhrmann/Klein/Fleischfresser (Ed.), *Arzneimittelrecht* (3rd Edition 2020 ed., pp. Rn. 20–38). Nomos.

Gallo, D., & Mariotti, C. (2017). The public financing of belgian hospitals and EU law: A core development in the field of state aid. In R. Mastroianni & A. Arena (Eds.), *Sixty years of EU competition law: Stocktaking and future prospects* (pp. 173–198).

Géradin, D. (2012). The new SGEI package. *Journal of European Competition Law & Practice, 3*(1), 1–3.

Gerber, D. J. (1994). The transformation of European Community competition law. *Harvard International Law Journal, 35*, 97.

Haas, T. (2017). *Die politische Ökonomie der Energiewende: Deutschland und Spanien im Kontext multipler Krisendynamiken in Europa*. Springer.

Hofmann, H., Micheau, C., & Mihaescu-Evans, B. C. (2016). *State aid law of the European Union*. Oxford University Press.

Jacobs, D. (2016). *Renewable energy policy convergence in the EU: The evolution of feed-in tariffs in Germany*. Routledge.

Kahles, M. (2015). Wegfall der EEG-Förderung bei negativen Preisen: § 24 EEG 2014, europarechtliche Hintergründe und Ausgestaltungsoptionen. *Stiftung Umweltenergierecht*.

Kanavos, P., & Mossialos, E. (1999). Outstanding regulatory aspects in the European pharmaceutical market. *PharmacoEconomics, 15*, 519–533.

Kortland, H. (2022). Vorbemerkung zu § 21 AMG. In Kügel/Müller/Hofmann (Ed.), *Arzneimittelgesetz* (3rd edn, 2022 ed.). C.H. Beck.

Kötter, M. (2011). BVerfG: Das Ende der "objektiven" Auslegungsmethode? VerfBlog, https://verfassungsblog.de/bundesverfassungsgericht-auf-methodisch-neuen-wegen/

Krapohl, S. (2008). *Risk regulation in the single market: The governance of pharmaceuticals and foodstuffs in the European Union*. Springer.

Kröll, R. (2017). *Das Europäische Arzneimittelrecht*. Springer.

Lavdas, K., & Mendrinou, M. (1999). *Politics, subsidies and competition: The new politics of state intervention in the European Union*. Edgar Elgar Publishing.

Malzahn, J., & Wehner, C. (2010). Zur Lage der Investitionsfinanzierung der Krankenhäuser–Bestandsaufnahme und Reformbedarf. *Krankenhaus-Report*, 107–125.

Möllers, T. M. (2017). *Juristische Methodenlehre*. CH Beck.

Permanand, G. (2006). *EU pharmaceutical regulation: The politics of policy-making*. Manchester University Press.

Permanand, G., & Mossialos, E. (2005). Constitutional asymmetry and pharmaceutical policy-making in the European Union. *Journal of European Public Policy, 12*(4), 687–709.

Röttger-Wirtz, S., & Eliantonio, M. (2019). From integration to exclusion: EU composite administration and gaps in judicial accountability in the authorisation of pharmaceuticals. *European Journal of Risk Regulation, 10*(2), 393–411.

Scharpf, F. W. (2008). Negative und positive Integration. In *Die politische Ökonomie der europäischen Integration* (pp. 49–87). Campus Verlag.
Schmidt, S. K. (2007). Mutual recognition as a new mode of governance. *Journal of European Public Policy, 14*(5), 667–681.
Senden, L. A. J. (2004). *Soft law in European Community law*. Hart Publishing.
Sinnaeve, A., & Slot, P. J. (1999). The new regulation on state aid procedures. *Common Market Law Review*, *36*(6), 1153–1194.
Smith, M. P. (1998). Autonomy by the rules: the European Commission and the development of state aid policy. *JCMS: Journal of Common Market Studies*, *36*(1), 55–78.
Soltész, U., & Köckritz, C. V. (2014). Das EEG im Fokus des EU-Beihilferechts. In Beiträge zum neuen EEG 2014. *GLEISS LUTZ Schriftenreihe zum deutschen und internationalen Wirtschaftsrecht*, 35–60.
Stefan, O. (2008). European competition soft law in European courts: A matter of hard principles? *European Law Journal, 14*(6), 753–772.
Szyszczak, E. (2012). Modernising state aid and the financing of SGEI. *Journal of European Competition Law & Practice*, *3*(4), 332–343.
Szyszczak, E. (2014). Time for renewables to join the market: The new guidelines on state aid for environmental protection and energy. *Journal of European Competition Law & Practice, 5*(9), 616–623.
Terpan, F. (2015). Soft law in the European Union-The changing nature of EU law. *European Law Journal, 21*(1), 68–96.
Treib, O. (2014). Implementing and complying with EU governance outputs. *Living reviews in European governance*, *9*(1).
Van Dam, C. (2017). Guidance documents of the European Commission: A typology to trace the effects in the national legal order. *Review of European Administrative Law, 10*(2), 75–91.
von Danwitz, T. (2009). Dienste von allgemeinem wirtschaftlichem Interesse in der europäischen Wettbewerbsordnung. In *Die Daseinsvorsorge im Spannungsfeld von europäischem Wettbewerb und Gemeinwohl* (pp. 103–130). Springer.
Wishlade, F. G. (2003). *Regional state aid and competition policy in the European Union*. Kluwer Law International.

CHAPTER 7

Conclusion: Not So Soft Law

7.1 Capturing Soft Law in Courts

In their role as decentralized enforcers of EU law and guarantors of the harmonization of national laws, national courts have made an important contribution to the deepening and widening of European integration (Maher, 1994). This development was, in part, possible because EU law is binding. But silently, EU soft law instruments, which are neither mere politics nor binding law, have become increasingly important at the EU level (Cappellina et al., 2022) and national level (Eliantonio et al., 2021). This book departed from the observation that we know little about the role of such non-binding instruments in national courts. The book asked how, why, and to what effect national courts use EU soft law. This led to three specific questions. First, how often courts use EU soft law, and what types of usage there are. Second, how the variation in judicial use of soft law can be explained. Finally, what the wider effects of the judicial usage of EU soft law on policy and actors at the national level are.

Soft law may not be binding, but the answers to these questions have important implications for our understanding of the nature of the EU legal framework in action, the role of courts in the EU multilevel system, and the democratic credentials of the increasing regulation through soft law. Chapter 1 introduced the phenomenon of the use of EU soft law in courts and reviewed the interdisciplinary literature on law and courts

A. Eick, *Soft Law and National Courts in the European Union*, European Administrative Governance,
https://doi.org/10.1007/978-3-032-04515-7_7

in the European Union. Most contributions on the role of EU soft law at the national level have focused on the administration (Copeland & ter Haar, 2013; López-Santana, 2006; Saurugger & Terpan, 2016), but I argued that these findings cannot be fully extended to courts because they are specific actors who are strongly bound by legal constraints and their adjudicative role in society. A few studies have already pioneered the study of the judicial use of EU soft law, but they have mostly engaged in systematic comparative legal analysis of judgments from a perspective that is rather internal to the law (Georgieva, 2017; Korkea-aho, 2015; Stefan, 2013). I then noted that the literature on judicial politics has proposed plausible explanations for courts' decision-making that are extra-legal and related to the characteristics of actors as actors and their institutional environment (Dyevre, 2010), but that these have not yet been applied to the decision to use soft law.

By merging these literatures, I developed a broad conceptual perspective on the national courts and their usage of soft law in Chapter 2. Courts were characterized as collective actors whose behavior is constrained and enabled by their institutional environment, legal culture of a country, characteristics of a judicial branch, and especially the law. There are also reasons to assume that the individual profile of judges matters, for example their knowledge of and attitudes towards EU law. I argued that the dependent variable, the judicial usage of soft law, cannot be fully captured by counting citations to soft law instruments in judgments, as citations do not equate to relevance to the reasoning or outcome of a case.

Therefore, the book conceptualized a graded dependent variable, which distinguishes several types of the judicial usage of EU soft law. Thereafter, it can take softer forms, where soft law carries only slightly more weight than a non-legal document, or harder forms, where soft law is used almost like hard law. It consists of the application of such instruments in a judgment and the recognition of their practical and legal effects. The book proposed that institutional factors related to the legal framework, policy area, country as well as actor-centered factors concerning the profile of judges may drive the judicial usage of EU soft law.

Obtaining systematic data on the use of EU law and soft law in national courts is difficult due to the unsystematic publication practices of courts and the difficult access to the judiciary. Thus, the book collected different kinds of data to approach the elusive phenomenon from multiple perspectives, which were introduced in Chapter 3. Two databases of judgments that feature soft law were collected to describe usage. The first, the main *judgment dataset*, was designed to capture, as far as possible, a complete universe of cases citing six soft law instruments from two policy areas in Germany and France to allow an in-depth study of the phenomenon—but for two 'steering' soft law instruments that are not connected to hard law no cases were found. The second dataset, SLDecNat, was designed to collect broader but less reliable judgment data across all countries, soft law instruments, and time periods to explore the generalizability of the patterns of judicial usage. Further, to test the proposed legal and extra-legal explanations for the phenomenon at the level of individual judges, I conducted a survey with French and German judges. Finally, four case studies in pharmaceutical policy and state aid based on in-depth reading of judgments, contextual documents, and expert interviews were conducted to illustrate mechanisms through which institutional factors lead to usage and to evaluate the wider implications of judicial usage. The case selection included relevant cases that vary in explanatory dimensions. France and Germany and typical soft law instruments from the areas of state aid and pharmaceutical regulation. All this led to the following key findings on the use of EU soft law in national courts.

7.2 Key Findings

Courts Rarely, but Increasingly, Use EU Soft Law. Chapter 4 found 111 French and German cases in the systematic *judgment data* in state aid and pharmaceutical regulation, while the exploratory but wider *SLDecNat* data included 102 cases in all Member States and policies. Considering the respective observation periods, this amounts to only about five cases per year in the first and two cases per year in the second dataset. While the poor publication and availability of judgments means that these figures are likely to underestimate the true number, it has become clear that cases involving soft law are very rare, compared to the thousands of cases in a policy area or involving EU law. The survey data corroborate these findings showed that only eight of the seventy responding judges reported having used soft law in the past. Most courts and judges don't seem to use EU soft law regularly, even in the likely policy areas of pharmaceutical regulation and state aid.

However, *usage increases over time*. The judgment data show that, in the second decade of observation (2012–2022), there were more cases citing the selected instruments in France than in the first decade (2002–2011). The wider SLDecNat data suggest an increase from 1975 to 2003, after which the data on the frequency of cases are unreliable. Although the use of soft law in relation to all cases appears to be low, the responses of judges to the survey show that they are in principle not reluctant to deal with soft law. While there is a small but notable proportion of respondents and judgments that reject the notion that soft law can have any legal relevance, Chapter 4 has shown that most judges responding to the survey recognize the legal relevance of such instruments, even if they have not yet applied them themselves. Given the increasing adoption of EU soft law (Cappellina et al., 2022), not least during the Covid-19 pandemic (Stefan, 2020), it seems likely that such instruments will be increasingly used by national courts in the future.

When Courts Use Soft Law, It Is Often Significant to the Judgment. But the analysis of judgments involving soft law in pharmaceutical regulation and state aid in Chapter 4 also showed that, when national courts use EU soft law, *medium-hard* and *hard uses dominate* over soft usage and non-usage. Such usage is likely to influence the argumentation, outcome, or wider policy and legal effects of a judgment. In particular, courts engage in what I have called *medium application* where they apply it in a judgment as an aid to interpret hard law or a supplementary standard of review together with hard law. In many cases, they even *recognize hard effects* of soft law by ascribing to it an indirect binding force in conjunction with hard law. Soft law can then become de facto binding for at least some of its addressees or, in some situations, as long as it does not deviate from its underlying hard law. The survey responses of judges from diverse policy areas presented in Chapter 4 show that this holds true beyond pharmaceutical regulation and state aid.

Case studies in Chapter 6 illustrated these typical cases of medium-hard and hard use. For example, a state aid case in which a German court ruled that wind farm operators and electricity suppliers must follow an interpretation of national law through the lens of the Environmental- and Energy State Aid Guidelines. In another case study, a court found that a public authority inspecting the safety of pharmaceutical manufacturing sites was obliged to examine evidence of the safety of a manufacturing site against the criteria of the GMP Guidelines, which concretize Directive 2003/94/EC. In such cases, soft law plays more than a purely non-legal role, the kind of role a political document or a scientific report would serve. Instead, soft law unfolds a non-binding legal effect in the former case, in that it provides an authoritative interpretation of hard law. In the latter case, soft law becomes indirectly binding in practice and the binding force of hard law spills over onto the adjacent soft law instrument that concretizes or interprets it (Goldmann, 2015, p. 59).

However, it has also become apparent that *soft law is never fully used like hard law*. The judgment and survey data show that courts never use soft law as a main standard of review or as an independent legal source, and—except for one survey respondent—never recognize a direct binding force of a soft law instrument in complete isolation from hard law. This confirms the findings of studies at EU level (Stefan, 2013) and national level (Georgieva, 2017) which found that courts may confirm that soft law has legal relevance, but they do not transform it into hard law. This book extends the generalizability of this finding. The analysis of patterns in the judgment data of Chapter 4 confirms it for the areas of pharmaceutical regulation and state aid at the national level. The complementary data sources presented in this chapter suggest that this also applies to a broader sample of policy areas (SLDecNat and survey data) and Member States (SLDecNat data).

Some Courts Use EU Soft Law More Frequently Than Others. We find that *German courts use EU soft law more frequently than French courts*. This became particularly clear in the analysis of systematic judgment data on the usage of six instruments that are likely cases for usage: in the judgment data, 86% of cases were from German courts and only 14% from French courts. The more exploratory but broader analyses in the complementary data confirmed this country difference, although Germany does not have quite the same margin over France in the more exploratory but broader SLDecNat judgment data and in the survey results. At the outset, this result was not clearly expected, as recent case law and legal debates in France have indicated a legal culture that is receptive to the legal relevance of EU soft law. However, the results suggest that the lengthy reasoning that is common in the German judiciary gives the courts more scope to use soft law more frequently than the French courts with their reserved legal style that produces short judgments.

Chapter 4 also found strong country differences across EU Member States. In particular, *the more a country's judiciary applies EU law in general, the more it uses EU soft law*. German courts engage both more with EU law in general and with EU soft law. This is also the case beyond these two countries, and the application of EU law is associated with the usage of EU soft law. Thus, cross-country variation is not specific to soft law factors, but rather to general trends of the Europeanization of the judiciary and the number of cases in a country.

The *frequency of usage also varies between court branches.* The case studies in Chapter 6 suggested that this is related to the actor's constellation and mode of regulation in a policy area. State aid and pharmaceutical policy are set up as areas where public authorities enforce administrative rules against other public authorities. They thus mostly end up in the administrative judiciary which controls the exercise of public power. This is similar in Telecommunications policy, which had the highest distribution administrative courts in the SLDecNat data. Competition policy dominated the civil judiciary, which corresponds to the dominance of civil litigation in the sector against anti-competitive behavior by companies or disputes between competitors. Although competition law covers a number of different areas of law, most concern the anti-competitive behavior of private actors or the relationship between competitors and therefore give rise to civil law claims. Thus, which judicial branch uses soft law depends on the mode of regulation in policy areas that feature soft law.

Usage is equally common in the two policy areas state and pharmaceutical regulation. These are indeed likely cases of judicial usage. But Chapter 4 showed that there are strong policy differences across the broader population of policy areas. Courts use EU soft law frequently in the areas of high EU competences: competition policy, state aid—which could also be characterized as part of the competition policy, and Telecommunications. This suggests that *courts use EU soft law more frequently in policy areas that of high EU competences.*

In contrast, there are no strong differences between the levels of the judiciary. Chapter 4 found slightly more usage in lower courts than in other branches of the judiciary in the judgment data, while the SLDecNat data found slightly more usage in apex courts. But the notable takeaway is that lower courts feature prominently in both datasets, against the expectation that the high workload would discourage them to engage in-depth with detailed non-binding instruments. All of this suggests that the *lower courts do not shy away from using EU soft law* despite potential bureaucratic constraints.

Institutional Factors Predict Harder Judicial Usages of EU Soft Law. Chapter 5 explained why judges use EU soft law in softer or harder forms. Several institutional explanations were proposed as reasons for harder forms of usage. Among them, factors at the level of countries and the judicial branch are associated with harder usage. What concerns country-factors, the data support the expectation that a *legal style of extensive reasoning in the judiciary is associated with harder usage*. Chapter 5 found harder usage in German than in French judgments in the judgment and survey data. The recognition of practical effects had the highest distribution among French survey respondents, while an indirect binding force of EU soft law had the highest distribution among German judges. In terms of the application of EU soft law, only French respondents indicated that they used EU soft law as an informal guide without citing it in the final judgment. This supports the argument that *legal style* matters. The extensive reasoning of German courts also provides more opportunities for harder judicial applications of EU soft law, requiring more argumentation or citations than is usually provided for in the brief and authoritative reasoning of French judgments.

Both the judgment and the survey data showed *harder use in the administrative branch than in the civil branch*, while non-usage dominated in the civil branch. This suggests that the administrative branch is particularly open to give legal relevance to EU soft law. I argued that this may be related to features of the characteristics of the administrative judiciary, such as experience of administrative judges with national soft law and the prominence of administrative EU soft law.

The case studies in Chapter 6 illustrate instances where EU soft law concretizes the criteria according to which public administrations take individual decisions and the administrative procedures that lead to such decisions. In the case of state aid, these are enforcement decisions by the European Commission, while in the case of pharmaceutical regulation, they are authorization decisions by national authorities.

But the book also found that several institutional factors are not associated with harder usage or only under certain circumstances. While the French legal culture is more receptive to soft law as manifested in recent academic debates and case law, this does not systematically translate into harder usage. The evidence for the argument that usage is harder in policy areas of high EU competence is mixed. While Chapter 5 found harder usage in state aid than in pharmaceutical regulation, the survey data found no significant association between competences and harder usage. Further, legal factors related to the nature of the instruments play a role, but only to some extent. 'Steering' soft law, which proposes policy and steers behavior independent of hard law, is wholly absent from the judgment data and survey data. It was expected that decisional soft law is particularly hard, as it concretizes the discretion of EU institutions. But Chapter 5 found no difference in the usage of these interpretative and decisional soft law instruments.

Actor-Centered Factors Only Have Limited Explanatory Power. Chapter 5 also probed several actor-centered factors relating to the profile of individual judges. The survey data showed that *positive attitudes toward soft law are associated with a recognition* of the effects of such instruments. Moreover, judges' knowledge of EU law is associated with the frequency of soft law usage. This suggests that where the judiciary is highly Europeanized, courts are more likely to engage with specialized instruments, such as soft law, which can contribute to the harmonization of EU law. However, *most actor-centered expectations were found to be irrelevant* both to explain the frequency of usage and harder levels of recognition.

The Governance Arrangement in a Policy Area Affects How Courts Use EU Soft Law. Further, Chapter 5 indicated the relevance of institutional factors based on the associations of the dependent variable with the explanatory factors, but it could not identify the mechanisms through which these institutional factors translate into individual court decisions in specific policy areas. Based on qualitative data, the case studies in Chapter 6 traced typical cases of usage in the areas of state aid and pharmaceutical regulation to uncover such mechanisms. The case studies found that *the governance arrangement in the EU multilevel system* translates into the judicial usage of EU soft law in national judgments.

The first set of cases focused on state aid policy and considered the usage of two prominent soft law instruments. In state aid, the *hierarchical governance*, which stems from the high level of competences at the EU level in the policy area, is the decisive overarching factor that leads to a harder forms of usage. The first case study concerned the usage of the *SGEI Communication* in the German ordinary judiciary as an aid to interpret EU state aid law. The high level of EU competence is reflected in the courts' recognition of powers of the Commission as the regulator and enforcer of EU state aid law. The Commission has the power to decide which measures are state aid and which are not, and it has wide discretion in interpreting the vague rules of hard law. While the CJEU reviews decisions by the Commission, national courts are not competent to do so. Against this background, national courts see the Commission's soft law in these sectors as an authoritative guide to interpret hard law.

The second case study concerned the use of the *Environmental and Energy State Aid Guidelines* 2014–2020 (EEAG). The case study diagnosed a *strong Europeanization of national law* in renewable energies support, which had evolved over time through negative integration, i.e., the adaptation of national law to EU state aid enforcement. In the legislative arena we can find an adaptation of national hard law to the criteria of state aid soft law, and thus the hardening of soft law. The case study showed how German courts use the EEAG as a tool to interpret national hard law in line with EU soft law. The courts recognize that the national legislator has adapted to EU soft law and therefore interpret the national rules in the light of this soft law.

In pharmaceutical regulation, the overarching institutional factor that led to usage of soft law in court was the *cooperative governance arrangement*, characterized by the entanglement of the national and EU levels of governance (composite administration). The soft law instrument *Notice to Applicants* is used against the background of a dense EU legal framework. Pharmaceutical soft law concretizes legal definitions and administrative procedures. German administrative courts invoke the Notice to Applicants to interpret legal terms of hard law, as they recognize the Notice to Applicants as a *harmonized legal interpretation of national and EU actors*. Soft law then draws its authority as common position of regulators at both levels of governance.

A German administrative court uses the *EU GMP guidelines* as a supplementary standard of review. In this case, national courts consider its requirements to be de facto binding because of their status as *accepted scientific knowledge*. Again, this is linked to the *inclusive formulation* of the instrument by experts from medicines authorities from all Member States. Thus, Chapter 6 confirmed that institutional factors explain usage. But which factors and their translation into usage are highly dependent on the governance arrangement and the division of competences between the levels in a policy area.

Judicial Use of Soft Law Has Important Wider Effects, But Their Direction Is Not Uniform. The case studies in Chapter 6 also evaluated the effects of typical cases of the judicial usage of EU soft law in state aid and pharmaceutical policy. They found that *judicial usage can substantively affect the legal reasoning* of the court, and it can *contribute to the outcome of a case*. Soft law was found to play a role as supplementary standard of review against which the facts of the case are tested, as in the cases concerning the SGEI Communication and the GMP Guidelines. Or it can shift the interpretation of EU and national hard law in a particular direction, as in the cases concerning the Environmental and State Aid Guidelines and the Notice to Applicants. But soft law was never entirely or alone responsible for a particular outcome of a case. But in all the case studies, it had a significant impact on the reasoning of the courts in a case and contributed to the outcome of the judicial proceedings.

The case studies have also shown that the *judicial use of soft law can contribute to the wider policy effects*, but the direction of those effects is not uniform. The case studies on state aid in Chapter 6 pointed to effects on the role of the state in the economy. The SGEI Communication was used in a judgment by the German apex ordinary court, and it probed the lawfulness of national subsidies for public hospitals. This ties into debates about the balancing of public goods against the European liberalization of services in the internal market. But the instrument does not systematically extend state aid law into areas of national competence; it can also strengthen national subsidiarity.

The application of the Environmental and Energy State Aid Guidelines 2014–2020 (EEAG), in a series of cases in the German ordinary courts concerned the question of which wind turbines could receive support under the national renewable energy support scheme during periods of negative prices. The court interpreted the national energy law in line with EU soft law and found that certain small wind parks should not receive renewable energy support in periods of negative prices. In this way, EU soft law contributes to the development of national energy policy effectively limiting renewable energies support in specific circumstances.

Chapter 6 also demonstrated how in pharmaceutical regulation, the judicial usage of EU soft law affects the harmonization of administrative practices and the density of regulatory requirements in risk regulation. A series of cases in the German administrative judiciary invoked the Notice to Applicants in order to interpret Europeanized national law on the authorization of medicines. In policy terms, the case concerned scope of national exceptions from the harmonization of medicines authorizations. Again, it became clear that the soft law instrument clearly affects the balancing between purely national practices and Europeanized administrative procedures, but different judicial instances drew diverging conclusions from the instrument. Finally, a case in the German courts has shown that EU GMP guidelines affect the regulatory requirements that a medicines manufacturer must meet, but also the standard of review that a national regulatory authority must apply. The case shows that soft law can bring detailed scientific standards into the courtroom. Overall, the judicial use of EU soft law can meaningfully constrain the actions of both public and private actors and influence national law and policy. However, its use does not always extend the influence of EU law over national law and policy, nor does it consistently favor one type of actor—such as public authorities or private litigants. Instead, the application of soft law remains more flexible, and its effects depend on the specific context and the court's reasoning in each case.

7.3 Wider Implications of the Findings

The results of the book contribute to three broader debates. First, about the legalization of the EU legal framework. Abbott et al. (2000) argue that law and policy are not two separate domains. Instead, there is a continuum of areas governed by law and areas where law is not relevant. In between, certain features of law are used to govern and regulate societies even in the absence of formal legal acts and binding force. The book finds that national courts contribute to the development of such a graded *continuum of legal normativity*. The judicial use of EU soft law in national courts falls and remains within such an intermediate space between law and non-law. On the one hand, courts do not treat soft law as something separate from the legal framework. Rather, they use it as a complement to hard law. Moreover, courts attribute interpretative effects and the concretization of legal obligations to it. Such effects can be close to those of hard law. Courts regularly 'harden' soft law to some extent when they recognize its legal effects or indirect binding force, as this confirms the place of such instruments in the legal framework. This finding is in line with several studies that observe a hardening of soft law at the EU and national level (Cini, 2000; Schoenefeld & Knodt 2020; Saurugger & Terpan, 2020). However, the results of the book also show that courts do not fully harden soft law, as they never transform soft law into hard law by declaring it binding in its own right and in isolation from binding legal acts. As already mentioned, this conclusion is consistent with previous findings in the EU courts (Stefan, 2013), and in national courts in a limited set of policy areas (Georgieva, 2017; Hartlapp & Hofmann, 2020) and confirms them for a broader population of policy areas and countries.

Second, in the context of the European Union and its Member States, legalization is closely related to the concept of *European integration through law* (Cappelletti et al., 1986), whereby EU law increasingly permeates politics, national legal orders, and societal conflicts. Such a dynamic would raise questions of democratic legitimacy, particularly in the case of soft law, as such instruments are not backed by legislative decisions. The findings of the book suggest that the judicial use of EU soft law may indeed have the potential to unleash such a dynamic in certain cases. Where EU competence is high and hard law is already in place, the use of EU soft law in judgments can intensify and extend the application of EU law. Soft law provides opportunities for courts and litigants to justify broad interpretations of EU law and to impose new obligations in the gaps of existing hard law. However, the book finds no evidence that soft law provides a basis for judicial decisions in policy areas where the EU has little competence and where little hard law exists.

Third, the findings of the book contribute to the description of the *role of the national judiciary in the EU multilevel system*. The case studies in Chapter 6 have shown that when national courts apply EU law and soft law, they do not merely mechanistically apply EU rules to national cases. Instead, they actively shape the enforcement of EU law at the national level and the interpretation of national law in line with EU law, even when the EU norms in question are soft law. Karen Alter (1998) argued that the lower courts play a central role in European legal integration, while more recent research suggests that it is now the higher courts that make a more decisive contribution (Dyevre et al., 2020, pp. 8–9; Pavone & Kelemen, 2019). The findings of this book suggest that courts at the lower level of the judiciary continue to play an important role in the day-to-day incorporation of EU law into the national legal order. The data on judgments and the case study on the Notice to Applicants show that lower courts are actively applying detailed soft law instruments to complex issues of EU law.

7.4 Scope of the Results

Several key findings of the book are generalizable to a broader population of cases. First, Chapter 4 mapped the frequency of judicial use of soft law across countries and policy areas and found that judicial use was rare overall, but more frequent in countries with many cases involving EU law and in policy areas with high EU competence. The survey data indicated the relevance of judges' attitudes and knowledge of EU law in seven different policy areas, which can be generalized to a broader population of policies.

While the ways in which soft law is used in judgments could only be conclusively identified in pharmaceutical regulation and state aid, these areas have close relatives to which the findings in these areas can be generalized. In state aid, the strong role of the Commission as an enforcer and issuer of soft law has influenced the judicial use of EU soft law by national courts. This is also likely to be the case in other areas with strong enforcement powers at EU level, such as monetary policy, where the European Central Bank enforces policy and issues soft law (Alberti, 2018). The inclusive adoption of soft law in pharmaceutical policy led to relevant cases in national courts. This finding is likely to apply to other areas of risk regulation that also have inclusive multilevel settings for the adoption of soft law and science-based safety standards. Areas such as food safety (Krapohl, 2008), aviation safety (Woodlock & Hydén, 2020), and financial regulation (van Rijsbergen, 2014) come to mind.

However, there are limitations to the findings of this book. Pharmaceutical regulation and state aid were identified as likely cases of judicial use of EU soft law. While the survey provided insights into the level of recognition in different policy areas, more detailed data collections of more diverse policy areas are needed to add nuance. Data collection on the role of soft law in the courts is still sparse. A more comprehensive mapping of types of use across qualitatively different policy areas would be a fruitful complement to the findings of this book.

Further, Chapter 6 pointed to policy-specific explanations for usage which have to do with the setup of the policy area. Due to the differentiated nature of EU governance, such there may be further policy-specific dynamics that could not be considered in this book. An interesting question for future research is how policy-specific dynamics affect the judicial usage of soft law. For example, the *Open Method of Coordination* and its successors in areas like social policy work through Council deliberations by political actors and country-specific recommendations to individual Member States which function through naming-and-shaming (Trubek & Trubek, 2005). If courts invoke such instruments, it is likely for different reasons and with different effects.

Similarly, the book identified the legal style of judgments as a likely explanation for country differences between Germany and France, and that the frequency of usage follows patterns of the general application of EU law across Member States. But there may be additional country-factors that could not be uncovered due to the limited selection of countries. It is worthwhile for future research to focus on the effect of country-level factors on judicial usage. For example, Hartley (2005) argues that EU law was initially an uneasy fit for courts in common law systems, but over time they found elaborate ways to incorporate EU law into their decision-making through mechanisms that differ from those in civil law courts. The specific mechanisms that lead to the judicial usage of EU soft law may be tied in similar ways to the legal system.

Finally, it should be pointed out that EU soft law is likely here to stay (Cappellina et al., 2022; Zhelyazkova et al., 2014). Soft law remains a go-to regulatory tool of the European institutions in times of crisis and in newly emerging areas of regulation and there are reasons to believe that it will increasingly find its way into national courts. In 2021, the CJEU has received several requests for preliminary rulings on the justiciability of EU soft law.[1] In the European courts, Advocate General Bobek has repeatedly called for judicial review of EU soft law.[2] All of this suggests that the judicial use of EU soft law in national courts will become more important in the future. As soft law permeates the legal system more and more, and as social conflicts are increasingly regulated by non-binding instruments, courts will likely have no choice but to address the status and effects of such instruments. Therefore, research on the judicial use of soft law will remain relevant.

References

Abbott, K. O. W., Keohane, R., Moravcsik, A., Slaughter, A.-M., & Snidal, D. (2000). The concept of legalization. *International Organization, 54*(3), 401–419.

Alberti, J. (2018). Challenging the evolution of the EMU: The justiciability of soft law measures enacted by the ECB against the financial crisis before the European courts. *Yearbook of European Law, 37*, 626–649.

[1] Judgment of the Court (Grand Chamber) of 15 July 2021. *Fédération bancaire française (FBF) v Autorité de contrôle prudentiel et de résolution* (ACPR). Case C-911/19; Judgment of the Court (Fourth Chamber) of 25 March 2021. BT v Balgarska Narodna Banka. Case C-501/18.

[2] Advocate General's Opinion in Case C-911/19. *Fédération bancaire française (FBF) v Autorité de contrôle prudentiel et de résolution* (ACPR).

Alter, K. (1998). Explaining national court acceptance of European court jurisprudendence: A critical evaluation of theories of legal integration. In *The European courts and national courts* (pp. 225–250). Hart Publishing.

Cappelletti, M., Seccombe, M., & Weiler, J. H. (1986). *Integration through law, volume 1: Methods, tools and institutions, Book 1: A political, legal and economic overview*. De Gruyter.

Cappellina, B., Ausfelder, A., Eick, A., Mespoulet, R., Hartlapp, M., Saurugger, S., & Terpan, F. (2022). Ever more soft law? A dataset to compare binding and non-binding EU law across policy areas and over time (2004–2019). *European Union Politics, 23*(4), 741–757.

Cini, M. (2000). From soft law to hard law?: Discretion and rule-making in the commission's state aid regime. *EUI Working Paper Series* European Forum Series (RSC No. 2000/35).

Copeland, P., & ter Haar, B. (2013). A toothless bite? The effectiveness of the European employment strategy as a governance tool. *Journal of European Social Policy, 23*(1), 21–36.

Dyevre, A. (2010). Unifying the field of comparative judicial politics: Towards a general theory of judicial behaviour. *European Political Science Review, 2*(2), 297–327.

Dyevre, A., Glavina, M., & Atanasova, A. (2020). Who refers most? Institutional incentives and judicial participation in the preliminary ruling system. *Journal of European Public Policy, 27*(6), 912–930.

Eliantonio, M., Stefan, O., & Korkea-aho, E. (2021). *EU soft law in the member states: Theoretical findings and empirical evidence*. Bloomsbury Publishing.

Georgieva, Z. (2017). *Soft law in EU competition law and its reception in member states' courts* (PhD Thesis). Tilburg University.

Goldmann, M. (2015). *Internationale Öffentliche Gewalt: Handlungsformen internationaler Institutionen im Zeitalter der Globalisierung*. Vol. 251. Springer.

Hartlapp, M., & Hofmann. A. (2020). The use of EU soft law by national courts and bureaucrats: how relation to hard law and policy maturity matter. *West European Politics*, 1–21.

Hartley, T. C. (2005). The European union and the systematic dismantling of the common law of conflict of laws. *International & Comparative Law Quarterly, 54*(4), 813–828.

Korkea-aho, E. (2015). *Adjudicating new governance: Deliberative democracy in the European Union*. Routledge.

Krapohl, S. (2008). *Risk regulation in the single market: The governance of pharmaceuticals and foodstuffs in the European Union*. Springer.

López-Santana, M. (2006). The domestic implications of European soft law: Framing and transmitting change in employment policy. *Journal of European Public Policy, 13*(4), 481–499.

Maher, I. (1994). National courts as European Community courts. *Legal Stud., 14*, 226–243.
Pavone, T., & Kelemen, R. D. (2019). The evolving judicial politics of European Integration: The European Court of Justice and national courts revisited. *European Law Journal, 25*(4), 352–373.
Saurugger, S., & Terpan, F. (2020). Normative transformations in the European Union: on hardening and softening law. *West European Politics*, *44*(1), 1–20.
Saurugger, S., & Terpan, F. (2016). Resisting 'new modes of governance': An agency-centred approach. *Journal of Comparative European Politics, 14*(1), 53–70.
Schoenefeld, J. J., & Knodt, M. (2020). Softening the surface but hardening the core? Governing renewable energy in the EU. *West European Politics, 44*(1), 1–23.
Stefan, O. (2013). *Soft law in court: Competition law, state aid and the court of justice of the European Union.* Kluwer Law International.
Stefan, O. (2020). COVID-19 soft law: Voluminous, effective, legitimate? A research agenda. *European Papers-A Journal on Law and Integration, 2020*(1), 663–670.
Trubek, D. M., & Trubek, L. G. (2005). Hard and soft law in the construction of social Europe: The role of the open method of coordination. *European Law Journal, 11*(3), 343–364.
van Rijsbergen, M. (2014). On the enforceability of eu agencies' soft law at the national level: The case of the European securities and markets authority. *Utrecht Law Review, 10*(5), 116–131.
Woodlock, J., & Hydén, H. (2020). (f) Lex avionica; How soft law serves as an instrumental mediator between professional norms and the hard law regulation of European civil aviation maintenance. *Safety Science, 121*, 54–63.
Zhelyazkova, A., Börzel, T. A., Schimmelfennig, F., & Sedelmeier, U. (2014). Beyond uniform integration? *MAXCAP Deliverable* 2.

Appendix Section 1. Judgment Database: Codebook

This codebook details the content of the main judgment dataset. The data comprises 111 judgments from Germany and France, spanning the years 2002 to 2022. It focuses on judgments that reference four relevant and typical EU soft law instruments within the domains of state aid and pharmaceutical regulation.[1] The following EU soft law instruments are covered: In State Aid, the 'Environmental and Energy State Aid Guidelines 2014-2020 (EEAG)' and the 'Communication on Services of General Economic Interest (SGEI Communication).' In Pharmaceutical Regulation, the 'Notice to Applicants' and the 'EU Guidelines for Good Manufacturing Practice (EU GMP Guidelines).' All variables in the dataset were manually coded based on the full text of the judgments. In addition to the coded variables, the dataset includes a dedicated field, 'info_SL_usage,' which contains relevant excerpts from the judgments where EU soft law is invoked or discussed. Table A.1 lists all variables along with their description and values they can take.

[1] During sampling, two additional steering soft law instruments were considered, the 'Pharmaceutical Strategy for Europe' and the 'State Aid Action Plan,' but no judgments citing these instruments were found. Several further searches for other steering soft law instruments also yielded no results.

A. Eick, *Soft Law and National Courts in the European Union*, European Administrative Governance,
https://doi.org/10.1007/978-3-032-04515-7

Table A.1 Judgment data: List of variables

Variable name	*Description*	*Values*
ECLI	ECLI number of judgments. Serves as id. If no ECLI exists, a fictional number is added in the form "ECLI:NaN:[number]"	ECLI number
date	Date of the judgment	DD.MM.YY
year	Year of the judgment	YYYY
court	Name of the court	–
filenr	National file number of the case	–
policy_area	Policy area of the soft law instrument	0 = Pharmaceutical Regulation 1 = State Aid
MS	Member State of the judgment	0 = Germany 1 = France
court_level	Level of the court	1 = low 2 = high 3 = apex
court_branch	Judicial branch in which the court operates	1 = civil 2 = administrative 3 = other
case_HL	Provisions of hard law relevant to the case: EU law, national law or both?	0 = national 1 = EU 3 = both
SL	Name of soft law instrument	1 = EEAG 2 = NtA 3 = SGEI 4 = GMP

(continued)

Table A.1 (continued)

Variable name	*Description*	*Values*
SL_function	Function of the soft law instrument *interpretative instruments* are "supporting and supplementing (…) EU law, in particular to ensuring the proper interpretation and—uniform—application thereof" (Senden 2004, 138–147) *Decisional instruments* "indicate in what way an EU institution will apply EU law provisions in individual cases when it has implementing and discretionary powers" (ibid. 119) Note that *steering soft law* would have been considered (=2), but the sampling found no such instruments. They are "measures of an encouraging nature" that "steer or guide action" and that are not connected to hard law (ibid. 156)	0 = interpretative; 1 = decisional; 2 = steering
recognition	The degree to which judges *recognize* soft law as a legitimate instrument of governance or act of law. We can assess their recognition by the extent to which they recognize practical and legal effects of such instruments	0 = no recognition 1 = practical effects 2 = non-binding legal effects OR indirect binding force 3 = direct binding force
application	Application of soft law refers to the function of soft law in the legal argument and the role of soft law within the judgment at large	0 = no application 1 = extra-legal information 2 = aid to interpret hard law OR supplementary standard of review 3 = main standard of review (ratio decedendi) OR object of a proceeding (judicial review)

(continued)

Table A.1 (continued)

Variable name	*Description*	*Values*
usage	Mean of application and recognition. Numerical	0 = no usage 0–1.5 = soft usage 1.5–2.5 = medium usage 2.5–3 = hard usage
usage_lev	Levels of usage as categorical variable	none = no usage soft = soft usage medium = medium-hard usage hard = hard usage
info_SL_usage	Text provisions of judgments that were used as a basis to code variables on the judicial usage of soft law	–
first_invoked_by	Soft law was first invoked by the parties to a case or the court?	Court; Parties
if_parties_invoke_court_reaction	If the parties invoke soft law, how does the court react? By rejecting, ignoring, or recognizing soft law?	ignores; recognizes; rejects
litigant	What type of actor is the litigant?	private; public
defendant	What type of actor is the defendant?	private; public

Appendix Section 2. SLDecNat Database: Sampling and Codebook

The SLDecNat database contains data on national judgments citing EU soft law from 1975 to 2019. It includes 102 observations. All judgments in this dataset were sourced from a broader third-party database 'Dec.Nat' which is jointly maintained by ACA-Europe and the Court of Justice of the European Union (CJEU) includes national judgments 'relevant to the development of EU law.' To identify from this source judgments citing soft law instruments, a systematic keyword search was conducted within Dec.Nat. The search focused on terms commonly used to label EU soft law in its narrow definition (see Cappellina 2022; Senden 2004, pp. 219–222). The following keywords were used: *Guideline, Recommendation, Communication, Notice, Conclusion, Declaration, Opinion, Resolution.* Thereafter, each judgment entry was reviewed to confirm whether it actually used an EU soft law instrument. Irrelevant entries were excluded. This was done by reading the case summary and metadata in Dec.Nat. Where necessary, the full text of the judgment or related CJEU rulings was retrieved and consulted. Table A.2 lists all variables, their description, and possible values.

A. Eick, *Soft Law and National Courts in the European Union*, European Administrative Governance,
https://doi.org/10.1007/978-3-032-04515-7

Table A.2 SLDecNat data. List of variables

Variable	*Description*	*Values*
id	Unique numberica id	–
date	Date of the decision of the national court	DD/MM/YYY
year	year	YYYY
MS	Member State	–
Court	Name of court	- civil - administrative - constitutional - other
court branch	Branch of the judiciary. Manually coded based on the name of the court	
court_ instance	Court instance	- peak - higher - lower - special - other
case	Name of the case	–
case_file	National file id	–
sl_id	Identifier of the soft law instrument. E.g. CELEX number	–
sl_type	Type of soft law instrument. This variable was manually coded based on the text of the soft law instrument	–
sl_provisions	Soft law instrument cited in the field 'provisions EU soft law' in Dec.Nat. This field lists all provisions of EU law that are applied in the national case as identified in Dec.Nat. As worded in Nat.Dec	Open text
sl_keyword	Soft law instrument cited in the field 'keyword' in Dec.Nat. According to the Dec.Nat codebook (ACA-Europe Newsletter 17) "this field provides an analyse by the Court's departments based on strings of keywords referring to the points of law covered by national decisions." As worded in Dec.Nat	Open text
sl_ instrument	Official name of the cited soft law instrument. As worded by the EU. The official instrument names were identified in Eur-Lex, Official Journal, or the EU publications office database	–
sl_CELEX	CELEX number or other official identifier of EU oft law. Identified in Eur-Lex, Official Journal, or the database of the publications office	–
sl_nr	Number of Soft law instruments cited in the judgment	–

(continued)

Table A.2 (continued)

Variable	*Description*	*Values*
sl_label	Self-label of the instrument (e.g. guideline, communication etc.)	communications conclusions declaration guidelines notice opinion recommendation resolution
sl_author	Author of the soft law instrument	Agency CJEU Commission Committee Council EUCO European Parliament High Authority
sl_function	Function of the soft law instrument. Definitions following Senden (2004, 138–147)	interpretative decisional steering

(continued)

Table A.2 (continued)

Variable	*Description*	*Values*
sl_policy	Policy area of the soft law instrument. Manually coded. This variable is instrument-centered and focuses on the author of the referenced soft law instrument	–

matter	Matters of law affected by the judgment. Captures the area of area law into which a national judgment falls. This variable was included in the Dec.Nat data
	cjeu = Court of Justice of the EU;
	comp = Competition;
	connect = Communications Networks, Content and Technology;
	ecb = European Central Bank;
	emp = Employme, Social Affairs, Inclusion;
	env = Environment;
	esa = European Supervisory Authorities (e.g. EBA, ESMA, EIOPA);
	euipo = EU Intellectual Property Office;
	ext = External Relations / Foreign Affairs;
	fisma = Financial Stability, Financial Services and Capital Markets Union;
	grow = Internal Market, Industry, Entrepreneurship and SMEs;
	home = Migration and Home Affairs;
	just = Justice and Consumers;
	near = European Neighbourhood and Enlargement Negotiations;
	sanco = Health and Consumer Protection
	sante = Health and Food Safety;
	staaid = State Aid;
	trade = Trade;
	trea = Treaty-related issues
		agri
		cjeu
		comp
		connect
		ecb
		emp
		env
		esa
		euipo
		ext
		fisma
		grow
		home
		just
		near
		sanco
		sante
		staaid
		trade
		trea

Appendix Section 3. Survey Questionnaire

The survey was conducted in the French and German judiciary using the web-based software Unipark[2] and ran from February to July 2022. A total of 70 judges responded to the survey. Questionnaire: The questionnaire contains a mixture of closed and open questions. The German version of the questions is displayed in normal font. The French questions are displayed in *italics*.

Questions:

1. **Please choose a language**
2. **Is your chamber/senate responsible for one or more of the following areas of law?** Financial market regulation, Common Foreign and Security Policy, Food safety, Sustainable agriculture, Police and judicial cooperation, Pharmaceutical regulation, State aid, Other (please specify)
3. **In which jurisdiction and instance are you active?**
   Administrative, civil, other (specify)
4. **What is your position in the court?**
   (open question)
5. **How long have you worked in the** judiciary?

[2] For more information, see https://www.unipark.com/en/, last accessed 10 July 2025.

A. Eick, *Soft Law and National Courts in the European Union*, European Administrative Governance,
https://doi.org/10.1007/978-3-032-04515-7

(in years)

6. **Do you regularly follow legal developments in EU law?**
   Scale from *1 (never) to 10 (often)*
7. **In approximately how many cases have you been involved in a decision?** *(open question)*
8. **In approximately how many of these cases did EU law play a role?**
   (open question)
9. **Did EU soft law play a role in at least one of these cases?**
   Yes / No / Don't know
10. **In how many cases did EU soft law play a role?**
    (open question)
11. **What type of EU soft law was relevant to your chamber?**
    Recommendation, Guideline, Communication, Declaration, Notice, Conclusion, Resolution, Opinion, Agency soft law, Other (please specify)

12 **Can you specify in what way EU soft law was relevant for your chamber?**

As informal guidance (but not cited in the decision text)
As a source of information
As an aid to interpret national law
As an aid to interpret EU law
As an additional standard of review
As the main standard of review or legal source
Other (please specify)

13. **Did your chamber use EU soft law to complement or support a specific Treaty article, EU directive or regulation, or use it independently of hard EU law?**

To complement hard EU law
Independently of hard EU law
Don't know

14. **What was the most important reason for your chamber to rely on EU soft law?**

Invoked by a party to the proceedings
Need for information

Need for clarification regarding a Directive/Regulation/ Treaty article
Need for interpretation of national law
Legal authority of soft law
Authority of the soft law's issuer
Other (please specify)

15. **In your opinion, does EU soft law have effects at the national level that are relevant for the judiciary?**

No
Practical effects for administration
Non-binding legal effects
Indirect legal force in connection with hard law
Independent direct binding force
Other (please specify)

16. **In your opinion, is judicial review of soft law possible?**
Yes/ No / Sometimes
17. **Some people believe the EU interferes too much in areas of national policy-making, while others highlight the benefits of closer European integration. What is your personal opinion?**
10-point scale from 1 (less EU involvement) to 10 (more EU integration)
18. **In discussions about soft law in general, some emphasize its advantages (e.g., flexibility, guidance), while others are more skeptical (e.g., lack of legitimacy, undermining legal certainty). Where would you personally place yourself on this continuum?**
10-point scale from 1 (very negative) to 10 (very positive)
19. **What other aspects of EU soft law do you consider important to mention?** *(Open question)*

Appendix Section 4. Overview of Interviews

Semi-standardized expert interviews were used as a source of qualitative information on the use of EU soft law by national administrations, agencies, social actors, and courts in the selected countries and policy areas. All interviews were conducted by the author of this book via phone or video call. Each interview was recorded, transcribed, and coded into substantive categories in MAXQDA for qualitative analysis. The transcripts were fully anonymized. Each interviewee was given information about the processing of personal data and data protection measures. Participants agreed to the scientific use of the data for this project. Table A.3 lists all interviews.

A. Eick, *Soft Law and National Courts in the European Union*,
European Administrative Governance,
https://doi.org/10.1007/978-3-032-04515-7

Table A.3 Overview of expert interviews

Abbreviation	*Institution*	*Department/ Role*	*Country*	*Date*
Min1	Federal Ministry for Economic Affairs and Energy (BMWi)	European Union Unit	Germany	04.03.2021
Min2	Federal Ministry for Economic Affairs and Energy (BMWi)	Energy Unit	Germany	13.04.2021
Min3	General Secretariat for European Affairs (SGAE)	Competition and State aid sector	France	11.05.2021
Min4	Regional Ministry of Economy	State aid Specialist	Germany	16.02.2021
IG1	Welfare association	In-house lawyer	Germany	25.10.2021
IG2	Law firm	State Aid Lawyer	Brussels	14.04.2021
IG3	Law firm	Pharmaceutical Lawyer	Germany	14.07.2021
AG1	National Medicines Agency	European Union Unit	Germany	15.10.2021
AG2	National Medicines Agency	GMP Unit	France	10.02.2021
IG5	Law firm	Pharmaceutical Lawyer	Germany	13.01.2022
IG4	Pharmaceutical Company	Public Affairs Department	Germany	16.12.2021
Min5	Federal Ministry of Health	Pharmaceutical Unit	Germany	16.11.2020
AG3	Inter-regional Agency	GMP Coordination Authority	Germany	21.01.2021
AG4	Regional agency	GMP Authority	Germany	18.11.2020
AG5	Regional agency	GMP Authority	Germany	02.02.2021
AG6	Regional agency	GMP Authority	Germany	21.02.2021
IG6	Association	Association of private hospitals	Germany	04.11.2021
IG7	Law firm	State Aid Lawyer	Germany	22.02.2022
IG8	Association	Renewable Energy Association	Europe	15.07.2021
IG9	Think Tank	State Aid law specialist	Germany	09.03.2021
Court1	Higher Regional Court	Judge	Germany	17.05.2022

Index

A. Eick, *Soft Law and National Courts in the European Union*, European Administrative Governance,
https://doi.org/10.1007/978-3-032-04515-7

FSC
www.fsc.org
MIX
Papier | Fördert gute Waldnutzung
FSC® C083411

Kolibri 360 GmbH
Ferdinand-Jühlke-Straße 7
99095 Erfurt, Deutschland
produktsicherheit@kolibri360.de